The Lunch Break Investor

The Lunch Break Investor

IDENTIFY WINNING STOCKS, BUILD YOUR WEALTH, AND RECLAIM YOUR TIME

THOMAS CHUA

Harriman House

HARRIMAN HOUSE
www.harriman-house.com

First published in 2026 by Harriman House, an imprint of Pan Macmillan
EU Representative: Macmillan Publishers Ireland Ltd, 1st Floor, The Liffey Trust Centre, 117-126 Sheriff Street Upper, Dublin 1, D01 YC43
Associated companies throughout the world
www.panmacmillan.com
www.panmacmillan.com/ai-at-pan-macmillan

Paperback ISBN: 978-1-80409-151-7
eBook ISBN: 978-1-80409-152-4
Audio ISBN: 978-1-80409-502-7

British Library Cataloguing in Publication Data
A CIP catalogue record for this book can be obtained from the British Library.

01 Printed and bound by CPI Group (UK) Ltd.

Cover design by Paul McCarthy. iStock image used.

CONTENTS

For my mother – the lights
will never go off again.

INTRODUCTION: MY JOURNEY FROM POVERTY TO FINANCIAL INDEPENDENCE

THE NIGHT EVERYTHING CHANGED

We are all a product of our environment, experiences, and the challenges we face. Growing up, two memories are etched into my mind.

The first is the dread I felt each time I opened the mailbox. It was always filled with overdue bills and final notices, their red lettering a stark warning of what was to come. One day, those warnings became reality. The lights held on to their last flicker before giving up, the fan spun its final oscillation before slowing down to a halt, and the silence fell. Our power had been cut off.

When I looked out the window, I saw brightly lit apartments and could hear my neighbors' televisions, their houses filled with conversations and laughter. As I sat in my room, the darkness and stale air reminded me of my family's financial situation.

Everything happened all at once. It was like a game of musical chairs, the music stopped and my family was left standing.

Oddly, the darkness didn't feel unfamiliar. Perhaps I was used to things not going well and I'd accepted that life is filled with speed bumps, or so I thought. I was 13 years old when this happened.

That night in the darkness, surrounded by the sounds of neighbors living their normal lives, something crystallized. Every unpaid bill, every embarrassed glance from teachers, every sacrifice my mother made – they weren't just hardships. They were lessons in what I refused to accept for my future. That helplessness I felt wasn't just pain. It became fuel. A determination to build wealth so solid that my family would never sit in darkness again.

Going to school wasn't much better. Teachers would discreetly pull me aside to discuss outstanding tuition fees, their concerned expressions, while well-intentioned, a source of shame and embarrassment. Thankfully, I was fortunate to live in Singapore, where early school education is compulsory and subsidized. Despite our financial circumstances, I was able to stay in school and get an education.

The second memory is the constant arguments between my parents, fueled by money worries. My dad, struggling with addiction to alcohol, gambling, and cigarettes, could never hold down a stable job. He'd often resort to borrowing from relatives or dipping into my mother's meager savings to fuel his vices. Every week, he'd buy lottery tickets, convinced this would be the one.

The most devastating blow came when my father pawned my mother's cherished wedding dowry. The jewellery told a story. Each piece was a chapter of their lives together, a testament to happier times. It was now reduced to a few crumpled pawn shop receipts and empty promises of redemption.

Though the collateral loan was modest, barely enough to sustain my father's vices for a fortnight, the emotional toll was immense. Witnessing my mother's quiet devastation, her eyes brimming with unshed tears, stayed with me. Through experiences like this, I made a promise to myself – I would build a different life for my family.

FINDING LIGHT IN THE LIBRARY

I didn't have traditional role models growing up, but I learned valuable lessons by observing my dad's mistakes. I saw the dangers of impulsive decisions, addiction, and living beyond one's means. I vowed to be different, to work hard, shun vices like alcohol, cigarettes, and gambling, and become the first in my family to earn a university degree.

But avoiding my father's mistakes was just playing defense. To truly change my life, I needed to go on offense.

The library became my refuge. At first, I went there for the air conditioning and quiet space to do homework. But gradually, I found myself wandering to the business section. I started with biographies – stories of people who built something from nothing. Andrew Carnegie. Sam Walton. Benjamin Franklin. People who understood that wealth wasn't found in lottery tickets or at the mahjong table, but built through hard work, ownership and patience.

The most important person I came to know through those books was Warren Buffett. Here was someone who became one of the richest people in the world not through speculation or trading, but through buying parts of businesses and holding them for decades. No daily price checking. No speculating on what would happen tomorrow. Just owning pieces of companies and letting them grow.

Everything clicked when I understood his approach. This wasn't about being smarter than everyone else or working 60-hour weeks. It wasn't about buying lottery tickets or speculating wildly in the stock market hoping to strike it rich. It was about finding good businesses, buying them at reasonable prices, and then – this was the revolutionary part – doing nothing. Just waiting. Letting the business do the work while you lived your life.

You bought ownership in solid businesses and held them. Boring, but effective.

The more I read, the more I realized that the stock market could be a casino for gamblers, or it could be a place to buy ownership in real businesses. The choice was yours.

Where my father clutched lottery tickets and his friends huddled around the mahjong table chasing the next winning hand, I would seek businesses with predictable earnings. Where they doubled down on bad hands hoping for a reversal, I would buy quality and hold it. They needed luck. I needed time.

That's when I discovered what I now call "steady compounding" – buying quality businesses and holding them for years, letting their growth do the heavy lifting. No daily price checking. No market timing. Just owning pieces of great companies and giving them time. It seemed almost too simple to work. But simple is exactly what works.

FROM SURVIVING TO FINANCIAL INDEPENDENCE

At 18, I eagerly opened my first brokerage account, ready to put my knowledge into practice. It wasn't always smooth sailing. I made mistakes, bought duds, and sometimes let my emotions get the better of me. But each setback was a learning experience, a chance to refine my strategy and understand my own risk tolerance.

As I navigated the complexities of the market, my passion for investing deepened. I knew I wanted a career in investment management. However, the realities of my family's situation demanded I put my dreams on hold.

By 22, I'd saved over S$30,000 – money originally meant for university tuition. It came from years of odd jobs and saving every dollar I could. But the real breakthrough came during my polytechnic days. While my classmates accepted school-arranged internships, I interviewed for opportunities outside until I found one willing to pay triple what my peers were getting. That single internship accelerated my savings dramatically.

Then came an opportunity – a government scholarship covering full tuition plus a living allowance, in exchange for a four-year bond in public service upon graduation.

The pen felt extremely heavy as I signed that scholarship. With each stroke, I was committing four years of my life after graduation. But it also meant something else – that S$30,000 could stay invested, compounding while I studied.

I took the deal. While classmates spent their allowances on parties and entertainment, I lived simply and invested almost everything. By the time I started my career, I had a six-figure portfolio – not from a high-paying job, but from letting compound interest do its work while I was still in school. Starting my compounding journey early and giving it time to work – that was the most important decision on my path to financial independence.

During those years, I continued to invest, letting the power of compounding work its magic. My portfolio grew steadily, fueled by contributions from my scholarship allowance and later my salary.

My first real winner was Starbucks under CEO Howard Schultz's leadership in 2011. At the time, paying $5 for coffee seemed absurd to most Singaporeans used to $1 coffees at most coffee shops. But I watched those stores every day, always packed. Often when someone bought Starbucks, they'd photograph it, post it, tag their location. The coffee cup had become a status symbol. The green mermaid logo wasn't selling coffee – it was selling identity.

That investment became my first multi-bagger – investor speak for a stock that multiplies several times over. It outperformed every "cheap" stock I'd bought based on traditional metrics. More importantly, it taught me that great businesses hiding in plain sight could compound wealth far better than complex bets. Buy right, sit tight, do nothing, and let it compound. Simple, boring, powerful.

One thing I'm grateful for is that delaying gratification and focusing on the long term came naturally to me. It's a trait that Charlie Munger, Warren Buffett's longtime business partner, once highlighted as crucial for successful investing. "It's waiting that helps you as an investor and a lot of people just can't stand to wait. If you didn't get the deferred-gratification gene, you've got to work very hard to overcome that."

Discipline, long-term thinking, and independent judgment became the cornerstones of my investment philosophy. These principles, developed through my early challenges, would serve me well in the years to come.

By 2021, after more than a decade of disciplined saving and investing, my portfolio had given me financial independence. I could leave my job, pursue my passion, and spend time with people who matter. The same steady compounding that lifted me from poverty now gave me freedom to choose.

THE LUNCH BREAK PROMISE

That independence led me to start *SteadyCompounding.com*, where I publish in-depth stocks research and share everything I've learned about investing in the stock market. I call the companies that make this possible "Steady Compounders" – businesses so strong they can build wealth while you build a life.

I also frequently give talks and post on all major socials under the handle @steadycompound, as I hope to pass it forward to the next person who's trying to figure out how to invest in the stock market. This book is the culmination of that mission – your guide to building wealth without sacrificing what matters most.

Let me be clear about what this book offers and what it doesn't.

This isn't a book for day traders or get-rich-quick seekers. If you're looking to double your money in six months or quit your job next year to trade full-time, you're in the wrong place.

This is a book for builders. For the executive climbing the corporate ladder who wants their money working as hard as they do. For the parent juggling soccer practices and piano lessons who refuses to add "portfolio babysitting" to their endless to-do list. For the sandwich generation caring for aging parents while raising children, who need wealth building that doesn't demand another full-time job.

Most investing books fall into two camps: academic theories that sound brilliant but offer no practical application, or aggressive strategies that require you to quit everything else and become a full-time trader. Both miss the point entirely.

Here's my promise: **You can build life-changing wealth with just one hour a day**.

That's what *The Lunch Break Investor* means. While your colleagues scroll social media or debate politics over lunch, you could be analyzing businesses, reviewing your portfolio, or simply reading annual reports. One focused hour. That's all.

Yes, there's a learning curve at the beginning – like learning to drive, the first few weeks require more attention. But once you understand the principles, maintaining and growing your wealth truly requires just your lunch break. The deep analysis happens upfront when you're learning and when you find new opportunities. After that, the businesses do the heavy lifting while you do the living.

From trader to owner

There's a transformation at the heart of this book, and I want to name it clearly before we begin.

Most people who buy stocks think of themselves as investors. But watch their behavior, and you'll see something different. They check prices daily. They celebrate small gains. They panic at small losses. They're always looking for the next opportunity, the next hot tip, the next thing to buy or sell.

They're not investors. They're traders in disguise.

I know because I was one of them.

In my early years, I'd buy a stock, watch it rise 20%, and sell triumphantly. "I made money!" I'd tell myself. Then I'd watch that same stock rise another 200% without me. I wasn't investing – I was picking up pennies in front of steamrollers, too focused on small wins to notice the fortunes I was leaving behind.

The transformation I'm going to guide you through is simple to describe and difficult to execute:

You're going to stop thinking like a trader and start thinking like an owner.

An owner doesn't celebrate when their business's stock price ticks up 5%. They celebrate when the business opens a new market, or renews a major contract, or hires a brilliant executive. An owner doesn't panic when the stock drops 30% – they ask whether the business itself has changed.

An owner measures wealth in decades, not days.

This shift sounds semantic, but it changes everything. How you research. How you buy. How you hold. How you react to bad news and good news alike. Once you genuinely see yourself as owning businesses rather than trading stocks, the entire practice of investing transforms.

By the end of this book, when you look at your portfolio, you won't see a collection of ticker symbols. You'll see businesses you understand, run by people you trust, protected by moats you can identify. You'll know what each one does, why it wins, and what would have to change for you to sell.

That's the transformation. Let's begin.

WHAT YOU'LL LEARN

This book is structured as a complete system, taking you from foundational concepts to advanced portfolio management:

Part I: The foundation

After discovering the millionaires nobody knew about in Chapter 1 and understanding the heart of steady compounding in Chapter 2, you'll master the three critical skills every investor needs. Chapter 3 reveals how to identify economic moats – those competitive advantages that protect a company's profits for decades. Chapter 4 unpacks the three drivers of capital appreciation, showing you exactly how businesses create shareholder value. Chapter 5 focuses on management, because even the best business fails with poor leadership.

Part II: Finding your winners

Chapter 6 teaches you how to find your first steady compounders – companies with the quality and durability to compound wealth over decades. Chapter 7 demystifies valuation, ensuring you never overpay no matter how great the business.

Part III: The mechanics

Chapter 8 covers buying strategies and the crucial written thesis you must create before every investment. Chapter 9 tackles the hardest decision in investing – when to sell. Chapter 10 shows you how to build a winning portfolio that balances concentration with diversification.

Part IV: The long game

Finally, Chapter 11 goes beyond the numbers to explore the psychology and philosophy of patient wealth building.

Throughout, you'll find real examples, not theories. When I explain how

Costco's membership model creates switching costs, you'll understand why renewal rates stay above 90%. When I show you how Microsoft transformed from selling software boxes to subscription services, you'll recognize similar patterns in other businesses. These aren't just case studies – they're mental models you'll use to evaluate every investment opportunity.

WHY THIS APPROACH WORKS

What gave me confidence that this approach could work for anyone was discovering I wasn't the first to figure it out. Throughout history, quiet millionaires have been hiding in plain sight, building enormous fortunes while working ordinary jobs. You'll meet them in Chapter 1.

The steady compounding approach works because it aligns with how wealth actually builds. Not through frantic activity, but through patient ownership. While others exhaust themselves checking prices daily, following hot tips, and jumping in and out of positions, you'll be quietly building wealth that can span generations.

But here's what breaks my heart. Most people never even start. They think investing is too complicated. They believe you need to be a math genius or have insider connections. They assume it takes all day to manage a portfolio. So they do nothing. And 20 years later, they're still talking about how they should really start investing "someday."

That someday never comes. Meanwhile, compound interest could have been working for them all those years. Building. Growing. Multiplying.

YOUR JOURNEY STARTS HERE

Twenty years from now, you'll face one of two realities.

You'll look back and realize you spent two decades waiting for the "perfect time" to start investing. Waiting for more money. Waiting for more knowledge. Waiting for the market to be "safer." And you'll see what that waiting cost you in compound returns that never happened.

Or you'll look back at a portfolio of wonderful businesses that grew quietly while you focused on what matters. Your career, your family, your life. And you'll realize you've built wealth that gives you true freedom. Not because you were brilliant or lucky, but because you took action. You learned. You put in the work. You invested. You waited.

The difference between these two futures? Starting. Today. With whatever you know and whatever you can save.

If you're ready to build wealth without sacrificing your life, if you believe your best investment is in your own experiences and relationships with your portfolio quietly compounding in the background, then turn the page.

Let me show you how ordinary people build extraordinary wealth, one lunch break at a time.

PART I

THE FOUNDATION

CHAPTER 1
THE MILLIONAIRES NOBODY KNEW

You might think my journey to financial independence was unique. That it required some special talent or lucky break. But I discovered many others who had done the same – ordinary people who built extraordinary wealth through this approach.

Steady compounding has been quietly making millionaires for decades. People you'd never notice. People who understood something most investors miss.

Let me introduce you to them.

FROM $5,000 TO $22 MILLION

In 1995, a lawyer handling an estate phoned Yeshiva University with news that stunned them. An elderly woman they'd never heard of had left her entire $22 million fortune[1] to Yeshiva University's Stern College for Women and Albert Einstein College of Medicine.

The woman was Anne Scheiber. And her story proved everything I'd been learning about patient wealth building.

Anne never earned more than $4,000 a year during her 23-year career as an IRS auditor. She never married. Never inherited money. Never won the lottery. She retired in 1944 with $5,000 in savings and a modest annual pension of $3,100 – her resources at age 51.

While many would have settled into a comfortable retirement on this income, Anne saw an opportunity to do more. She took that $5,000 and started buying shares of companies she understood.

In 1950, with her profits, she bought 1,000 shares of Schering-Plough Corporation, the pharmaceutical company, for about $10,000. And she just held on. Through stock splits, those original 1,000 shares eventually became 128,000 shares, worth $7.5 million at her death.

Another of her longtime holdings, Coca-Cola, increased in value from $28,000 to $720,000 in just the last 15 years of her life. That doesn't even include $62,000 in dividends.

Here's what Anne didn't do: trade. When Schering-Plough dropped 20%, she held. When Coca-Cola surged, she didn't "take profits." When brokers called with the next sure thing, she ignored them. For five decades – she died at 101 – she just kept buying and holding.

Her broker, William Fay, later told *The New York Times*: "She was never looking for a quick buck. Her whole idea was to get performance on a long-term basis. She felt over the long run the value would grow."

Think about that. Fifty years of not selling. Through the Cuban Missile Crisis. Through Vietnam. Through the 1973 oil crisis. Through Black Monday in 1987. Every time the world was "ending", Anne Scheiber did nothing. And that nothing turned $5,000 into $22 million.

When I read about Anne in *The Washington Post*, it reinforced what I'd been discovering – ownership in good businesses, given enough time, creates extraordinary wealth. The same principle I'd stumbled onto, but proven over a lifetime.

The $22 million she left behind went to educating young women and advancing medicine – her way of helping others overcome the discrimination she'd faced. Her money is still working today, decades after her death. That's the power of patient capital.

THE JANITOR WHO LEFT $8 MILLION

Then there's Ronald Read, whose story I find equally remarkable.

Read worked as a gas station attendant and mechanic for about 25 years. After retiring for a year, he took a part-time janitor job at JCPenney where he worked for 17 years until 1997. His friends knew him as the guy who held his coat together with safety pins to avoid buying a new one. When he died in 2014 at age 92, his family prepared for a modest estate. Maybe $50,000 if they were lucky.

The actual number was $8 million.[2]

Mr. Read left behind a five-inch-thick stack of stock certificates in a safe-deposit box. He had been quietly buying shares for decades with whatever he could save from his paycheck, never selling, just accumulating.

According to *The Wall Street Journal*, Ronald Read owned at least 95 stocks at the time of his death, many of which he had held for years, if not decades. His top holdings show what decades of steady compounding can do to a janitor's modest savings: Wells Fargo worth $510,900, Procter & Gamble at $364,008, Colgate-Palmolive at $252,104, American Express at $199,034, J.M. Smucker at $189,722, and Johnson & Johnson at $183,881.

Each of these positions likely started with just a few hundred dollars from his paycheck. But held for 20, 30, even 40 years, they compounded into six-figure fortunes. That's the power of time plus steady compounding – turning a janitor's savings into millions.

These weren't speculative bets. They were established businesses spread across railroads, utilities, banks, healthcare, telecom and consumer products. He avoided technology stocks entirely.

His method was remarkably simple. When he got paid, he bought shares. When he had extra cash, he bought more shares. When stocks went up, he held. When stocks went down, he held.

Mr. Read's portfolio wasn't perfect. He owned shares of Lehman Brothers Holdings, which collapsed in 2008. But it didn't need to be perfect. He was diversified and he let his winners run.

Because here's the thing in investing: we don't have to get everything right, and there's no way anyone can get everything right. We need to be diversified and let winners run. If 5% of your portfolio was Apple when the iPhone launched, you won. If 5% was in Blackberry, it's a rounding error. That's why we'll talk about the importance of diversification and letting winners run later in this book.

Read's generosity matched his patience. The local Brooks Memorial Library received $1.2 million – its largest bequest ever. Brattleboro Memorial Hospital received $4.8 million – also its largest gift in the institution's history. This janitor who everyone overlooked had quietly built an extraordinary fortune.

When people ask me about diversification, I think about Ronald Read. When they worry about picking the perfect stock, I remember his five-inch stack of certificates. He didn't need to be right about everything. He just needed to be patient with the right ones.

WHAT THEY ALL HAD IN COMMON

Anne Scheiber and Ronald Read weren't alone. Once I started looking, I found them everywhere.

Gladys Holm, a secretary who never made more than $15,000 a year, left $18 million to Children's Memorial Hospital for research[3] – the largest bequest in the institution's 115-year history, surpassing even the McDonald's founder's previous record of $10 million. Unlike many investors who trade frequently, Holm practiced true buy-and-hold investing.

Gilmore and Golda Reynolds, a small-town couple, shocked everyone with a $23 million bequest. Jay Jensen, a teacher, accumulated $4 million on an educator's salary. Grace Groner, who bought three shares of Abbott Laboratories in 1935 for $60 and never sold, left behind $7 million.[4]

These people had nothing in common on the surface. Different jobs. Different cities. Different eras. But dig deeper, and there was a clear pattern.

They bought shares in companies they understood – usually companies whose products they used. They held those shares for decades, not months. They ignored market predictions and hot tips. They never tried to time the market. Most importantly, they never interrupted the compounding.

They didn't have finance degrees. They didn't use complex models. They didn't subscribe to expensive financial data services. They just bought ownership in good businesses and waited.

What strikes me most is their remarkable emotional control. While financial TV screams about what to buy today and sell tomorrow, these investors held the same shares for decades. Through every crash, every boom, every headline predicting disaster – they simply held on. They understood that volatility is the price of admission for long-term returns.

I realized something profound. My journey to financial independence was following a path that Scheiber, Read, and dozens of others had already proven.

This is the opportunity sitting in front of you. To build the wealth that gives you the freedom to live life on your terms. To have the privilege of drawing your own canvas – whether that's traveling the world, pursuing your passion, supporting causes you believe in, or simply having the security to pursue work you love rather than work that pays the bills.

Through patience. Through ownership. Through what I call steady compounding – an approach that's deceptively simple but profoundly powerful. In the next chapter, let me show you exactly what it means.

LUNCH BREAK SUMMARY

- **Ordinary people, no finance training, extraordinary results**: Anne Scheiber was an IRS auditor. Ronald Read was a janitor. No MBAs, no Wall Street connections. If they could build millions through steady compounding, so can you.
- **The pattern is consistent**: They bought companies they understood, held for decades not months, ignored market predictions, and never interrupted the compounding.
- **Let your winners run while staying diversified**: Ronald Read owned 95 stocks. When Lehman collapsed, it didn't matter – his other positions kept compounding. You don't need to be perfect, just diversified enough to let winners overwhelm the losers.

- **Emotional control beats intelligence**: These investors held through every crisis for 50+ years. Their secret wasn't genius-level analysis but the discipline to do nothing when everyone else was panicking.
- **Wealth is the means, not the end**: Notice how every quiet millionaire gave their fortune away. They built wealth to support causes they believed in, to leave legacies that mattered. That's the heart of the lunch break investor: building wealth that empowers you to live the life you actually want.

YOUR NEXT STEP

You've seen the proof – ordinary people building extraordinary wealth through patient ownership. But what exactly is this "steady compounding" approach that made it possible? In Chapter 2, I'll show you the mechanics behind the magic. Why compound interest becomes unstoppable given enough time, why time in the market beats timing the market, and why doing nothing is often the most profitable action you can take. The stories are inspiring, but the investing principles we're about to visit are what will transform your wealth.

CHAPTER 2
THE HEART OF STEADY COMPOUNDING

WHAT EXACTLY IS this steady compounding approach that transformed my life and created the quiet fortunes of the people we met in Chapter 1?

Let me show you why it's so powerful.

When you buy a stock, you're not buying a lottery ticket or a trading card. You're buying partial ownership in an actual business. If you owned a rental property, would you check real estate websites every morning to see its estimated value? Would you sell it because someone offered you 20% less than yesterday's estimate? Of course not. You'd focus on whether tenants were paying rent, whether the property was being maintained, whether it was generating steady income.

That's steady compounding. You become a business owner, not a stock trader.

You don't need to check prices daily. You don't need complicated strategies. There's no need to babysit these businesses. Just ownership and patience.

This approach is far less demanding than the strategies that consume people's lives, yet it produces better results for most investors. You don't need to analyze microcaps by visiting factories and calling suppliers. You don't need to find turnaround situations or special events. You don't need to day trade or follow every Fed announcement. By owning great businesses that are able to reinvest their earnings and grow over time, your portfolio grows with them.

You need to find good businesses, buy them at fair prices, and then – this is the crucial part – do nothing.

Of course, doing nothing goes against everything we're taught about success. Work harder, analyze more, stay ahead of the competition. The investment legends must have done exactly that to achieve their incredible returns, right?

HALL OF FAME RETURNS – AT WHAT COST?

I spent years in the library studying the greatest investors. Warren Buffett's partnership years delivered 31.6% annual returns before fees from 1957 to 1968.[1] Peter Lynch at Fidelity achieved 29.2% annual returns from 1977 to 1990.[2] Mind-blowing numbers.

But here's what the books don't emphasize – those returns came at a cost most of us aren't willing to pay.

In *The Snowball*, Alice Schroeder reveals the true price of Buffett's success. The man who started selling gum door-to-door at age six never stopped his quest to amass wealth – but not to spend it, as his license plate, THRIFTY, suggested. This quest would take him all the way to being the richest man in the world, but it would cost him dearly.

Buffett was consumed by his work – the kind of man who'd leave the dinner table mid-meal to go upstairs and work. As he later admitted of his wife Susie, "She kept me together for a lot of years, and she contributed 90% to raising the kids." She kept hoping that once they had enough money – $8 to $10 million, she figured – he would finally slow down. She was wrong. After the kids were grown, Susie moved to San Francisco. They lived apart for 27 years. Buffett was crushed, calling it the biggest mistake of his life.

Lynch's account is equally revealing. He worked six days a week at Fidelity, visiting more than 200 companies a year and reading hundreds of annual reports.[3] In *Beating the Street*, he admits choosing vacation spots based on time zones and phone booth locations. His favorite ski resort was Balsams in Dixville Notch, New Hampshire, because it had a phone at the bottom of the lift. He'd ski down, call the trading desk, rattle off a page of buys and sells, then ride back up. His daughter Mary played in seven soccer games one year. He made it to one. His approach had only two modes: "overdrive and off. No in-between."

At 46, Lynch walked away. "Nobody on his deathbed ever said, 'I wish I'd spent more time at the office,'" he reminded himself. He chose his daughters over another decade of jaw-dropping returns.

Buffett and Lynch's approaches delivered legendary performance, but there's a price to pay, one that can't be measured in dollars and cents.

Even they eventually recognized this. Lynch chose family over fortune. Buffett, in his later years, shifted his approach, saying he's not looking to jump over seven-foot bars anymore – he's looking for one-foot bars he can step over.

The whole point of building wealth was to live a better life, not to sacrifice my life on the altar of compounding. The truth is, you don't need hall of fame returns to build life-changing wealth. You need consistent, sustainable returns that let you sleep at night and enjoy your days.

Howard Marks, the legendary investor behind Oaktree Capital, discovered this truth from studying pension fund performance. In his memo "The Route to Performance," he described a fund that never ranked above the 27th percentile in any single year, yet ended up in the top 4% over 14 years.[4]

As Marks explained, "Attempting to achieve a superior long-term record by stringing together a run of top-decile years is unlikely to succeed. Instead, striving to do a little better than average every year – and through discipline, to have highly superior results in bad times – is more likely to work."

That's the steady compounding philosophy. Not swinging for the fences. Not trying to be a hero. Just consistently hitting singles and doubles while avoiding the strikeouts that destroy wealth. As Marks proved, sustainable above-average performance – even if it never looks spectacular in any single year – becomes exceptional over time.

The challenge is that early on, this approach feels painfully slow. Most people quit during these frustrating early years, not realizing they're about to witness the true power of compound interest.

SLOWLY, THEN ALL AT ONCE

I was walking through Arashiyama, the famous bamboo forest in Kyoto, when our guide shared something that perfectly reflected how I think about wealth building.

"Do you know how bamboo grows?" he asked. For the first three years after planting, you see nothing above ground. But underground, the bamboo is storing energy and nutrients, building an extensive root system that will support massive growth. A gardener might water and fertilize for years, seeing only tiny shoots or nothing at all.

Then, almost overnight, it explodes. The bamboo rockets up a meter per day, transforming empty land into a towering forest.

Your wealth works the same way. The first years feel slow. You're building, accumulating, reinvesting – and it feels like nothing's happening.

But underneath, the foundation is strengthening. Each year of patient investing adds another layer to your base. The compounding machine is quietly building momentum.

Then the breakthrough comes. The same patience that seemed to produce little in the early years becomes the engine driving exponential growth. What felt like crawling becomes sprinting, not because you changed your approach, but because time transformed your foundation into a fortress.

Warren Buffett perfectly illustrates this principle. At age 65 in 1995, he was worth $12 billion according to *Barron's*.[5] By his mid-nineties, his net worth had grown past $140 billion. More than 90% of his fortune was created after the age most people retire. The compounding machine that took 65 years to build $12 billion needed just three more decades to add ten times that amount. Same investor, same philosophy, just more time for the snowball to gather mass.

Buffett himself compares wealth building to a snowball rolling down a hill. The longer the hill, the bigger it gets. "The trick is to have a very long hill," he says, "which means starting very young or living to be very old."

The mistake most investors make is giving up during the root-building years. They don't see immediate results, so they try something else. New strategy. New approach. New asset class. They keep ripping up their bamboo and replanting, wondering why they never see a forest.

YOUR EDGE OVER THE PROFESSIONALS

Hold stocks for one month and you'll lose money 40% of the time. Hold for 20 years and your odds of loss drop to essentially zero.

Schroders analyzed 148 years of US stock market data and uncovered something that should fundamentally change how you think about investing risk. They looked at every possible holding period from 1871 to 2020 and calculated how often investors in the broad market index would have lost money after adjusting for inflation.[6]

These results are for the US stock market as a whole – a diversified basket of America's largest companies.

Figure 2.1: The longer you hold, the safer it gets

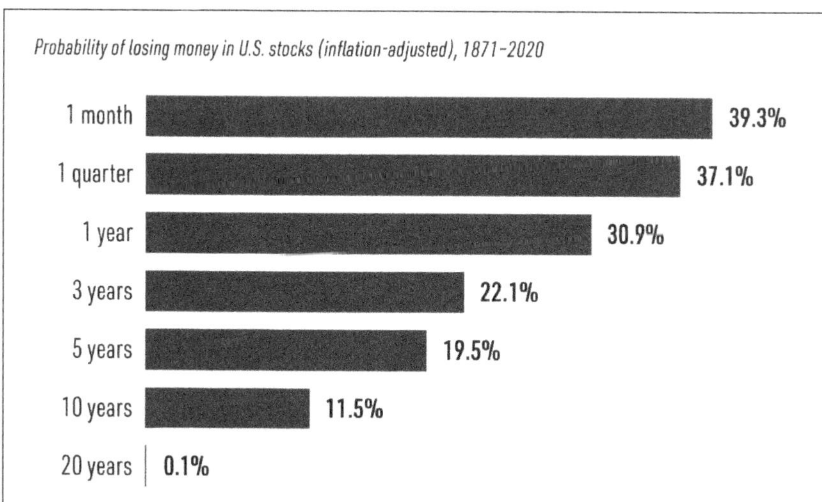

Source: Robert Shiller, Schroders. Analysis based on rolling periods for S&P 500 index. Data: January 1871–March 2020.

Figure 2.1 tells the story. Out of 1,551 rolling 20-year periods between 1871 and 2020, there was exactly ONE where investors lost money after inflation – July 1901 to June 1921, with a barely negative -0.2% annual return. In the other 1,550 scenarios, your returns would have beaten inflation.

This isn't luck. Short-term volatility and long-term returns are completely different phenomena. In the short term, stocks bounce around based on sentiment, news, and noise. Over decades, they reflect human progress, innovation, and economic growth.

Here's the beautiful part: While Wall Street fund managers are forced to play the short-term game – reporting quarterly results, managing redemptions, justifying every move to impatient investors – you can play an entirely different game. You can sit in the long term where the odds are overwhelmingly in your favor.

The professionals with Bloomberg terminals and million-dollar research budgets can't do what you're about to do. They're trapped in quarterly cycles, punished for holding "boring" stocks that take years to pay off. Time horizon is the one advantage money can't buy – and you have it in abundance.

This is why steady compounding works. You're not trying to outsmart the market day by day. You're positioning yourself where the odds are stacked in your favor.

THE LUNCH BREAK INVESTOR WAY

This philosophy is for people who genuinely enjoy studying businesses and understanding what makes them tick. You love the intellectual challenge of investing – analyzing moats, evaluating management, finding opportunities others miss. You want to be an engaged owner who makes thoughtful decisions, not a prisoner to daily price movements.

But you also recognize a crucial truth: great businesses, once purchased at fair prices, reward patient owners far more than active traders. The deep work happens upfront. After that, the business does the heavy lifting while you do the living.

Plant the seeds. Then do the living. The patience that seems boring in year one becomes your superpower by year 10.

You're not interested in Wall Street's quarterly obsessions. You're building generational wealth while actually enjoying the generation you're in.

THE PATH FORWARD

The stories of Anne Scheiber and Ronald Read prove something crucial. Ordinary people achieved extraordinary results through the right approach and patience. You need the discipline to let steady compounding work, not genius-level talent or complicated strategies that usually do more harm than good anyway.

Academic research has since validated what Anne and Ronald discovered through decades of quiet conviction. Professor Hendrik Bessembinder studied nearly a century of stock market data and found that wealth creation is extraordinarily concentrated – just 4% of stocks were responsible for all of the stock market's gains above Treasury bills. The other 96% collectively matched what you'd earn from government bonds.[7]

Let that sink in. If you owned a randomly selected stock, you had a 96% chance of matching what you could have earned with zero risk. The entire case for stock investing – all of it – rests on finding and holding that exceptional 4%.

We'll explore this research deeply in Chapter 9, but the implication shapes everything that follows: finding and holding exceptional businesses isn't just a nice strategy. It's mathematically essential.

In the chapters ahead, I'll show you exactly how to implement steady compounding. How to identify businesses with durable moats. How to spot great management. How to determine fair prices. How to build a portfolio that compounds wealth without consuming your life.

But it all starts with a simple shift in mindset. You're not a trader. You're not a speculator. You're a business owner who happens to buy those businesses through the stock market.

Once you embrace that mindset, everything else falls into place.

LUNCH BREAK SUMMARY

- **You're an owner, not a trader**: When you buy stocks, you're buying businesses. Like a rental property owner focuses on rent not daily valuations, focus on business quality not stock prices.
- **Consistency beats brilliance**: Howard Marks proved that steady, unspectacular performance becomes exceptional over time. You don't need to be a hero – just consistently above average.
- **Compound growth works like bamboo**: Years of invisible foundation-building, then explosive growth. Warren Buffett built over 90% of his wealth after 65 – patience in the early years enabled the spectacular later ones.
- **Time is your shield against risk**: The longer you hold, the safer investing becomes. Short-term volatility is noise; long-term ownership captures human progress and economic growth.
- **Hall of fame returns come with a terrible price**: The investing legends achieved incredible results but at tremendous personal cost. You can build life-changing wealth with sustainable returns that preserve what matters most.

YOUR NEXT STEP

In the next chapter, we'll dive into the first crucial skill: identifying economic moats – the protective barriers that separate great businesses from mediocre ones. Because steady compounding only works if you own businesses that can actually compound. You need companies with sustainable competitive advantages that protect their profits year after year.

Let me show you exactly how to spot them.

CHAPTER 3

ECONOMIC MOATS

DURING THE PANDEMIC, Zoom Video Communications looked like a company that had won the future.

"Zoom" had become a verb. The thesis seemed bulletproof: how people work has changed permanently, remote work is here to stay, and Zoom is the platform everyone already knows. Between 2020 and 2022, the numbers were extraordinary – gross margins of around 70–80%, revenue grew 560% to $4.1 billion, operating margins swung from 2% to 26%, operating income exploded 8,277% to $1.1 billion.

On paper, this was the perfect growth story. But there was a fatal flaw hiding in plain sight.

While Zoom had the best product, Microsoft and Google had the distribution. They bundled video conferencing within Office 365 and G-Suite – tools that enterprises were already paying for. Corporate CIOs, looking to cut costs post-pandemic, defaulted to the "good enough" bundled option rather than paying extra for the "best" option.

Zoom lacked the barriers to prevent enterprise customers from turning to competitors who gave away video conferencing as a feature, not a product. The company is still profitable, but it failed as a growth investment. As I write this in 2025, Zoom is down over 75% from its highs in 2021.

Great product. Incredible growth. No protection. The returns got competed away.

Warren Buffett has a name for what Zoom was missing: an "economic moat" – the invisible barriers that protect a business from competition.

It's the reason Coca-Cola still dominates after over 130 years, while hundreds of beverage startups fail annually – even though die-hard fans can't tell it from Pepsi in blind taste tests.

It's the moat.

Every investment decision hinges on this question: can this business keep winning? Before we talk valuations or portfolios or any other aspect of investing, you need to recognize what protects a company's profits from being competed away. Master this, and everything else becomes clearer.

The secret to wealth is surprisingly boring: find businesses that can compound capital at high rates for decades, then do absolutely nothing.

Let them work while you live your life.

The best businesses are profit generators. They take every dollar invested and turn it into steadily growing profits, year after year. A business earning 20% returns on invested capital (ROIC) will, over the long run, deliver similar returns to its shareholders, if it can reinvest all its earnings at similar rates. This relationship between business returns and investor returns is the foundation of wealth creation.[1]

The problem is, high returns attract competition like bees to honey. Competitors smell opportunity and will do everything possible to grab a piece of those profits. Without protection, even the most profitable business will see its returns eroded down to average levels. Sometimes it happens slowly. Sometimes overnight.

That's where economic moats come in. Think of your business as a castle with treasure inside – the treasure is the right to earn above-average returns. The moat is the water-filled trench that keeps invaders from storming your walls. In business terms, it's the barrier that protects a company's ability to sustain high returns decade after decade.

WHY HIGH RETURNS DON'T LAST (WITHOUT A MOAT)

Before we dive into the mechanics, let me explain why this concept deserves an entire chapter so early in this book. It's because moats determine whether a business can keep the wealth it creates.

The best way to see this is through how businesses naturally evolve. Michael Mauboussin's research reveals the complete picture of competitive dynamics.[2]

Mauboussin identified that the typical company moves through four phases:

1. **Innovation**: Young companies with genuine breakthroughs see rapid rises in returns and massive investment opportunities. This phase is chaotic – substantial entry and exit as everyone tries to capture the opportunity, but few survive.
2. **Fading returns**: High returns attract competition, and those spectacular returns start their inevitable march downward toward the industry average – basically what any decent company in that business can earn. Companies still earn excess returns, but the trajectory is unmistakably down. The gold rush mentality fades as the market matures.
3. **Maturity**: The business reaches competitive equilibrium. Returns settle around the industry average. Nothing special anymore – just another player in a stable market.
4. **Decline**: Some businesses see returns drop below average – they're actually destroying value. This forces hard choices: restructure the business, shift the model entirely, sell to someone else, or face bankruptcy.

This framework explains everything about competitive dynamics. Without protection, businesses race through these phases at breakneck speed. But with a strong moat, they can maintain high returns for decades, resisting that gravitational pull toward average.

Mauboussin's framework then goes deeper. He shows that sustainable value creation has two dimensions: the magnitude of returns above average, and the duration those returns can last. **A business earning massive returns that quickly fade isn't nearly as valuable as one earning solid returns for decades. The depth of the moat matters, but so does its permanence**.

Competition is relentless. The moment competitors sniff out excess returns, they attack. We see this pattern everywhere: trends rise, experience a boom-bust cycle, then settle into brutal competition.

You might remember the bubble tea craze in the early 2000s. When those Taiwanese tea-based drinks with tapioca balls first hit cities like Singapore, New York, and Los Angeles, the novelty and unique taste created instant demand. Long lines snaked outside the few shops that offered them.

With such high demand, those early bubble tea stores must have been printing money – classic Innovation phase, earning fantastic returns on their capital. Naturally, this encouraged rapid expansion. More stores opened. Then more. Then even more. The Fading Returns phase had begun.

But here's the thing about low barriers to entry – competition floods in like water through a broken dam. Before long, bubble tea shops appeared on every corner. The market hit Maturity almost overnight. Oversaturation, coupled with the next trendy drink, quickly eroded profits. As fast as they appeared, many shops began to close – straight into Decline. The entire cycle, from Innovation to irrelevance, took just a few years.

The bubble tea boom and bust illustrates how fleeting success can be without a durable competitive advantage. **A business with no moat races through all four phases, unable to maintain either the magnitude or duration of its returns.**

Quick check: Do you see the pattern?

Before we go further, let's make sure the foundation is solid. Think about a business you've watched rise and fall – maybe a restaurant chain that was everywhere and then vanished, a tech product everyone used until they didn't, or a retailer that dominated until it didn't.

Can you map it to the four phases?

- **Innovation**: When did it seem like they'd discovered something special?
- **Fading returns**: When did competitors start copying them?
- **Maturity**: When did it become just another option?

- **Decline**: When did the economics turn truly ugly?

If you can see this pattern in businesses you've personally witnessed, you're already thinking like an investor. The framework is a lens for understanding the business stories happening around you every day.

Capitalism is brutal. The privilege of earning attractive returns must be continually earned. This is exactly why economic moats are so crucial. Warren Buffett didn't choose the castle metaphor by accident – like medieval fortresses surrounded by water-filled trenches, the best businesses build multiple layers of protection against competitive assault.

That's why the moat must be both wide and deep. As Buffett famously put it: "We want to throw crocodiles and sharks and everything else – gators, I guess – into the moat to keep away competitors." Multiple layers of protection that make competitors think twice before even trying.

A well-fortified moat ensures that competing leads to unsatisfactory returns and, more importantly, the fear of failure. It slows – or even stops – that inevitable progression through the four phases.

But moats are never static – they're either widening or narrowing. Robert Vinall, in his 2016 co-investor letter, captures this perfectly: "Widening the moat is more important than the width of the moat. Everyone is attacking a company's moat, so the question is not how wide it is, but whether it is widening at a faster pace than competitors are filling it up."

The best companies have executives who focus on expanding their moats, not just delivering short-term results. These businesses compound wealth over the long term because they resist the gravitational pull toward average returns.

This obsession with durability shows up repeatedly in Buffett's writings. In his 2007 letter, he wrote: "A truly great business must have an enduring 'moat' that protects excellent returns on invested capital. The dynamics of capitalism guarantee that competitors will repeatedly assault any business 'castle' that is earning high returns… Our criterion of 'enduring' causes us to rule out companies in industries prone to rapid and continuous change."[3]

The lesson is clear: "The key to investing is not assessing how much an industry is going to affect society, or how much it will grow, but rather determining the competitive advantage of any given company and, above all, the durability of that advantage." Businesses with expanding, sustainable moats reward investors over the long run.

But what exactly creates a wide, durable moat? What keeps competition at bay and allows a company to generate strong returns year after year? What specific defenses can keep a business in the Innovation or Fading Returns phase instead of sliding inevitably toward Maturity and Decline?

Over my 17 years of investing, I've learned to look for six specific types of moats. Some will seem obvious once I point them out. Others might surprise you. But here's what matters: once you know what to look for, you'll start seeing these patterns everywhere – in the brands you buy, the services you use, even in the companies that frustrate you but somehow keep your business.

THE SIX SOURCES OF COMPETITIVE ADVANTAGE

There are six main sources of competitive advantage. Think of them as the crocodiles and gators in your moat, protecting your business from marauding competitors. These are:

1. Branding
2. Network effects
3. Switching costs
4. Cost advantages
5. Distribution networks, and
6. Regulatory protection

Let's dive into each one.

1. BRANDING

Ask any great marketer, and they'll tell you something many investors struggle to grasp. Most consumers buy on emotion, then justify with logic. Let me repeat this because it matters: we buy with our hearts and justify with our heads.

Take Starbucks – a company everyone knows. When Howard Schultz first pitched the idea of selling high-priced specialty coffee in the 1980s, investors thought he was insane. Coffee is a commodity. Why would anyone pay more when they can make it at home? Of the 242 investors Schultz approached, 217 rejected him.[4]

Today, Starbucks has over 41,000 stores worldwide, raking in over $36 billion in sales. That's a lot of expensive coffee.

But is Starbucks coffee truly worth the price? Ask any coffee connoisseur, and they'll likely tell you it's over-roasted, with better alternatives available at similar prices, and certainly cheaper options too. So what's the X factor? How has Starbucks managed to charge premium prices for a commodity and dominate the market?

It boils down to two powerful branding effects: status signaling and reducing search costs.

Status signaling

One key driver of Starbucks' success is its ability to leverage status signaling. When you buy a cup of Starbucks, you're not just buying coffee. You're buying an image. The iconic green mermaid logo signals sophistication. More importantly, it implies you have disposable income. Carrying that cup says you belong to a certain social group, the one that has "made it."

This is the same reason you see Ferraris in cities like New York or Singapore, where speed limits and traffic make it impossible to unleash the car's full power. A Toyota would work just fine. But a Ferrari isn't just transportation. It's a status symbol that screams "Look at me, I've made it!"

Reducing search costs: A shortcut to trust

Beyond status signaling, Starbucks excels at reducing search costs – the time, effort, and mental energy consumers spend making decisions.

Here's a perfect example. In *Game of Thrones* season 8, episode 4, eagle-eyed viewers spotted a modern coffee cup sitting on a medieval feast table. The internet immediately erupted. Without missing a beat, everyone assumed it was a Starbucks cup. Social media and major news outlets ran wild with the story, giving Starbucks massive free publicity.

HBO later clarified that the cup wasn't from Starbucks at all. But the fact that people instantly associated a random coffee cup with Starbucks shows how deep their mindshare runs. It's so engrained in our consciousness that even a generic cup conjures up the green mermaid.

This familiarity gives Starbucks a significant edge. Customers know what to expect – quality, service, ambiance. Whether you're in an unfamiliar neighborhood needing a quick coffee fix or looking for a place to meet friends, that familiar brand provides comfort.

Coca-Cola dominates for the same reason. It's not necessarily about taste (although die-hard fans will disagree). It's about trust and familiarity. When you see that iconic red label, you know exactly what you're getting. No surprises. No cognitive effort needed. Brands that reduce search costs have a clear advantage because consumers gravitate toward the familiar in a world full of choices.

Brands that capture hearts, capture wallets

See's Candies is one of Warren Buffett's all-time favorite investments. He frequently praises the company while munching on its peanut brittle during Berkshire Hathaway's annual meetings. But Buffett's fondness goes beyond the sweet treats – it's a lesson on how great brands create pricing power.

Speaking to students at the University of Florida in 1998, Buffett explained what makes See's so special.

"Every person in California has something in mind about See's Candies, and overwhelmingly it was favorable. They had taken a box on Valentine's Day to some girl, and she had kissed him. If she slapped him, we would have no business. As long as she kisses him, that's what we want in their minds. See's Candies means getting kissed. If we can get that in the minds of people, we can raise prices."

The joy of giving and receiving See's chocolates is about more than candy. It's about shared experiences and feelings of love and appreciation. Brands that evoke such warm feelings can raise prices without losing customers. The brand becomes more than just a product – that's where pricing power lies.

Disneyland Hotels are another example of a brand that taps into emotion. Hotels are typically commodities, with prices fluctuating based on the economy, business travel, and holidays. Yet Disneyland Hotels defy this norm. As I'm writing this in mid-2025, they're fully booked months in advance. Junior suites cost over $1,000 a night. Signature suites like the Mickey Mouse Suite go for more than $5,000 a night.

Disneyland Hotels can charge these astronomical prices for a simple reason. The rational mind might point to early park entry and convenience. But that doesn't justify a $5,000 price tag.

The real answer is simpler. Disneyland brings smiles and laughter to children's faces (and let's be honest, adults too). Visitors call it "The Happiest Place on Earth," where dreams come true. Companies that capture a piece of your heart will get a piece of your wallet too. This emotional magic allows Disneyland to command premium prices, no questions asked.

If a brand can't price, the moat's on thin ice

Here's a common mistake investors make: assuming that a well-known brand automatically has an economic moat. In reality, a brand only becomes a true moat if it enhances customer loyalty and provides pricing power. Without the ability to charge a premium without losing market share, a brand doesn't have an economic moat.

Consider consumer electronics. Samsung, LG, and Sony are household names. Yet they can't charge significantly more than competitors without sacrificing market share. Ironically, when it comes to electronics, most consumers suddenly become rational, basing decisions on specs, reviews, and value for money.

Apple tells a different story. Apple's brand loyalty is so strong that fans camp out overnight just to be first to get the latest iPhone. Unlike other brands, Apple has created an emotional experience around its products. Owning an iPhone or MacBook isn't just about function. It's about status, identity, and belonging to an exclusive group.

Apple's magic lies in its attention to detail. Every aspect is carefully designed, from launch events to product aesthetics to the unboxing ritual. Apple even holds a patent on its iPhone packaging to ensure the perfect amount of friction between the box's cover and base. This extends the moment of anticipation as the lid slowly drops.

While Android users compare specs like dual-SIM capability, 50MP cameras, or storage, Apple users often think simply, "I want this because it's an iPhone." Apple's ability to foster this emotional attachment allows it to charge premium prices and maintain its moat.

Some argue that Google's brand is so powerful it became a verb. People say "I'll Google it" instead of "search the web." But that's not necessarily a moat indicator.

Here's a classic example from every statistics class. Ice cream sales and drowning incidents are statistically correlated – when ice cream sales go up, so do drownings. But ice cream doesn't cause drowning (if yours does, you're eating the wrong ice cream). The real factor is warm weather, which drives both ice cream cravings and swimming.

Just because two things happen together doesn't mean one caused the other. Google being a verb would be meaningless if it didn't provide the best search results.

History proves this point. All these brands became the default term for their entire product category. People said "Xerox this" instead of "photocopy this." Polaroid meant any instant photo. Tupperware meant any plastic container. Where are they now? Xerox's revenue has more than halved since 2011. Polaroid filed for bankruptcy in 2001. Tupperware filed for bankruptcy in 2024.

When your brand name replaces the product category in everyday speech, it seems like ultimate success. But without pricing power, even this level of dominance means nothing.

Ultimately, a brand only contributes to a company's moat if it enables premium pricing relative to competition without losing market share.

When brands lose their shine

Even the most iconic brands can lose their luster if they're not carefully nurtured.

Warren Buffett's 1999 letter to shareholders shared a powerful lesson on this. He mentioned that GEICO could spend as little as $50 million annually on advertising and maintain its current business. Instead, Tony Nicely, GEICO's CEO at the time, was keeping his foot on the advertising pedal. Buffett's foot was on Tony's. They committed to spend $300–350 million in 2000 on advertising and related expenses.

The goal? Achieve significant growth and "extend and solidify the promise of the GEICO brand in the minds of Americans."

Buffett understood something crucial. Cutting advertising might boost short-term profits, but it would undermine long-term brand strength. Cementing GEICO's brand in consumers' minds was critical for maximizing shareholder value over the long haul.

Not all companies follow this approach. After Howard Schultz stepped down as Starbucks CEO in 2000, the coffee giant lost its way. It became too focused on expansion and short-term profits at the expense of customer experience.

To cut costs, Starbucks began shipping pre-ground coffee instead of whole beans, sacrificing freshness. Baristas started steaming milk in bulk and reheating it rather than preparing each cup individually. The company introduced automated espresso machines. Sure, they improved efficiency. But they destroyed the handcrafted nature that made Starbucks special.

The profit obsession didn't stop there. Stores began selling CDs, books, and DVDs, straying from their core mission. The final blow came when Schultz visited a store to find piles of stuffed animals for sale. When he questioned the manager, the response was simple: "They have high profit margins."

The consequences were stark. Starbucks' stock plummeted 42%. Many stores struggled. Some cannibalized sales from neighboring Starbucks locations. The relentless pursuit of growth and profits had eroded the very customer experience that fueled initial success.

On February 14, 2007, Schultz sent a now-famous email titled "The

Commoditization of the Starbucks Experience." He lamented how the brand had lost its soul. The company needed swift action to salvage its identity before it was too late.

Starbucks had become a soulless corporation motivated by the bottom line rather than quality and experience. This massive moat erosion allowed competitors to chip away at market share.

By January 2008, Schultz returned as CEO to save Starbucks. He immediately closed 660 stores – about 4% of the chain – resulting in $267 million in restructuring costs. In a bold move, he temporarily closed all 7,100 US outlets for a day, costing $6 million, to retrain baristas on pouring the perfect espresso. His mission was clear: bring back the authentic Starbucks experience and restore brand integrity. The turnaround wasn't quick or easy. Customer surveys didn't show renewed engagement and loyalty until the end of 2009.

The Starbucks story serves as a potent reminder: brand stewardship isn't a one-time effort but an ongoing commitment. Even the most powerful brands can falter if they lose sight of core values and customer experience.

What I look for in brand moats: Can they raise prices without losing customers? Do customers feel emotional attachment beyond rational benefits? Is management investing to strengthen the brand even when profits are strong? These signals tell me whether the moat is widening or narrowing.

2. NETWORK EFFECTS: THE POWER OF CONNECTIONS

Not all moats rely on capturing hearts or minds. Some businesses become irreplaceable simply because everyone else is already there. The value isn't in the product itself but in the connections it enables.

The telephone is a classic example of network effects in action. AT&T figured this out back in 1908, writing in their annual report: "A telephone – without a connection at the other end of the line – is not even a toy. It's one of the most useless things in the world. Its value depends on the connection with the other telephone – and increases with the number of connections."

They'd discovered something fundamental about certain businesses.

Every additional user makes the service more valuable for everyone else. Once these networks reach critical mass, they become incredibly difficult to displace. New competitors face a brutal reality. Why would anyone switch to a smaller, less valuable network?

Let's break down the different types of network effects that create enduring value.

Direct network effects: More users, more value

Direct network effects occur when the value of a product increases directly with the number of users. This is especially true of social networks like Facebook, Instagram, and LinkedIn. The more users join, the more creators are incentivized to produce quality content. This in turn attracts and retains even more users. It's a flywheel effect where each new user amplifies the network's value for everyone.

Because their strength lies in numbers, social networks often offer their services for free. They monetize by serving targeted ads to users who may be interested in the products or services.

These ad revenues are then reinvested back into the platform. They improve the ecosystem by ensuring low latency, evolving algorithms to adapt to content consumption preferences, regulating content, and adding new functionalities. All this ensures it remains the platform of choice.

Constant improvement and adaptation to changing consumer behavior are essential. Without them, network effects can unravel surprisingly quickly.

But direct connections between users aren't the only way to build network effects.

Indirect network effects: Value through complements

Indirect network effects work differently. The product itself doesn't get better with more users. Instead, it gets better when more stuff is built for it.

Think about gaming consoles. PlayStation doesn't become a better machine when more people buy it. But when millions own PlayStations, game developers rush to create titles for it. More games mean more reasons to buy a PlayStation. Which attracts more developers. Round and round it goes.

Try launching a new console today. Even with superior hardware, you face an uphill battle. Gamers won't buy a console with no games. Developers won't make games for a console with no gamers. Classic chicken-and-egg problem.

Apple plays this game masterfully. Millions of iPhone users attract app developers. More apps make the iPhone more useful. Which sells more iPhones. Which attracts more developers. The cycle reinforces itself endlessly.

Two-sided network effects: Everyone needs everyone

The next type of network effect involves marketplaces. These businesses need both buyers and sellers on their platform – and neither side will show up without the other.

Take Booking.com. When you're booking a hotel online, you gravitate toward platforms with the most options. Hotels know this, so they list where the travelers are. Each side draws in the other.

Booking Holdings (the parent company behind Booking.com, Priceline, and Agoda) cracked this puzzle brilliantly. Europe's hotel scene is fragmented – thousands of small, family-run hotels. These small hotels couldn't afford to build their own booking platforms or marketing campaigns. Travelers wanted one place to compare all their options. Booking.com became the bridge between them.

The result is powerful. Travelers naturally check Booking.com because it has the most comprehensive listings. Hotels – even massive chains – have to list there because that's where millions of travelers look. The platform becomes a tollgate that's hard to avoid.

Visa mastered the same game. You carry a Visa because every merchant accepts it. Merchants accept Visa despite the fees because every customer carries one. Both sides are locked in. Try launching a new payment network today. Even if you can get regulatory approval to start a payment network, you still face the chicken-and-egg problem. Merchants won't accept it without customers. Customers won't carry it without merchants. You're stuck.

The beautiful part is how Visa monetizes this position. They take a cut of every transaction just for maintaining this network. In 2024, Visa processed $13.2 trillion in payment volume, generating $35.9 billion in revenue – a take rate of roughly 0.27%.[5] No inventory, no credit risk, no customer service for consumers. When someone defaults on their credit card, that's the bank's problem, not Visa's. They've built a tollgate on global commerce. Every swipe makes them money, which they pour back into security, convenience features, and rewards programs that keep both sides happy.

When you look at these examples – Facebook, PlayStation, Booking.com, Visa – you notice a pattern. The winners take almost everything.

Network dominance: Winner-takes-most dynamics

The difficulty of competitive entry creates winner-takes-most dynamics. Network-based businesses tend to create natural monopolies and oligopolies. This usually results in juicy profit margins and majority market share capture.

This makes sense. If the value of a product or service increases with the number of users, the most valuable network will be the one that attracts the most users. This creates a virtuous cycle that squeezes out smaller networks while increasing the size of dominant networks. As dominant networks grow, they also become stronger. This makes network effects a powerful competitive advantage.

This *winner-takes-most* dynamic highlights the critical importance of establishing a strong network early on. Once established, it's incredibly challenging to unseat.

How the internet supercharged network effects

The winner-takes-most reality has only intensified with the internet. Networks can now consolidate around the leader faster than ever before.

The internet has supercharged network effects by eliminating much of the friction of onboarding users and businesses. Take Meta, for instance. Facebook and Instagram attract millions of users without requiring a dedicated team to sign them up. There's no additional cost for each new user. Businesses can independently run ads on these platforms without direct assistance from Meta's staff.

Thanks to the internet, we're seeing more network-driven businesses on an unprecedented scale. YouTube connects creators and viewers. Amazon links buyers and sellers. LinkedIn matches professionals and recruiters. Uber links riders with drivers. Booking Holdings connects travelers with accommodations.

For a new competitor to break into such markets, they have two choices. Try to replicate the existing network's value – which is extraordinarily difficult since users have no reason to switch to a smaller network. Or find a completely different angle, a niche the incumbent isn't serving. But even that requires something special to work.

David versus Goliath: How TikTok challenged Meta's network

TikTok took the different angle approach and turned it into one of the most spectacular David versus Goliath stories in tech history.

The platform for short videos officially landed in the United States in 2018. This impressive growth occurred despite Meta's near-dominance in social media, with close to three billion monthly active users in 2020. Yet TikTok became the most downloaded app in the world in 2020, 2021, and 2022. It grew its user base from 55 million in January 2018 to over 1 billion by September 2021.[6]

Meta's castle was under siege. CEO Mark Zuckerberg acknowledged in the company's Q4 2021 earnings call that TikTok was growing very quickly. It was crucial for Meta to double down on short-form video content with Reels to fend off the rising star.

The threat was clear. TikTok's rapid growth and engaging format posed a serious challenge to Meta's dominance. It could potentially lure away users and erode its network effect. Investors worried about Meta's network unraveling in the face of this formidable competitor. When Meta's revenue growth slowed significantly, the company's share price plummeted by 80% between late 2021 and late 2022.

So how exactly did TikTok penetrate the market despite Meta's dominance?

First, they found their niche – short-form, engaging videos. This format was underserved by existing platforms. Instagram focused on posts and stories. YouTube dominated long-form content. TikTok filled the gap in between. If their value proposition had been simply connecting people, similar to Facebook, they would likely have failed. That need was already well-served. This novelty attracted a younger audience and created a unique content space.

Second, TikTok's rapid success came from its ingenious "For You" page algorithm. It excelled at recommending relevant and engaging content to users without relying on their existing social connections. This greatly reduced friction in content consumption. New users didn't have to rely on a pre-existing network. They could be entertained without curating which content creators to follow.

Third, TikTok provided content creators with extremely user-friendly creative tools. This made it easy for anyone to create and share video content. It democratized content creation and fueled rapid growth of user-generated content.

Fourth, TikTok had deep pockets, backed by its parent company ByteDance. They spent an estimated $3 million per day on user acquisition marketing in the US alone. That totaled around $1 billion in advertising expenditures throughout 2018.

It required herculean effort and big investment, but TikTok demonstrated something important. While network effects are mighty, they're not impossible to overcome. The key is figuring out how to acquire users and lower friction for both sides of the network. Users and creators both need reasons to join. By combining a differentiated product, frictionless user experience, and aggressive marketing, TikTok successfully penetrated the market despite Meta's formidable stronghold.

Meta's counterattack to defend its castle

Meta wasn't sitting idle, waiting for TikTok to dismantle its moat. Recognizing the changing landscape, it introduced Reels and invested heavily in artificial intelligence.

During this period, margins decreased. Meta postponed monetizing Reels with advertising while fine-tuning the product and pushing users to adopt it. This cannibalized its lucrative Stories and feed advertising revenue.

On the creator side, Facebook and Instagram prioritized their algorithms to push out Reels. They encouraged creators to produce more short videos. This strategic pivot initially impacted profitability. But it demonstrated Meta's commitment to adapting to evolving user preferences and preserving its long-term network effect.

Eventually, Meta's efforts paid off. Revenue growth accelerated, profitability regained ground, and the stock reached new all-time highs.

Maintaining the edge with network effects

Network effects create formidable barriers to entry. They often result in a winner-takes-most dynamic where leading companies enjoy substantial market share and enviable profitability.

However, even the most entrenched players can be unseated by new technologies, shifting consumer preferences, and bold challengers. I look for management teams who demonstrate commitment to continuous innovation and adaptability. This ensures the long-term resilience of their competitive advantage.

3. SWITCHING COSTS: THE PAIN OF CHANGE

Not all moats rely on the power of the crowd. Some businesses keep customers because switching is incredibly painful – whether they planned it that way or not. The product might frustrate you daily, but the thought of changing is even worse.

Few things are as universally dreaded as dealing with legacy banks. It's riddled with inefficiencies, endless forms, and long customer service wait times. Resolving an issue often means hours on hold or waiting at a branch. It can feel like a journey through red tape.

Although there are alternatives ranging from traditional banks to digital banks, most legacy banks continue to maintain their customer base and profitability despite terrible service. This is partly due to the overwhelming pain of changing banks. The forms, the adjustments to direct deposits and bill payments, the potential disruptions to our busy lives. The prospect of transferring accounts, updating payment information, and navigating potential disruptions creates formidable inertia. It keeps customers tethered to their existing banks.

Unless the inconvenience with a bank becomes unbearable, most of us would rather put up with the inefficiencies of our current bank.

This pain is essentially switching costs. When a product or service is so ingrained in our lives that switching feels like more trouble than it's worth, companies can raise prices or lag on innovation without losing customers.

That's a competitive advantage.

I look for businesses where switching costs create customer lock-in. The best have multiple layers – financial costs, time investment, learning curves, and operational disruption. When I see 95%+ retention rates despite average products, that's switching costs at work.

Let's dive deeper into the different ways companies create this stickiness.

A steep learning curve

It may seem counterintuitive, but sometimes a product that's difficult to master can actually work in a company's favor. You might wonder how a company can get away with making its products challenging to use.

Adobe provides a compelling example. The company actively supports educational institutions by providing students and educators with free or heavily discounted access to its software. But they don't stop there. Recognizing that mastering these tools can be a significant undertaking, Adobe collaborates with educators to develop course materials and resources that incorporate its software. This ensures students become proficient in industry-standard tools like Photoshop, Illustrator, and After Effects. It increases their familiarity and reliance on these products as they enter the workforce.

Adobe also offers certification programs that validate students' skills in using its software. These certifications enhance resumes and make students more attractive to potential employers. Employers often prefer candidates familiar with Adobe's tools. This gives students extra motivation to master Adobe's software despite the steep learning curve.

Adobe's products are not easy to use. They require months to master. But once creative professionals learn them, they're unlikely to switch unless a significantly better product comes along. By investing in education and fostering a generation of Adobe-proficient professionals, the company creates a pipeline of sticky customers with high switching costs. This ensures a steady stream of revenue for years to come. It allows Adobe to continue raising prices routinely and earn extremely high margins with low customer churn.

Sometimes the switching cost isn't about learning new skills. It's about breaking deeply ingrained habits.

The chains of habit: When familiarity breeds loyalty

I've been an Android user my whole life. Switching between brands – Samsung, LG, Pixel – has never been a big deal for me. After all, they all run on Android, so there's really not much friction.

But iPhone users? They're a different breed. If you've ever met an iPhone user, you know they're fiercely loyal to the brand. It's almost to the point where the mere thought of switching to Android feels like betrayal. iPhone users sometimes even tease Android users, calling them "peasants." This happens despite the fact that some Android phones now cost more than an iPhone. What fuels this deep-seated loyalty?

There are several reasons behind it. A major one is how accustomed iPhone users have become to Apple's iOS. Apple has cleverly cultivated this "stickiness" by creating a closed ecosystem that discourages switching and fosters exclusivity. Many iPhone users have invested heavily in the Apple ecosystem. They've purchased apps, accessories, and services like iCloud or Apple Music that often aren't transferable to Android devices.

For a long time, even seemingly minor details like charging cables reinforced this lock-in. Apple insisted on using the Lightning cable, incompatible with the USB-C cables used by most Android phones.

Beyond that, cognitive biases play a crucial role. Social identity theory suggests that we derive part of our self-image from the groups we belong to. For many, being an iPhone user has become part of their identity. Switching away from Apple could feel like losing a part of themselves.

Consistency bias leads people to stick to their publicly stated positions, even when presented with contradictory evidence. Since many iPhone users have proclaimed the iPhone's superiority, they're more likely to stick with it. They want to appear consistent and avoid the discomfort of cognitive dissonance.

But the most inescapable switching costs come when a product becomes the backbone of your operations.

Tight integration into a business process

SAP is a leading provider of enterprise resource planning (ERP) software. It's integral to running some of the world's largest businesses and governments. These systems integrate all aspects of a company's operations, including finance, human resources, manufacturing, and sales. The company claims that 77% of the world's transaction revenue touches an SAP system.[7]

To see how customers really feel about a product, we can look at the Customer Net Promoter Score (NPS). This widely used metric measures customer loyalty and satisfaction based on their likelihood to recommend a company, product, or service to others. The score goes to a maximum of 100 points. The higher it is, the more likely existing customers are to recommend your product to others.

In 2019, SAP reported an NPS of -6. Yes, you read that right. It came in negative. This means customers not only won't recommend SAP to others, they actively want to leave. It's perhaps why some refer to SAP as "Suffer and Pay."

But here's the thing. Revenue increased 11.5% to a new all-time high of

€27.6 billion that year. That's wild. These software contracts don't come cheap, easily costing millions of dollars for mid to large enterprises. Yet unsatisfied customers found it hard to switch products.

Basically, SAP's software solutions are so deeply integrated into organizations' operational processes that switching becomes nearly impossible. Once implemented, these systems become critical to daily operations. Any transition to a different platform would be highly disruptive. Changing ERP systems is like ripping out the plumbing of a business. It's not only complex but also risky for ongoing operations.

Of course, not all switching costs are about operational necessity. Some companies manufacture them through clever incentive structures.

Loyalty program costs

Loyalty programs are an effective way to retain customers by rewarding their continued patronage. Starbucks, for example, has reported that a Rewards member spends two to three times more than a non-member. Remember that humans do not make all decisions rationally. When a customer starts down the slippery slope of points collection, they become reluctant to switch to a competitor. This happens even when a potential new provider offers better prices or services.

Loyalty programs, while seemingly designed to reward customers, cleverly increase switching costs. They make it painful for customers to abandon their accumulated benefits.

The most potent loyalty programs go beyond simple points collection where customers redeem free gifts after accumulating points: they offer tiered programs. Customers who spend the most are given a higher tier with generous benefits. It creates a strong lock-in effect on customers in the highest tier. It insulates them from competition as they strive to maintain their status and continue enjoying the perks.

Because of loss aversion, customers are motivated to maintain their status and avoid losing the perks they've worked hard to achieve.

Take the Hilton Honors program, which has multiple tiers from Silver up to Diamond and beyond. To reach the higher tiers, you might need 50 or more nights per year. For most people, this means choosing Hilton hotels for almost every vacation or work trip.

It isn't easy to reach that level. But once you've reached this oasis, you get free room upgrades to suites where available, executive lounge access, free continental breakfast, extra bonus points on stays, and more. It takes effort, money, and time to reach this level. Once customers taste these perks, they're usually reluctant to let go.

Airlines employ similar tactics through frequent flier programs. They reward top spenders with free upgrades, priority check-in, and access to exclusive lounges. These programs turn loyalty into a habit, making customers stick around, often for life.

Then there are switching costs created by sheer financial commitment.

Sunk costs: Heavy initial investment

We can see this playing out in the medical industry. Take Intuitive Surgical, the company behind the da Vinci Surgical System. This sophisticated robotic platform enhances a surgeon's capabilities in minimally invasive procedures.

The surgeon operates from a console, manipulating robotic arms with EndoWrist instruments. These instruments offer superior dexterity and range of motion compared to the human hand. The technology can even balance out a surgeon's natural tremor. This translates to smaller incisions, reduced trauma to surrounding tissues, and faster patient recovery.

Interestingly, the company doesn't make most of its money from selling these machines. It's the consumables – the accessories and instruments – that drive revenue.

Recurring revenue: The razor and blade model

These instruments and accessories include the EndoWrist attachments, which act as the surgeon's robotic hands. Each attachment is used for 10 to 18 surgeries before needing replacement. Accessories also include staplers, vessel sealers, sterile drapes, sensors, lights, and cameras. These recurring add-ons allow the company to continue making revenue long after the sale of a da Vinci system. In fact, Intuitive Surgical's recurring revenue accounted for 84% of its total revenue in 2024.[8]

This is a classic razor-and-blade business model. The company earns recurring revenue after it has sold the da Vinci system. The system itself costs north of $2 million. Hospitals that have invested this significant sum want to ensure these systems are well-utilized. Surgeons receive extensive training early on in how to operate these machines.

These two factors make switching to a competitor's system extremely difficult. As long as Intuitive Surgical incrementally improves its instruments, hospitals and surgeons have little reason to switch.

When trapped customers become a time bomb

Switching costs are extremely powerful. But there's a potential downside. If a business thrives solely because the pain of changing is greater than the pain of using the product, it might be extracting more value than it provides. In essence, it's punishing customers for their initial trust. And in the long run, it's a dangerous game.

If customers hate a product or service but are trapped by switching costs, the business becomes a sitting duck. Eventually, the bill comes due. Competitors may find ways to overcome these switching costs, and dissatisfied customers will flee in droves.

Cable television is the perfect example. For decades, cable companies had customers locked in through bundled contracts, installation hassles, and a simple reality: there was no alternative. If you wanted live sports or HBO, you paid whatever they charged.

Because customers couldn't leave, cable companies stopped trying. Bills crept up every year with unexplained fees. Customer service became notoriously awful. The product barely improved while prices doubled. Why innovate when your customers are trapped?

Then Netflix, YouTube, and streaming arrived. Suddenly there was a way out – and the exodus was swift. Customers weren't loyal. They were hostages. And hostages escape when opportunities present themselves.

For this reason, I avoid investing in companies with products or services that customers dislike but are forced to use due to high switching costs. These businesses are vulnerable in the long run.

However, when a product genuinely adds value and customers are happy to stay within the ecosystem, switching costs become a formidable moat. Businesses are constantly striving to outperform each other and capture market share. Here, switching costs buy you time. Not only to innovate but also to stay ahead while capturing healthy profits.

4. COST ADVANTAGES

While some moats trap customers through switching costs or network effects, others win through a more straightforward advantage. Some companies are able to profitably sell at prices that would bankrupt their competitors.

Jeff Bezos has remarked that he has often been asked what would change in the next decade. His response flipped the question. "I almost never get the question: What's not going to change in the next 10 years? And I submit to you that that second question is actually the more important of the two – because you can build a business strategy around the things that are stable in time."

In retail, he knew customers would always want low prices. As he put it, "It's impossible to imagine a future 10 years from now where a customer comes up and says, Jeff I love Amazon; I just wish the prices were a little higher."

When you know something won't change, you can bet the company on it. And that's exactly what Amazon did. They built their entire strategy around delivering the lowest prices profitably.

This creates a different kind of moat. Companies that can consistently offer better value without compromising their own profitability hold a lasting edge. They don't trap customers – they make them never want to leave.

Amazon's flywheel: How scaled economics shared creates dominance

When most companies get bigger, they keep the savings. Their costs drop with scale, but they pocket the difference. Savings go straight to their profit margins. Shareholders rejoice.

But Nick Sleep, who ran the Nomad Investment Partnership, noticed something different about Amazon. They were taking those savings and giving them back to customers through lower prices. He called this "scaled economics shared."

It sounds crazy. Why give away your profit advantage? But here's the genius – lower prices bring more customers, more customers bring more scale, more scale brings lower costs, which enables even lower prices. Bezos famously sketched this on a napkin:

1. Lower prices lead to increased customer visits.
2. Increased customer visits lead to higher sales volume.
3. Higher sales volume leads to a lower cost structure per unit.
4. Lower cost structure enables further price reductions.

Bezos's diagram shows Amazon's virtuous cycle. Each element feeds the next: lower prices > more customers > more sellers > greater selection > better customer experience > more traffic > back to lower prices. Note that Bezos did not include an arrow showing profits leaving the cycle – it's a closed loop.

Each turn of this wheel makes Amazon harder to compete with. While traditional retailers were protecting their margins, Amazon was building an unstoppable flywheel.

Typically, as a company scales and matures, growth slows down. This often happens because the company becomes less agile than its younger competitors. Those competitors are attracted by the older company's high profit margins. However, scaled economics shared turns size, normally an anchor to growth, into an asset.

Nick Sleep observed in his letters to his fund's shareholders that e-commerce companies have a capital advantage over traditional brick-and-mortar businesses. However, the Achilles' heel for internet companies is their operating costs, which are particularly high in the early stages. By adopting scaled economics shared, Amazon quickly ramped up revenue. They drove down operating costs as a percentage of revenue until they were even lower than those of established players like Walmart.

The diagram below shows how Amazon's operating costs as a percentage of revenue dropped below competition – including established players like Walmart – by pursuing scaled economics shared. While traditional retailers kept their cost savings as profit, Amazon passed them to customers as lower prices, fueling further growth.

Figure 3.1: How Amazon's operating costs dropped below traditional retailers

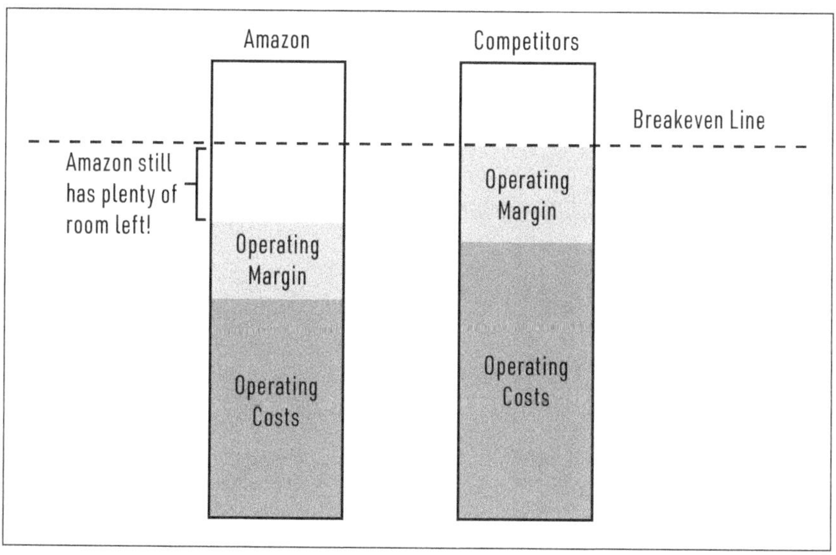

Source: Created by Thomas Chua.

Let's pause for a moment. When a company can sustainably price its competitors out of the market while remaining profitable, it's hard to imagine a more powerful moat. After all, who doesn't love low prices? And by turning size into strength, Amazon has built a cost advantage that not only attracts customers but makes it incredibly difficult for rivals to break through.

Netflix: The streaming flywheel

Netflix shows how cost advantages work differently in the digital age. They don't compete on being the cheapest option – in fact, their monthly subscription often costs more than competitors. But by spreading massive content costs across 260 million subscribers, they deliver unbeatable value per hour of entertainment.

Let me show you how this model becomes stronger with every new subscriber.

The chart below illustrates Netflix's massive content investment over the years. Between 2016 and 2023, Netflix invested roughly $118 billion in content.[9] They were all-in on building the world's best content library.

Figure 3.2: Netflix's $118 billion content investment (2016–2023)

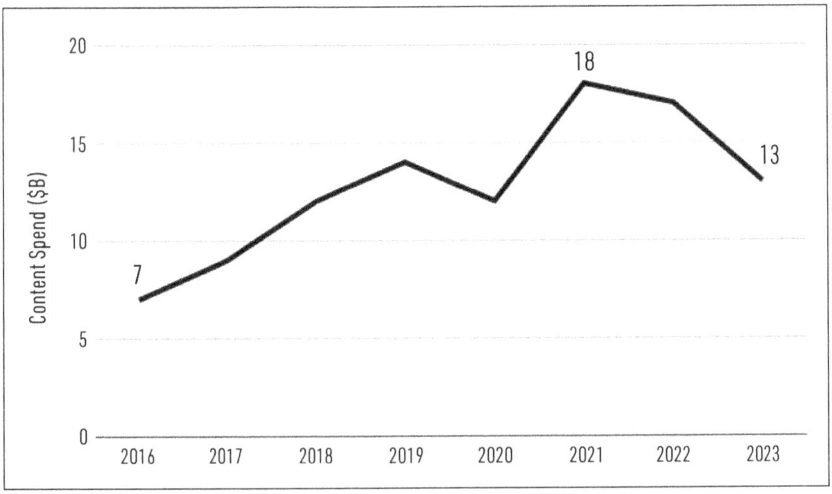

Source: Data from Netflix's annual report, chart created by Thomas Chua.

As you can see from the spending pattern above, content investment briefly dipped in 2020 due to Covid-19 and again in 2023 amid the Hollywood writers' strike, but Netflix's focus on compelling, original content has remained steadfast.

Here's the key insight: Much of this spending is a fixed cost. Whether Netflix serves 100 million or 200 million subscribers, the expense of creating hits like *Squid Game* or *The Queen's Gambit* doesn't change. Every additional subscriber is almost pure profit on content that's already made.

This creates extraordinary economics. The average user watches 31.5 hours monthly. At $17.99/month, that's just $0.57 per hour of entertainment. Compare that to a $15 movie ticket for two hours ($7.50/hour) or traditional cable at $100+ monthly. No competitor can match this value proposition while remaining profitable.

The transformation has been remarkable. In 2008, Netflix had fewer than nine million subscribers. After introducing streaming directly to TVs and launching a streaming-only service in 2010, growth exploded. By 2023, they'd amassed 260 million paid subscribers – the largest streaming service worldwide.

This scale creates powerful operating leverage. In 2016, Netflix earned $93 per user while spending $77 on content – a margin of just $16. By 2023, revenue per user had climbed to $129 while content cost per user dropped to $50 – a margin of $79. As shown in Figure 3.3, where the shaded area between these lines represents this expanding cushion.

Figure 3.3: Netflix's operating leverage (2016–2023)

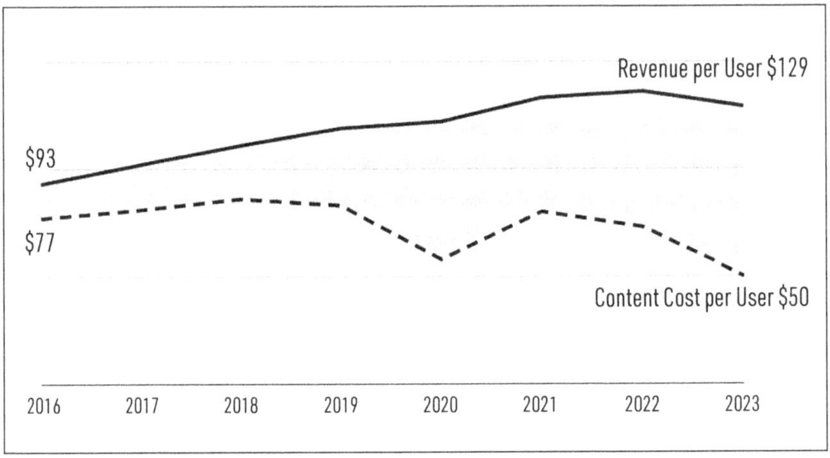

Source: Author's calculation.

This is fixed-cost leverage at work. Total content spending nearly doubled from $7 billion to $13 billion, yet cost *per user* fell because 260 million subscribers now share that expense. Revenue growth from new members and price increases flows almost directly to profit. This reflects the growing value subscribers find in its platform and its ability to support periodic price increases.

With 260 million subscribers sharing fixed content costs, the financial results speak for themselves. As Figure 3.4 shows, operating margins expanded from just 4% in 2016 to 21% by 2023.

Figure 3.4: Netflix's margin expansion (2016–2023)

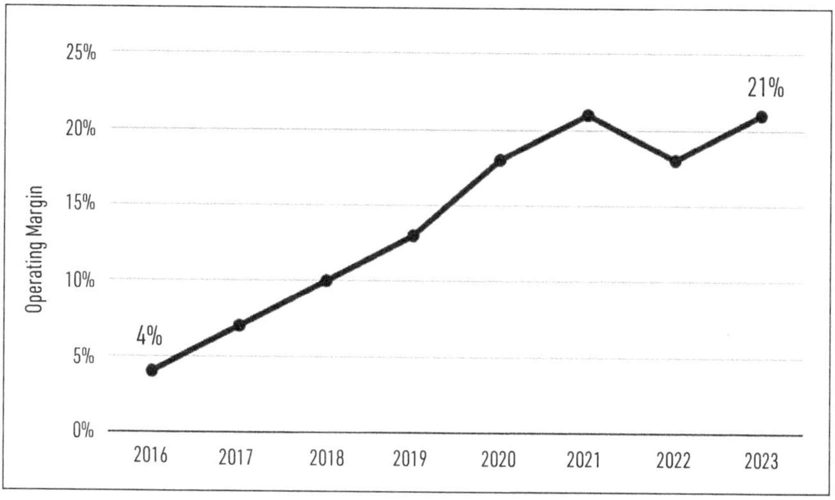

Source: Author's calculation.

Notice the dip in 2022 – margins pulled back to 18% amid post-Covid normalization and cost pressures. But Netflix recovered quickly, demonstrating the resilience of the model. This is fixed-cost leverage at work: more subscribers without proportionally more costs equals expanding margins.

The beauty of this model is its self-reinforcing nature. More subscribers fund more content, which attracts more subscribers, which justifies even more content investment. Unlike traditional TV networks that hit ceiling constraints, Netflix's content library can grow indefinitely. Every dollar spent on content becomes more efficient as it's amortized across an ever-larger base.

This is scaled economics at its finest – but instead of sharing the benefits through lower prices like Amazon, Netflix shares it through more value. Subscribers get an ever-expanding library of content for roughly the same price. Competitors trying to match Netflix's content spending would burn through cash, while Netflix prints money. That's a cost advantage that compounds with scale.

5. DISTRIBUTION POWER: GREAT PRODUCT AIN'T ENOUGH

There's a popular saying in venture capital. "First-time founders are obsessed with product. Second-time founders are obsessed with distribution."

You can have the best product in the world, but if no one can access it, it's irrelevant. Building a great product is essential. But great distribution is often what separates the winners from everyone else.

Gillette: Ruling the razor game – until the internet

Gillette entered the razor business in 1903 with the patented double-edged safety razor. It revolutionized shaving. Even after the patent expired in 1921, Gillette remained king. This wasn't because of patents anymore. It was because of distribution dominance.

Gillette made its products impossible to miss. They were in every supermarket, pharmacy, and big-box store. They paid for prime shelf space at eye level. They bought expensive TV ads during sports games. In the pre-internet era, this was the only game in town. If you couldn't afford these channels, you couldn't compete.

This strategy worked brilliantly. By the early 2000s, Gillette had captured around 70% of the US razor market.[10] But there was a hidden problem. Gillette's dominance came at a cost that consumers reluctantly paid. They grumbled about razor prices but had no alternatives. Then the internet changed everything.

The internet dulls the razor's edge

It's easy to mistake Gillette's success for brand loyalty. But the internet exposed the truth – customers hated the high prices.

In the early 2010s, Dollar Shave Club and Harry's bypassed retail entirely. They sold directly to consumers online, cutting out the middleman and slashing prices.

Dollar Shave Club's launch video, shot for just $4,500, went viral with millions of views. It crashed their site from the traffic and spoke directly to frustrated customers. The message was simple. Why pay $20 for razor cartridges when you can get them for a few bucks?

By 2015, Dollar Shave Club had two million subscribers. Unilever bought the company for $1 billion in 2016.

Here's what many investors missed. They thought Gillette's moat was brand power – that customers were loyal to the name. But customers weren't loyal, they were trapped. Gillette's real moat was distribution dominance. When the internet made that irrelevant, Gillette's pricing power vanished overnight. Investors who mistook distribution for brand loyalty were blindsided by how quickly the moat crumbled.

But the internet isn't the only way distribution moats can fail. Sometimes your biggest distributor becomes your biggest competitor. Just ask any brand facing Costco's Kirkland.

Nike: Scoring an own goal

Sometimes companies don't lose their distribution moat to disruption – they voluntarily surrender it. Nike's catastrophic strategy under CEO John Donahoe (2020–2024) shows how quickly decades of distribution dominance can evaporate when you forget what made you powerful.

Donahoe, a former tech executive, looked at Nike's wholesale partnerships and saw inefficiency. Why share profits with retailers? Why not sell directly to consumers and capture those margins? In 2021, he set an aggressive goal: shift direct-to-consumer sales from 40% to 60% of revenue. In other words, he was telling wholesale partners: you aren't important to us anymore.

The wholesale exodus was swift and brutal. In 2021, they cut ties with DSW, Urban Outfitters, and Macy's. They dramatically reduced presence at Foot Locker, their most important partner. The company that once dominated every sporting goods store's premium shelf space – the displays at eye level, the dedicated Nike sections – began pulling out.

Here's what Donahoe didn't understand: those wholesale partnerships weren't just sales channels. They were Nike's physical omnipresence. When you needed running shoes, Nike was there. When you browsed for basketball gear, Nike dominated. That constant availability reinforced the brand's dominance in consumers' minds.

The abandoned shelf space became a feast for hungry competitors. Hoka, On Running, Brooks, and New Balance filled the gaps and deepened the relationships Nike had neglected. By 2024, Nike found itself positioned *behind* these upstarts in the very stores it once dominated.

But the distribution disaster was only half the problem. Donahoe also abandoned Nike's legendary brand marketing – the emotional athlete stories that made people willing to pay premium prices. Instead, he shifted to performance marketing, treating Nike like a direct-response company optimizing for clicks and conversions.

The company that created "Just Do It" and "Find Your Greatness" became weirdly disconnected from sport itself. Nike's marketing became algorithmic rather than emotional, focused on retargeting pixels instead of cultural moments. When Elliott Hill took over as CEO in 2024, he admitted: "We've shifted investments away from creating demand for our brand to capturing demand through performance marketing for our Nike digital business."

The financial carnage was brutal. Gross margins fell from 46% in fiscal 2022 to just 40% by Q4 fiscal 2025. Why? Nike had to resort to heavy discounting in its direct channels to move product. By late 2024, half of Nike's digital sales were promotional versus full price.[11] The strategy meant to increase margins destroyed them instead.

By the time Elliott Hill took over in October 2024 – a 32-year Nike veteran brought back from retirement – the damage was done. Hill admitted bluntly: "We lost our obsession with sport" and needed to "earn back" shelf space from competitors. The company was now fighting to regain positions it had voluntarily abandoned.

The lesson cuts deep: Distribution isn't just about where you sell – it's about being unavoidable. When Nike retreated to its own channels, it became avoidable. Competitors weren't just taking shelf space; they were taking mindshare. Every time a sales associate recommended On instead of Nike, every time a runner discovered Hoka at their local store, Nike's moat eroded.

Donahoe treated Nike like a tech company that could "disrupt" itself through digital transformation. But athletic gear isn't tech. It's physical products that people want to see, touch, and try. It's community validation when others see your brand choice. It's cultural relevance that algorithms can't manufacture.

The most painful irony? Nike didn't lose its distribution moat to innovation or disruption. They gave it away, thinking they were being smart about margins and digital transformation. They learned what Gillette learned, just differently: controlling distribution means nothing if you abandon the channels where customers actually shop.

Costco's Kirkland: When your distributor becomes your competitor

In a CNBC interview, Warren Buffett acknowledged that Berkshire Hathaway "overpaid for Kraft." They misjudged the resilience of its brands in a rapidly changing consumer landscape. The mistake became clear in February 2019. Kraft Heinz announced a staggering $15.4 billion write-down, acknowledging its diminished brand value. The company's stock plummeted 27% the following day.

Buffett highlighted Costco's Kirkland brand as a prime example of this shift. While Kraft Heinz had spent billions on advertising over the past century, generating $26.3 billion in sales, something remarkable happened. Costco's Kirkland brand, launched in 1995, achieved $39 billion in sales in 2018 with only 750 or so outlets. Kirkland had become a dominant force in consumer packaged goods.

Buffett remarked on the contrast. "Here they are [Kraft Heinz], 100 years plus, tons of advertising, built into people's habits and everything else. And now, Kirkland, a private-label brand, comes along and with only 750 or so outlets, does 50% more business than all the Kraft Heinz brands."

Buffett pointed to a new reality. "The ability to price has changed, and that's huge."

To be fair, Kirkland isn't the only reason Kraft Heinz struggled. Consumers were shifting to fresh foods, the company was drowning in debt from its merger, and they'd underinvested in innovation for years. But Kirkland represents something every brand now fears – when your distributor knows exactly what sells, has your customers' trust, and decides they don't need you anymore. They can offer comparable quality at 20–30% lower prices without spending a dollar on advertising. It's not just Costco either. Walmart, Amazon, and Aldi have all strengthened their private labels. Today, distributors hold the keys to reach. Companies without strong consumer loyalty are finding themselves outpaced by the very distribution channels they once relied on.

But distribution power isn't always vulnerable. Some companies have turned distribution into an offensive weapon rather than a defensive moat. They don't just reach customers – they embed themselves so deeply that leaving becomes unthinkable.

Microsoft: The king of land and expand

The "land and expand" strategy is common in software. A sales representative secures a small deal with an organization, earns their trust, then expands the relationship. They sell more products or increase user licenses. This strategy leverages an initial point of distribution to entrench the customer within the company's ecosystem.

And no one executes this strategy better than Microsoft. After all, almost every non-Mac computer comes pre-installed with the Windows operating system. Windows still holds over 70% of the desktop PC operating system market share. This massive installed base provides a powerful launchpad for Microsoft's land and expand strategy.

Microsoft Teams, a communication and collaboration platform, exemplifies this approach. During the Covid-19 pandemic, Teams experienced explosive growth. By August 2021, it had surpassed 250 million monthly active users. This dwarfed its competitor Slack, which had 32 million users that same year. This happened despite Slack having a three-year head start and arguably a superior product. Slack consistently receives higher user ratings on platforms like G2.

Microsoft's incredible distribution network, however, gave Teams a decisive advantage.

Similarly, Microsoft has made significant inroads in the crowded endpoint security market. This market was traditionally dominated by players like

Symantec and McAfee. In 2017, Microsoft held a mere 1% market share. By 2021, it had become the leader with a commanding 18.9% share, generating $2.5 billion in revenue. By 2023, this had grown to 25.8% and $3.2 billion.

Microsoft's strategic bundling of products within Microsoft 365 has been key to its success with Teams and Defender for Endpoint, despite being a late entrant in both markets. These tools are often included in Microsoft 365 subscriptions, especially higher-tier enterprise plans like E5. Companies subscribing to Microsoft 365 for essential productivity tools like Word, Excel, and Outlook also gain access to Teams and Defender.

This bundling strategy is brilliant. Customers get more value for their money. Organizations deal with one vendor instead of many. Everything works together seamlessly. Meanwhile, Microsoft undercuts its competition by including what others charge separately for.

Microsoft has perfected bundling as a growth strategy. They get in with Windows, expand with Office, then bundle in Teams, Defender, and everything else enterprises need. Companies love this because they get multiple solutions from a single vendor, streamlining procurement and ensuring everything works together. Why pay for Slack when Teams is included? Why buy separate security when Defender is already there? This bundling strategy creates a dual moat – distribution power combined with switching costs. Once companies build their operations around Microsoft's integrated ecosystem, the cost and disruption of switching to multiple vendors becomes prohibitive.

So far we've seen moats built on emotion, networks, pain of switching, cost advantages, and distribution power. But there's one more source of competitive advantage – the law itself.

6. REGULATORY PROTECTION: WHEN GOVERNMENT BECOMES YOUR MOAT

This last type of moat is the most controversial because it has nothing to do with being the best. You don't need superior products, loyal customers, or operational excellence. You just need the government on your side.

Some investors love regulatory moats because they're incredibly hard to attack. Others avoid them because what the government gives, the government can take away. The key is knowing which type you're dealing with.

Bond rating agencies: Gatekeepers of the credit market

The bond-rating business perfectly illustrates regulatory protection, dominated by Moody's, S&P, and Fitch. In the US, bond rating agencies must be designated as Nationally Recognized Statistical Rating Organizations to truly matter. Why? Because many institutional investors are legally required to use NRSRO ratings. Obtaining this status is a rigorous, complex process that creates a high entry barrier for new firms. This has limited competition to just three major players.

Even after the 2008 financial crisis – where their overly optimistic ratings of toxic mortgage securities helped crash the global economy – they rebounded quickly. They remained the go-to sources for credit assessments. Moody's, for example, continues to achieve operating margins north of 40%, thanks largely to its regulatory moat. Regulations have effectively made bond rating agencies the gatekeepers of the credit market. This gives them significant pricing power and a reliable revenue stream.

But not all regulatory moats are created by design. Sometimes the most powerful protection comes from rules meant to restrict companies, not help them.

Tobacco: When regulation helps incumbents

For decades, tobacco companies were the biggest advertisers in America, spending billions to fight for market share. Then in the 1970s, cigarette ads were banned from TV and radio. The 1998 Master Settlement Agreement restricted marketing even further.

You'd think this would hurt Big Tobacco. Instead, it was a gift.

Without advertising, consumers stuck with brands they already knew – especially Marlboro (owned by Philip Morris). New competitors couldn't build awareness, while established brands lived on in consumers' habits and memories. Existing players saved billions in advertising costs while their market share stayed locked in place. The regulations meant to hurt them became their protection.

Not all regulatory moats provide the same level of protection. Regulations intended to protect consumers but that incidentally shield incumbents from competition often form much stronger moats. Those crafted primarily to encourage initial investment tend to be weaker.

Airlines: When deregulation destroys moats

Airlines show what happens when regulatory protection disappears.

Before the 1978 Airline Deregulation Act, airlines enjoyed controlled routes and fares. Regulations gave them exclusive rights to specific routes, limited competition, and guaranteed steady profits. This protected environment encouraged investment. But it also created problems. Airlines essentially had monopolies on various routes, with little incentive to compete on price or innovate. Consumers grew frustrated with high fares and subpar service.

When deregulation arrived, the competitive floodgates opened. New entrants surged in, airfare costs plummeted, and consumer choice expanded. For travelers, it was a win. But for airlines and their shareholders, the story changed dramatically. Carriers faced volatile fuel prices, unsustainable price wars, and eventual consolidation. Many went bankrupt or were acquired by larger rivals.

Without regulatory protection, most airlines today are price takers in an intensely cyclical industry. Profitability swings wildly with economic conditions. The industry now offers notoriously low returns on capital. This shows how fragile regulatory moats can be when they exist mainly to protect investment rather than serve consumers.

Airlines learned that regulatory protection can vanish overnight. Other businesses face a different challenge – their legal protection comes with an expiration date from day one.

Patents: A moat with an expiration date

Wouldn't it be great if there were a law that said, "No competition allowed"? That's basically what patents do. They grant companies exclusive rights to profit from their creations for a set period. Sounds perfect for investors. Except patents come with an expiration date, and this moat often springs leaks sooner than expected.

Consider Ozempic, the diabetes medication that became a weight-loss phenomenon. Novo Nordisk charges upwards of $900 per month in the US. Why? Because patents block generic competitors.

But that protection expires December 5, 2031. Worse, profitable patents attract legal challenges. In October 2024, Novo Nordisk settled a patent lawsuit that could let generics enter even sooner.

And there's no guarantee companies can keep creating new blockbusters. You're betting on constant innovation and favorable court rulings.

As a long-term investor seeking businesses with enduring competitive advantages, patents offer limited appeal. I don't want to depend on hitting the jackpot with new discoveries or winning legal battles. You're stuck on a treadmill – constantly needing new patents to replace expiring ones, with no guarantee you'll find them. That unpredictability makes patents less attractive than other economic moats.

How to spot these moats yourself

Now that you've seen all six moat types in action, let me show you how I identify them in real companies.

Throughout this chapter, we've explored how companies like Starbucks, Amazon, and Meta built their fortresses. But how do you spot these advantages in companies you're evaluating today? After 17 years of investing, I've developed a simple framework for each moat type – specific signals that tell me whether a moat is strengthening or starting to crack.

The one question that matters

Before diving into specific moats, I always start here: Is this company's advantage getting easier or harder to attack?

Amazon gets harder to compete with every year – more products, more warehouses, more Prime members locked into the ecosystem. Newspapers got easier to disrupt every year until anyone with a blog could compete. This single question cuts through the noise and forces you to think about trajectory, not just current position.

WHAT I LOOK FOR IN EACH MOAT TYPE

Let me walk you through exactly how I evaluate each type of moat, using the same companies we've discussed as reference points.

Branding power

Remember See's Candies and their ability to raise prices because customers associate them with romance? That's what I'm hunting for in any brand investment.

The key test is simple: Can they raise prices 5% without losing customers? You don't need insider information – watch for price increase announcements, or better yet, notice when you're shopping. That $5 Starbucks coffee that was $4.50 last year? That's pricing power in action.

Then I dig into the numbers. Gross profit margins tell the story. When margins stay steady despite inflation, the company is successfully passing costs to consumers. When margins expand over time, they're raising prices faster than costs – that's a widening moat. But declining margins are a warning shot. Either the company can't pass on rising costs (weak brand) or competition is forcing prices down (no differentiation). When consumers see no difference between their product and cheaper alternatives, there's no moat, just a commodity business heading for trouble.

Network effects

Meta's battle with TikTok taught us that network effects can be both powerful and fragile. Here's how I spot the difference.

First, I check if both sides of the network are growing. It's not just total user count – Meta needs both users and content creators, Airbnb needs hosts and guests, Uber needs drivers and passengers. When one side stagnates, the flywheel stutters. I learned this watching MySpace collapse – users left because creators moved to Facebook, and creators moved because users were leaving. The unraveling happened in months, not years.

The clearest signal of network strength? Marketing expenses as a percentage of revenue. Strong networks sell themselves – each user brings more users. When Airbnb was scaling rapidly, their marketing expenses as a percentage of revenue dropped from 35% in FY 2020 to 19% in FY 2024. The network was doing the selling for them. But when you see marketing expenses rising to maintain growth, the network effect is weakening.

Management usually reports user engagement and retention metrics. What I want to see is engagement increasing with scale – more users making each user more active. And watch revenue per user. If it's climbing as the network grows, the moat is widening.

Switching costs

Unlike network effects that can unravel quickly, switching costs create individual prisoner situations. Even unhappy customers stay trapped.

I look for annual customer retention above 90% – anything less suggests switching is too easy. Above 95%? That's fortress-level lock-in. SAP customers might hate the software (remember that negative Net Promoter Score?), but they renew anyway because the pain of switching would shut down their operations.

The stickiness comes in many forms. Sometimes it's training – Adobe knows that designers who spent years mastering Photoshop won't easily switch to alternatives. Sometimes it's operational integration – hospitals with million-dollar DaVinci surgical systems and specially trained surgeons aren't shopping for alternatives. Sometimes it's just habit – iPhone users are accustomed to iOS and dread learning Android.

But here's the critical warning: regulations can destroy switching costs overnight. Telecoms enjoyed powerful moats because customers couldn't switch without losing their phone numbers. Then regulators introduced number portability in the late 1990s. Within months, customer defection rates doubled. The lesson? When evaluating switching costs, always ask what could make switching suddenly painless.

Cost advantages

Amazon and Netflix showed us two paths to cost advantage – one shares savings through lower prices, the other through more value. Here's how to spot similar advantages.

Start with industry position. Cost advantages typically belong to the biggest players – they spread fixed costs over more units and negotiate better terms with suppliers. If a company isn't in the top three by revenue, question whether they really have sustainable cost advantages.

Then compare operating margins to competitors. Amazon's thin margins are by design – they're profitably selling at prices that would bankrupt competitors. Netflix's expanding margins show the opposite approach – fixed content costs spread across a growing subscriber base. Both models create self-reinforcing fortresses that get harder to attack as they grow.

Watch for early warning signs of erosion. Sears once had sizeable cost advantages in retail, but with the rise of Walmart and later Amazon, its supply chain, scale, and operational efficiencies fell behind. Its inability to keep up with the low-cost models of competitors led to margin erosion and loss of relevance. When you see an industry's cost structure changing fundamentally, yesterday's advantages become tomorrow's anchors.

Distribution power

Distribution moats are the easiest to spot but hardest to evaluate, because they're often hiding in plain sight.

You know a company has distribution power when you can't avoid them.

Gillette at eye-level in every store. Microsoft pre-installed on every PC. The products that consultants and salespeople push because they get the best commissions. If you don't have to look for them because they find you, that's distribution power.

But here's what Gillette's collapse taught me: watch where customers are actually buying. When Dollar Shave Club bypassed retail entirely, Gillette's shelf space became irrelevant. The strongest distribution moat means nothing if customers shop somewhere else.

Red flags appear when market share declines despite stable or increased marketing spend. The company is pushing harder but selling less – distribution is failing. Also watch for exclusive arrangements ending or premium shelf space going to competitors. These changes happen gradually, then suddenly.

Regulatory protection

I'll be honest – I mostly avoid these. Not because they aren't powerful, but because they depend on forces beyond the company's control.

Patents expire. Regulations change with new administrations. What seems like permanent protection can vanish with one court ruling or legislative session. The airlines learned this when deregulation destroyed their route monopolies. Tobacco companies actually benefited when advertising restrictions prevented new competitors from building awareness, but that could change with one FDA decision.

If you do invest in regulatory moats, you need to watch the shifting sands closely – not the final court rulings or legislative votes, but the political currents that precede them. By the time a regulation actually changes, it's too late. You need to spot when public sentiment turns, when lobbying intensifies, when political rhetoric shifts. Every earnings call, every investor presentation, management will emphasize their regulatory advantages – right until the moment those advantages disappear.

Which is why, as a Lunch Break Investor, I don't like businesses that require me to watch these shifting sands constantly. The whole point is to find companies you can own for years without constant monitoring.

Regulatory moats demand the opposite – vigilant attention to every change in the political winds.

THE TRAJECTORY OF THE MOAT MATTERS MORE THAN ITS SIZE

Economic moats are never static. They either expand or contract over time. And it's the trajectory of the moat – not its current size – that ultimately determines a company's longevity. A wide moat today can quickly shrink if neglected. Meanwhile, a narrow but growing moat can evolve into an impenetrable fortress. The rise of Netflix and the fall of Blockbuster perfectly illustrate this dynamic.

Blockbuster's peak in 2004 was nothing short of spectacular. With over 9,000 stores worldwide and 60 million members, it reigned supreme in the video rental market. It raked in $5.9 billion in revenue and $400 million in profit. Its business model, though simple, was incredibly effective. Customers rented movies or video games, and late fees bolstered the bottom line. Blockbuster's moat was built on brand dominance, convenience, and scale. This gave it a significant edge in a pre-digital world. Its vast inventory and studio partnerships ensured the newest releases were always available. Smaller competitors couldn't replicate this.

But success bred complacency. Blockbuster dismissed customer complaints about rigid late fees. It stubbornly clung to VHS tapes long after DVDs became the standard. When Netflix introduced DVD-by-mail with no late fees, it didn't just solve customer pain points. It began chiseling away at Blockbuster's moat. Despite this warning shot, it took Blockbuster six years to launch its own DVD-by-mail service in 2004. By then, Netflix was gearing up for its next big move.

In 2007, Netflix launched streaming, reimagining the entire rental experience. Instant, on-demand access to movies and shows changed everything. Blockbuster dismissed it as a passing fad while Netflix went all-in. They invested heavily in technology and licensing deals to expand their library.

By the time Blockbuster finally entered streaming with Blockbuster On

Demand in 2010, it was too late. The service had a limited library, technical glitches, and felt like an afterthought. It was a stark contrast to Netflix's polished platform.

Between 2007 and 2010, Netflix grew from 7.5 million to 20 million subscribers while Blockbuster floundered. The wide moat had become a trap – Blockbuster was so confident in their position they couldn't see it eroding beneath them.

This is why smart investors look beyond current moat size. They study how management allocates capital, whether they're investing in tomorrow's advantages or protecting yesterday's. The managers who obsess over strengthening their competitive position, even when business is good, are the ones who ensure their moat keeps widening.

Management quality can make or break even the best business models – something we'll explore in detail later. But for now, remember this. The moat that matters isn't the one you have today. It's the one you're building for tomorrow.

YOUR LUNCH BREAK SUMMARY

- **Every business moves through four phases from innovation to decline** – moats protect both the magnitude of returns (how high above average) and duration (how long they last)
- **Six moat types exist**: branding (pricing power), network effects (winner-takes-most dynamics), switching costs (pain of leaving), cost advantages (economies of scale), distribution (channel control), and regulatory (legal protection)
- **Even the strongest moats have vulnerabilities** – network effects can be beaten by finding unserved niches, not competing head-on with established players
- **Distribution advantages erode when channels shift** – controlling traditional channels means nothing when competitors create entirely new paths to customers

- **Moat trajectory beats current size** – a narrow but widening moat will outlast a wide but narrowing one, making the direction of change more important than today's position

---

YOUR NEXT STEP

Now that you can identify economic moats, you need to understand how these translate into actual investment returns. In Chapter 4, we'll explore the three drivers of capital appreciation – the forces that turn a company's competitive advantages into real wealth for shareholders.

A NOTE ON WHAT'S AHEAD

In the next chapter, we'll shift from concepts to numbers. You'll see terms like P/E multiples, operating margins, and cash flows. Don't worry if these feel unfamiliar – I'll explain each as we go. The Meta case study will show you exactly how these metrics work in practice. Remember, you don't need an accounting degree to be a successful investor – just the willingness to understand a few key numbers that reveal whether a business is truly creating value.

CHAPTER 4
THE THREE DRIVERS OF CAPITAL APPRECIATION

IN THE PREVIOUS chapters, we explored economic moats – the competitive advantages that protect a company's profits. But here's something that confused me for years: a strong moat doesn't automatically mean a strong investment return.

I've owned businesses with wide moats that went nowhere for a decade. I've watched companies with seemingly unassailable positions trade sideways while the market marched upwards. What was I missing?

It took me years to understand that moats are necessary but not sufficient. A moat protects the *ability* to earn attractive returns. But three other forces determine whether those returns actually show up in your portfolio.

In this chapter, I'll show you the three drivers of capital appreciation: earnings growth, share buybacks, and multiple expansion. Once you see how they interact, you'll understand why some well-protected businesses make disappointing investments – and why patience with the right business at the right price is so richly rewarded.

This is where the theory starts translating into money. Let me show you how all three drivers came together in one of my own investments.

It was 2022, and the financial news headlines couldn't have been more dire.

"Meta shares collapse 26% in biggest one-day wipeout in history."

"Facebook owner Meta has lost more than $500 billion in market value."

"Zuckerberg's pivot to the metaverse is destroying shareholder value."

Investors were fleeing in panic. If you'd owned Meta, you'd have watched nearly 80% of your investment evaporate, as the share price fell from about $384 to a low of $88. By year-end, it had only partially recovered to $120, valuing the company at just 14× trailing earnings. Investors were paying only $14 for every dollar of actual profits, a valuation typically reserved for companies whose best days are over.

Wonderful businesses almost always trade at a premium. It usually takes several major problems to make them this cheap.

As the share price drops and negative headlines mount, the market's investment horizon shrinks. This is precisely when opportunities emerge for investors who can stay level-headed while others panic.

There were five main problems plaguing Meta in 2022:

1. **Signal Loss from Apple's iOS Changes**: Apple's App Tracking Transparency (ATT) changes limited Meta's ability to target and measure ads effectively. During Q1 2022, Meta's management estimated this would cause a $10 billion revenue loss in 2022.[1]
2. **Shift to Short-Form Video (Reels)**: To counter the TikTok threat, Meta rolled out Reels, which cannibalized higher-monetizing ad formats like Feed and Stories.
3. **Slowdown in Active User Growth**: Growth decelerated due to increasing competition from TikTok, tough comparisons to pandemic numbers, and the loss of users in Russia (following Russia's invasion of Ukraine).
4. **Macroeconomic Challenges**: Reduced advertiser demand and economic uncertainty led to a slowdown in advertising revenue growth, particularly in North America and Europe.
5. **Massive Investments in the Metaverse**: Meta was pouring billions into Reality Labs – over $13 billion in 2022 alone – with no clear path to profitability.

It's only when there's a perfect storm of negativity that a company like Meta becomes this cheap. Remember, in investing, a rosy outlook and an attractive valuation never come hand-in-hand.

But step back from the headlines and look at what Meta had built. In the five years before this crisis, the company nearly tripled its revenue from $40.7 billion to $118 billion, growing at roughly 30% per year. It maintained operating margins of around 40% – keeping over 40 cents of every dollar of revenue as profit – and generated over $186 billion in operating cash flow. This wasn't a struggling business – it was a cash machine with strong network effects as its moat.

And at the helm was Mark Zuckerberg, a founder CEO who was only 36 years old, with a long runway ahead and significant skin in the game.

While Wall Street had essentially declared game over for Meta, I saw a company that wasn't lying down after getting punched.

Despite the negative headlines, several factors gave me conviction to invest.

First, the company still generated massive cash flow. After accounting for all debts, it had $32 billion in cash. It had plenty of ammunition to meet its challenges head-on.

Second, this wasn't Zuckerberg's first rodeo. The ATT changes and shift to short-form video were less threatening than Facebook's pivot from desktop to mobile at its 2012 IPO. Back then, Facebook generated zero revenue from mobile advertising – an existential threat. Yet Zuck successfully overhauled the organization and transitioned to a "mobile-first" strategy.

Third, with ATT, Meta was the largest social media company with the biggest pool of data and resources. If Meta, with more data than any competitor, was having targeting problems, then its competitors would face even greater challenges capturing ad dollars.

Fourth, and most importantly, Zuck was crystal clear and candid with shareholders about the path forward. Meta attacked each problem head-on:

- **Addressing ATT's Signal Loss**: Meta invested in privacy-enhancing technologies and AI-driven tools to improve targeting while respecting privacy.
- **Monetizing Reels**: By Q2 2022, Reels had reached a $1 billion annual revenue run rate.

- **Launching a "Year of Efficiency"**: Meta aggressively reduced expenses, implemented layoffs, and announced a broad hiring freeze.
- **Investing in AI Infrastructure**: Significant investments were made to improve ad ranking, recommendations, and video monetization.

But that's not all. As Meta's share price declined, management aggressively bought back shares. They spent $27.9 billion in 2022 to repurchase shares at an average price of roughly $173 per share, retiring approximately 161 million shares, a 4.5% reduction.[2]

These facts gave me conviction to buy Meta while everyone else was selling.

Beneath the chaos, I saw the potential for all three drivers of capital appreciation to work powerfully in my favor.

Understanding these drivers is what separates great investments from mediocre ones. After years of investing – and plenty of mistakes – I've learned to focus on the forces that actually move stock prices. Once you see them clearly, everything else clicks:

1. Earnings growth.
2. Share count reduction (through buybacks).
3. P/E multiple expansion.

Yes, dividends provide returns too. But great compounder companies reinvest profits to drive growth at attractive returns, or buy back shares opportunistically when conditions are right – both of which are more tax-efficient than scheduled dividend payments.

My Meta investment ultimately delivered exceptional returns because all three of these drivers worked together in concert.

HOW THE THREE DRIVERS PLAYED OUT IN META

Fast forward to 2024, and Meta had successfully navigated its challenges. The company that Wall Street left for dead had transformed itself.

From 2022 through 2024:

- Revenue grew 41% to $164.5 billion.
- Operating profits surged 140% to $69.4 billion.
- Daily active users rose 18.8% to 3.35 billion.

But the stock price recovery was even more dramatic. Three drivers compounded together:

- **Driver 1 – Earnings grew 169%**: Net income rose from $23.2 billion to $62.4 billion as Meta cut costs and monetized Reels.
- **Driver 2 – Buybacks amplified the per-share gain**: Management spent $49.8 billion buying back shares over 2023 and 2024, shrinking the share count by 3.3%. Combined with the earnings recovery, this pushed earnings per share up 178%, from $8.59 to $23.86.
- **Driver 3 – P/E multiple expanded 75%**: From 14× at the end of 2022 to 24.5× as fear turned to optimism.

By the end of 2024, Meta traded at $585 per share, nearly fivefold its 2022 year-end price, with all three drivers working in its favor.

The difference between panic and opportunity comes down to understanding these three forces. While headlines screamed disaster, the three-drivers framework revealed something else entirely: a profitable business with recoverable earnings, management deploying billions at distressed prices, and a multiple compressed to levels that assumed Meta would never grow again.

When you can see these drivers clearly, chaos becomes an opportunity. The same framework that worked for Meta can work for any quality business.

Let me walk you through each driver in turn, starting with the foundation – earnings growth.

DRIVER 1: EARNINGS GROWTH AS THE FOUNDATION

Benjamin Graham said it best – in the short run, the market is a voting machine, but in the long run, it's a weighing machine.

And what it weighs is earnings. A company's share price will track its earnings over time, and this is the one engine that can run the longest if you're invested in a good company.

That said, a company can boost its earnings in two primary ways.

First, by enhancing operational efficiency – cutting costs to retain more profit for every dollar of sales. While beneficial, cost-cutting has its limitations. There's only so much fat you can trim.

Second, and more critically, a company can reinvest its earnings to fuel revenue growth. Whether opening new stores, expanding into new markets, or developing new products, companies with a long runway for revenue growth possess the potential to significantly increase earnings over time.

True Steady Compounders don't just grow earnings for a few years. They continue doing so over decades. This is why reinvestment opportunities are essential for identifying companies that can compound your wealth.

In his 1992 letter, Buffett nailed it: "The best business to own is one that over an extended period can employ large amounts of incremental capital at very high rates of return."

Companies can grow earnings through four primary paths:

1. Reinvesting at high returns.
2. Expanding geographically.
3. Creating new products.
4. Raising prices.

Some companies excel at one of these paths; the best companies combine several.

Let me walk you through each path and show you what to look for.

Path 1: The power of reinvestment

Why reinvestment runways matter

In our previous chapter, we discussed economic moats – those competitive advantages that protect high returns on invested capital. But a moat alone doesn't guarantee a company will become a compounding machine.

To become a true compounder, a company needs both high returns on invested capital and somewhere to reinvest this money.

Let me give you a simple example.

A tale of two companies

Imagine two companies, both valued at $15 million. Both earn $1 million in net profits. Both can reinvest capital at 20% returns. Both trade at a constant 15x earnings multiple. The only difference? What they do with their profits.

Company A pays out all profits as dividends**. Company B** reinvests everything back into growth.

Let's see how this plays out over 10 years.

The dividend machine

Company A earns $1 million annually but reinvests nothing. It distributes all profits as dividends – a 6.7% yield. Not terrible, right?

After 10 years:

- Dividends received: $1m annually x 10 years = $10m.
- Ending value: $15m (no profit growth).
- Total return: $25m (1.7x your money).

Not bad – until you see what happens with Company B.*

---

* For simplicity, this assumes dividends are received as cash.

The reinvestment machine

Company B reinvests all profits at 20% returns on invested capital – meaning every dollar reinvested generates 20 cents of additional annual profit. That $1 million from year one grows into $1.2 million by year two. The entire $1.2 million is reinvested, generating $1.44 million the following year.

The compounding snowball keeps rolling. This is where it gets exciting.

After 10 years:

- Earnings: Have grown to $6.2 million annually.
- Company Valuation: $6.2m earnings x 15 P/E = $93m.
- Total Shareholder Return: $93m (6.2x your money).

Same starting point. But Company B returned nearly 4x as much wealth.

The lesson isn't that dividends are bad – companies without reinvestment opportunities should return cash to shareholders. But dividend-heavy companies are often signaling they've run out of runway. The best compounders rarely pay meaningful dividends because they have better uses for the money.

The power of compounding

These two examples showcase the extremes, but the lesson is clear – a long runway for reinvestment is transformative.

Compounding does the heavy lifting when businesses reinvest at high returns over time, driving exponential growth.

And I haven't even factored in taxes. Dividends are taxed when distributed, while reinvested profits compound tax-free until the shareholder realizes gains. This would further tip the scales in favor of reinvestment-heavy companies.

For us long-term investors, finding businesses with both high returns on invested capital and ample reinvestment opportunities is like finding the holy grail – a true Steady Compounder.

Path 2: Geographic and market expansion

Market expansion through existing products

Once a company has product-market fit – meaning customers love what they're selling – it's much easier to sell more of the same to similar customers than it is to develop something new from scratch.

Expanding across geographies

The United States is a dream market for ambitious businesses. With 335 million people, high spending power, and a single common language, the US offers a massive, unified market.

Its lack of internal trade barriers and relatively homogenous consumer preferences makes scaling across states far easier than in more fragmented regions like Europe or Southeast Asia.

Peter Lynch noticed this pattern in *One Up on Wall Street* – successful companies replicate their formula city by city. Here's what to ask yourself: is there evidence that the business model works in one market before the company attempts to scale to others?

Starbucks goes global

Starbucks exemplifies successful geographic expansion. Starting in Seattle, it methodically expanded throughout the Pacific Northwest. Then it moved to other major markets like Chicago and California, proving its concept's viability beyond its initial city.

The company went public in 1992 with $93.1 million in revenue and 140 outlets, valued at $271 million. By 2024, it generated $36 billion in revenue across over 40,000 outlets with a market capitalization of $114.2 billion. That's a 421-fold increase from its initial valuation.

This is the power of a long growth runway – the ability to replicate what works, city by city, country by country, decade after decade. But physical expansion looks almost quaint compared to what digital businesses can achieve.

Digital expansion and borderless growth

The internet has obliterated traditional geographic boundaries. Digital-first businesses can now expand globally at unprecedented speeds.

Take Netflix. It launched its streaming service in 2007 with a modest library serving only the US market. By 2010, streaming had overtaken DVD rentals as Netflix's primary revenue source, reaching 20 million US subscribers. Confident in its domestic success, Netflix expanded into Canada that same year. It then rapidly rolled out to 43 Latin American countries in 2011.

By the end of 2024, it operated in over 190 countries with more than 302 million paying subscribers.

Digital platforms are rewriting the rules of expansion. As high-speed internet becomes ubiquitous, user acquisition happens at speeds that would have seemed impossible just a decade ago. ChatGPT hit 100 million users in two months. Less than a year later, Meta's Threads beat that record – reaching 100 million in just five days.

Have you ever witnessed such explosive growth in the physical world? This is the digital advantage – when you nail product-market fit, you can scale at rates traditional businesses could only dream of. For investors hunting compounders, a digital business with global product-market fit can grow earnings for decades without the capital expenditure that physical expansion demands.

Demand creation through innovation

Some companies grow by fighting for market share. Others grow by expanding the entire market. This happens when innovation transforms a product so fundamentally that it unlocks a much larger Total Addressable Market (TAM) – creating new use cases and expanding the pool of potential customers.

Uber redefines transportation

Take Uber. It didn't just compete in the taxi market. It redefined the market entirely.

In 2014, a public debate erupted between investor Bill Gurley and valuation expert Aswath Damodaran. Damodaran valued Uber based on the existing taxi market. Gurley saw something bigger – Uber wasn't just replacing taxis, it would capture a much larger transportation market that didn't even exist yet.

And Gurley was right.

Back in 2008, Uber's seed pitch deck pegged its total addressable market (TAM) at just $4.2 billion, based on the size of the taxi market. By 2024, the company generated over $23 billion in revenue from ride-hailing alone – more than five times their entire original market estimate.

Uber didn't just steal market share from taxis. It created an entirely new market for on-demand transportation – expanding access to underserved areas, removing the friction of cash payments, and lowering prices through better driver utilization. In 2024, Uber generated over $25 billion in mobility revenue – more than five times the entire market they originally pitched to investors.

That's the power of TAM expansion. Companies that genuinely redefine their markets don't fight for share – they grow the pie.

When I evaluate expansion potential, the key question is simple: has this company proven the model works somewhere before trying to replicate it everywhere? Starbucks proved Seattle, then Chicago, then the world. Netflix proved the US before going global. The best expansion stories follow this pattern – dominate one market, then methodically repeat.

Of course, expanding the market for existing products is just one path. The most ambitious companies don't stop there – they create entirely new products and businesses from scratch.

Path 3: Creating new revenue streams

The spawner advantage

Some companies don't just grow their existing business – they spawn entirely new ones from within. In investing, these are popularly known as "spawners."[3] They have the DNA to consistently incubate new products and revenue streams that become their next growth engine.

These companies embrace failure as part of the process. They experiment, accept that most ventures won't succeed, and double down when something works.

They also enjoy a tax advantage. By reinvesting pre-tax earnings into new ventures, they compound intrinsic value without triggering immediate tax liabilities.

Amazon is the ultimate example.

Amazon: The ultimate spawner

Amazon started in 1994 as an online bookstore. If it had stopped there, its growth runway would have been short-lived. Instead, it became "The Everything Store." It quickly expanded into music, videos, electronics, software, and virtually everything else imaginable.

But that was only the beginning.

It introduced Amazon Prime, creating a loyal customer base with benefits like free shipping, video streaming, and other perks. This drove both retail sales and subscription revenue.

The company also developed Amazon Web Services (AWS). It initially built AWS to address its own IT infrastructure needs. Recognizing that other businesses faced similar challenges, Amazon leveraged its internal expertise to create a cloud computing solution for the broader market. By 2024, AWS was the dominant cloud infrastructure provider, generating over $100 billion in revenue with 35% margins. Jeff Bezos himself called AWS's head start "the greatest piece of business luck in history."

But as the saying goes, luck is what happens when preparation meets opportunity.

Amazon's history is also littered with failures: Fire Phone ($170 million write-down), Amazon Destinations (lasted six months), Amazon Restaurants (couldn't compete), Amazon Wallet (six months), Amazon Local (four years of losses). The list goes on.

Yet Amazon keeps experimenting. In his 2017 letter to shareholders, Bezos captured this philosophy: "Experiment patiently, accept failures, plant seeds, protect saplings, and double down when you see customer delight."

What separates spawners from diworsifiers?

Not every company has the DNA to successfully expand. The Hour Glass, Singapore's premier luxury watch retailer with over 60 outlets and S$1.1 billion in annual revenue in 2024, shows what happens when management ventures beyond its competence.

In 1989, Hour Glass acquired a 51% stake in Milano Pizza. The venture bled money for years before shutting down in the mid-1990s. Undeterred, management tried watchmaking – acquiring Gerald Genta in 1996. Watch manufacturing requires specialized skills Hour Glass lacked. Facing mounting losses, they divested in 2000.

Peter Lynch called this "diworsification" – the destruction of shareholder value through misguided expansion.

So what separates Amazon's long list of failures from Hour Glass's? It comes down to three things.

First, strategic logic. Amazon stayed close to home. AWS grew from solving the company's own infrastructure problems. Advertising leveraged customer data they already had. Logistics extended fulfillment capabilities they'd already built. Each move connected to what came before. Hour Glass jumped from luxury watches to pizza with nothing linking them.

Second, track record. When a company announces a new venture, I look at their history. How often have their expansions succeeded? Amazon's failures are well-documented – Fire Phone, Destinations, Restaurants. But so are their wins: AWS, Prime, Advertising, Logistics. The wins dwarf the failures in value created. AWS and advertising alone generate tens of billions in profits annually. Hour Glass tried pizza and watchmaking, failed at both, and gave up. There's no pattern of learning, iterating, and eventually winning.

Third, asymmetric payoffs – which explains why Amazon's wins dwarf their losses. Each experiment had genuine upside if it worked. AWS didn't become a nice side business – it became one of the most profitable enterprises in tech. Advertising didn't add incremental revenue – it created an entirely new profit engine. What's the ceiling for a watch retailer succeeding at pizza? A regional chain, at best.

When I evaluate potential spawners, I ask: Do their experiments connect to existing strengths? What's management's hit rate on new ventures – and are they learning from failures? Is there genuine upside if the bet works? Companies that can show a pattern of strategic expansion, with wins that justify the inevitable misses, have earned the right to keep experimenting.

Path 4: Pricing power

Raising prices – the ultimate profit driver

Warren Buffett once said that the most important factor in evaluating a business is pricing power. "If you've got the power to raise prices without losing business to a competitor, you've got a very good business. And if you have to have a prayer session before raising the price by 10%, then you've got a terrible business."

Why does Buffett care so much about pricing power? Because of how dramatically it impacts profits.

Consider a simple business selling 1,000 widgets annually at $100 each, with $60 in variable costs per widget and $10,000 in fixed costs. Operating profit: $30,000.

Now raise the price 10% to $110. Revenue jumps to $110,000. But costs don't change – same number of widgets, same production costs, same fixed overhead. That extra $10,000 in revenue flows straight to profit. Operating profit: $40,000.

A 10% price increase just drove a 33% profit increase.

	Before	**After 10% Price Increase**	**Percentage Change**
Price per widget	$100	$110	+10%
Units sold	1,000	1,000	0%
Revenue	$100,000	$110,000	+10%
Variable costs	$60,000	$60,000	0%
Fixed costs	$10,000	$10,000	0%
Operating profit	**$30,000**	**$40,000**	**+33%**

This is why I'm always on the lookout for companies with pricing power. Small price increases, compounded over years, create enormous value. But not many businesses can raise prices consistently without losing customers. To succeed, a company needs a strong economic moat – usually built on a brand that customers feel emotionally connected to. See's Candies shows exactly how this works.

See's candies – a sweet lesson in pricing power

One of Buffett's favorite examples of pricing power is See's Candies. He and Charlie Munger acquired it in 1972. Back then, See's sold its candies for $1.96 per pound. By 2024, the price had risen to $25 per pound – a roughly 13-fold increase over 52 years.[4]

That's an average annual price increase of 5%, outpacing inflation, which averaged approximately 4% over the same period.

When speaking to students at the University of Florida in 1998, Buffett explained the psychology behind See's pricing power. "There was something special. Every person in California has something in mind about See's Candies and overwhelmingly it was favorable. They had taken a box on Valentine's Day to some girl and she had kissed him… See's Candies means getting kissed. If we can get that in the minds of people, we can raise prices."

What makes See's remarkable isn't just its ability to raise prices – it's retaining customers while doing so. Look at the numbers from 1972 to 1983:

- Candy sales volume grew at an unremarkable 3.8% annually.
- Revenue grew at 15.6% annually – driven almost entirely by price increases.
- Earnings after tax grew at 20.7% annually.

Sales volume grew at a slow rate, but earnings compounded at over 20% a year. That's pricing power in action.

Of course, pricing power always comes back to value creation. Is the company delivering as much value as it's charging? A strong moat allows a business to generate excess profits, but without providing sufficient value, even beloved brands face a reckoning. Customers will abandon the brand the moment a better alternative comes along.

Netflix – pricing power meets operating leverage

Netflix shows what happens when you combine pricing power with massive scale.

In 2017, Netflix offered over 30,000 hours of content for just $9.99 per month – an irresistible value proposition compared to paying $9 for a single movie ticket. This immense value allowed Netflix to raise prices significantly without losing customers. Between 2017 and 2023, Netflix increased its standard plan price from $9.99 to $15.49, yet its subscriber base grew from approximately 118 million to 260 million.

But here's where it gets interesting. During this period, revenue grew 188% from $11.7 billion to $33.7 billion. Operating income grew 729% – from $839 million to $6.95 billion.

How does profit grow so much faster than revenue?

Operating leverage. Netflix pays the same for a show whether one person or 100 million people watch it. Each new subscriber adds revenue with minimal incremental cost. Price increases flow straight to the bottom line.

This dynamic isn't unique to Netflix. Tech companies excel at operating leverage because their costs are largely fixed. Meta builds its ad platform once – then serves billions of ads at near-zero marginal cost. Visa processes payments through the same network whether transaction volume doubles or triples. Once the infrastructure is built, additional revenue flows almost entirely to profit.

But growing earnings is only the first piece of the puzzle. What companies do with those earnings – whether they pay dividends, buy back shares, or reinvest – can dramatically impact your returns. This brings us to our second driver: the power of shrinking the share count through strategic buybacks.

DRIVER 2: HOW SHARE BUYBACKS CREATE OR DESTROY VALUE

So far we've seen how companies grow earnings. But what about the second driver – using those earnings to shrink the share count?

Share buybacks, when done right, are another great way to increase intrinsic value for remaining shareholders. Buybacks reduce the total number of outstanding shares. This increases each remaining shareholder's proportional ownership in the company.

Warren Buffett succinctly puts it: "When the share count goes down, your interest in our many businesses goes up."

But the caveat is that buybacks only create value when done correctly. They can destroy value under the wrong circumstances.

Buffett offers clarity on this subject in his 1999 letter to shareholders. "There is only one combination of facts that makes it advisable for a company to repurchase its shares: First, the company has available funds – cash plus sensible borrowing capacity – beyond the near-term needs of the business and, second, finds its stock selling in the market below its intrinsic value, conservatively-calculated."

In other words, share buybacks only make sense when:

1. The company has enough funds to maintain its competitive position.
2. There's nowhere else to reinvest at attractive returns.
3. The company's stock is selling below intrinsic value.

A business's number one priority is to invest in building or enhancing its economic moat. A strong moat grants the business the ability to earn attractive returns on the money it invests. If the business has opportunities to keep reinvesting at those attractive returns, we want it to do so – that's how intrinsic value compounds.

But if the company has spent sufficiently to maintain its competitive position and has nowhere to reinvest at attractive returns, then it should consider buying back shares to return value to shareholders.

When buybacks create or destroy value

To understand how buybacks can go either way, let's walk through a straightforward example.

Imagine ABC Cupcakes: 1,000 shares outstanding, each worth $100 in intrinsic value, giving the company a total intrinsic value of $100,000. Management has $50,000 in cash to buy back shares. The question is: at what price?

	Buyback at $80	**Buyback at $120**
Price versus intrinsic value	Below	Above
Shares repurchased	625	416
Shares remaining	375	584
Remaining intrinsic value	$50,000	$50,000
New value per share	$133	$86
Shareholder outcome	+33% richer	−14% poorer

Same company. Same cash spent. Opposite outcomes.

When management buys below intrinsic value, they're acquiring $100 of value for $80 – and remaining shareholders capture the difference. When they buy above intrinsic value, they're paying $120 for $100 of value – and remaining shareholders absorb the loss.

The lesson is simple: buybacks at the right price create wealth. Buybacks at the wrong price destroy it. When I evaluate a company's buyback program, I look for management that demonstrates discipline – buying aggressively when shares are cheap, holding back when they're expensive.

Few companies have demonstrated this discipline better than AutoZone.

AutoZone: The buyback champion

AutoZone, America's leading auto parts retailer with over 6,000 stores across the US and Mexico, has executed one of history's most successful buyback strategies.

Between 1998 and 2023, the company grew its net income by nearly 11-fold, from $228 million to $2.5 billion – roughly 10% per year. The P/E multiple remained relatively flat at 20x.

Despite growing net income by 11-fold, AutoZone's stock price increased nearly 86-fold. It rose from $30.12 in 1998 to $2,585.61 in 2023 – a compound annual growth rate of 19.5% over the 25-year period.

What drove these meteoric returns?

The company reduced its total shares outstanding by an astonishing 88% during this period. It spent $33.8 billion to bring its shares from 152 million in 1998 to just 18 million in 2023.

While net income grew at 10% annually, earnings per share grew at nearly 20% annually. The difference was driven by the shrinking share count, which effectively doubled the growth rate that accrued to each remaining share.

This disciplined capital allocation strategy enhanced per-share intrinsic value. It also drove exceptional stock price appreciation, making AutoZone a standout example of effective buybacks.

AutoZone was able to execute this aggressive strategy because of its unique business model. The company generates strong free cash flow year after year. Its capital-efficient operations require just 4–5% of revenue in capital investment. And it actually collects cash from customers before paying suppliers, creating negative working capital – meaning the business funds itself as it grows.

Businesses with these characteristics will likely have the ammunition to buy back shares aggressively when it makes sense for shareholders.

When I'm analyzing potential investments, I look for companies that generate strong free cash flow – the cash left over after running the business and maintaining equipment – and demonstrate a track record of intelligent capital allocation through disciplined share repurchases.

But not all management teams understand these principles. Some prioritize financial engineering over the business itself, destroying value in the process. Starbucks shows exactly where this approach leads.

Starbucks: When buybacks backfire

We saw in Chapter 3 how Starbucks diluted its brand after Howard Schultz stepped down. Under former CEO Kevin Johnson, the buyback story is equally cautionary – a case study in how share repurchases, poorly executed, can undermine a company's future.

Johnson committed to returning $25 billion to shareholders through buybacks and dividends by fiscal year 2020. Between 2017 and 2022, Starbucks spent over $25 billion on repurchases, reducing shares outstanding by approximately 20%. Yet despite this massive shrinkage, earnings per share barely kept pace with revenue growth – both around 7.5% annually. Operating margins had collapsed from 18.5% to 14.3%, swallowing the benefit of a smaller share count.

Twenty billion dollars spent, and per-share earnings grew no faster than revenue. Three problems lurked beneath.

First, valuation discipline disappeared. Starbucks bought back shares at 18x forward earnings – the price relative to next year's expected profits. That's reasonable. But they kept buying as the multiple climbed to 30x. Repurchasing overvalued shares transfers wealth from remaining shareholders to those who sell. It's the opposite of value creation.

Second, debt funded the buybacks. Long-term debt ballooned from $3.9 billion to $14.6 billion during Johnson's tenure – not out of necessity, but to amplify repurchases. The justification was low interest rates. But as Pulak Prasad writes in *What I Learned About Investing from Darwin,* "debt diminishes strategic flexibility and hence long-term value creation." When Covid hit in 2020, Starbucks suspended buybacks to preserve liquidity. A stronger balance sheet might have let them go on offense while competitors struggled.

Third, buybacks came before the business. A company's first priority is investing in its moat. For Starbucks, that meant the baristas who create the "third place" experience. Instead, chronic understaffing and excessive workloads fueled unionization efforts at over 130 stores by early 2022. By 2024, comparable-store sales were declining. Customers faced long wait times. The stock, which had peaked above $126 in mid-2021, fell below $73 by mid-2024.

The market eventually brought in Brian Niccol as CEO – known for his Chipotle turnaround. But years of underinvestment will take time to repair.

As an investor, I view Starbucks as a powerful reminder: never invest in companies that prioritize financial engineering over strengthening their competitive advantage. The companies that create the most long-term value maintain a laser focus on nurturing their economic moat.

AutoZone and Starbucks illustrate the stark difference between disciplined and destructive buybacks. But even the best earnings growth and smartest buybacks won't deliver exceptional returns if the market never recognizes the company's value. This brings us to our third and final driver – changes in how much investors are willing to pay for those earnings.

DRIVER 3: MULTIPLE RE-RATES

The third driver of returns is changes in the P/E multiple – how much investors are willing to pay for each dollar of earnings.

Here's a simple way to think about it. If a stock trades at $100 per share and earns $5 per share, the P/E multiple is 20x. Investors are paying $20 for every $1 of earnings.

This multiple reflects expectations. When investors are optimistic about a company's future, they'll pay more for each dollar of current earnings. When they're pessimistic, they pay less. A company earning the same $5 per share might trade at $150 (30x) when loved by the market or $50 (10x) when hated – same business, wildly different prices.

A common misconception is that a lower P/E multiple automatically means a stock is "cheap." Likewise, a higher P/E multiple doesn't necessarily mean it's "expensive." The P/E multiple is based on historical earnings, while the market is forward-looking.

True valuation involves assessing future earnings potential, a topic we'll explore in detail in the chapter on valuation.

Generally, businesses with strong growth prospects, high returns on capital, and long-term viability command higher P/E multiples than businesses lacking those qualities. High-quality businesses tend to have higher P/E multiples.

But the market isn't always efficient.

There are times when high-quality businesses experience temporary P/E multiple compression due to investor overreactions to short-term negative news.

These situations present opportunities for astute investors. When a high-quality business's P/E multiple is temporarily depressed, you can benefit not only from earnings growth, but also from multiple expansion as the market recognizes the company's true worth.

Warren Buffett's investment in Apple demonstrates this perfectly.

Buffett's home run with Apple Inc.

Warren Buffett began building Berkshire Hathaway's position in Apple in 2016. He ultimately invested $36 billion by the end of 2018. By 2023, that stake had ballooned in value to approximately $174 billion.

This investment shocked the financial world. For decades, Buffett had famously avoided tech stocks. He cited the sector's rapid pace of change and the difficulty in predicting long-term winners.

What prompted Buffett to change his mind?

He saw Apple differently from other investors. To him, it wasn't a hardware company but a consumer products company with a powerful brand.[5] The ecosystem created customer loyalty and high switching costs. Tim Cook's capital allocation strategy – focused on returning excess capital through dividends and buybacks – aligned perfectly with Buffett's philosophy.

But what truly sweetened the deal was Apple's valuation.

Beyond these qualitative factors, Apple's valuation was compelling. It was trading at a forward P/E multiple of only about 11×, compared to 17× for the S&P 500.

The company had a net cash position of approximately $150 billion at the time. Excluding this cash, Apple's forward P/E was roughly 8×.

The prevailing narrative surrounding Apple at the time focused on its hardware business. Many overlooked the strength of its ecosystem and the growth potential of its services segment. Many investors compared Apple to Nokia and Blackberry – companies that had collapsed when their markets shifted.

Apple's ecosystem proved far stickier than anyone anticipated. Its services segment, with its recurring revenue streams, grew rapidly. Apple's aggressive share buyback strategy further enhanced its per-share value.

Between 2016 and 2023, Apple reduced its shares outstanding by 27%. This, combined with increased profitability from its high-margin services segment and operational efficiencies, drove diluted earnings per share from $2.08 to $6.13 – a 195% increase.

But the most significant driver of returns was multiple expansion. Apple's forward P/E multiple increased from about 11× to 29×, a remarkable 165% increase.

Buffett's investment in Apple was a home run. It was a classic example of an investment that benefited from all three value creation engines – growth, share buybacks, and multiple expansion.

How to spot multiple expansion opportunities

How do you spot these opportunities before the market catches on? Let me share what I look for.

The setup usually looks the same: a quality business hit by temporary problems, with headlines suggesting permanent decline. Meta in 2022 had all the markers – compressed multiple, extreme pessimism, but fundamentals that told a different story. The company was still generating billions in cash. Management was taking decisive action. The problems were fixable, not fatal.

I ask myself three questions.

First, is this a broken business or a broken stock? Meta's advertising platform still worked. Users weren't leaving. And while the iOS changes hurt everyone in digital advertising, Meta had more data and resources than any competitor. If Meta couldn't navigate the changes, no one could – and ad dollars would continue flowing to whoever performed best on a relative basis. The business wasn't broken – just temporarily impaired.

Second, is management responding or denying? Zuckerberg didn't pretend everything was fine. He launched a "year of efficiency," cut costs aggressively, and invested heavily in AI to rebuild ad targeting capabilities lost to iOS changes. He communicated a clear path forward. When management acknowledges problems and attacks them head-on, that's when multiples can re-rate quickly.

Third, how much pessimism is already priced in? At 8.7x forward earnings – the price relative to next year's expected profits – the market was treating Meta like a dying business. Any improvement – not perfection, just improvement – would force a reassessment.

You can't predict exactly when multiples will expand. But you can recognize the conditions: a quality business, temporarily misunderstood, with management taking visible action. When you find that setup alongside earnings growth potential and disciplined capital allocation, all three drivers can work in your favor simultaneously. That's the opportunity worth waiting for.

CONCLUSION – PUTTING IT ALL TOGETHER

While all three drivers matter, earnings growth is the foundation. Buybacks and multiple expansion can amplify returns, but without earnings growth, there's nothing to amplify. The strongest compounders grow earnings for decades – and that growth overwhelms almost everything else.

Consider what Terry Smith uncovered when he examined historical returns of quality businesses over long holding periods. Investors could have paid 281 times earnings for L'Oréal in January 1973, 126 times for Colgate, or 100 times for PepsiCo – valuations that seem absolutely insane – and still earned roughly 7% annually through 2019, beating the global market's 6.2% return. Despite these extreme entry prices, the quality and durability of these companies' earnings growth eventually overcame even the most unfavorable starting point.[6]

Charlie Munger explained why this happens: "Over the long term, it's hard for a stock to earn a much better return than the business which underlies it earns. If the business earns 6% on capital over 40 years and you hold it for that 40 years, you're not going to make much different than a 6% return even if you originally buy it at a huge discount. Conversely, if a business earns 18% on capital over 20 or 30 years, even if you pay an expensive looking price, you'll end up with a fine result."

This doesn't mean valuation is unimportant – we still need discipline about price. But it reveals that for long-term investors, correctly assessing business quality and the sustainability of competitive advantages matters even more than precision on entry multiples. The difference between paying 20x or 25x earnings for a true compounder becomes almost irrelevant over decades, while the difference between a business earning 6% versus 18% on capital shapes your entire outcome.

Consistent earnings growth generates the cash for buybacks and builds the track record that often leads to multiple expansion when the market finally recognizes the company's quality.

Share buybacks amplify returns when done at the right price. Multiple expansion provides a powerful boost when the market recognizes undervalued quality.

The most powerful investments – like Buffett's Apple stake or my Meta investment – benefit from all three drivers working in concert. Earnings grew. Management bought back shares at attractive prices. And the market eventually recognized what it had missed, driving multiples higher.

When evaluating potential investments, I always ask:

- Does the business have sustainable competitive advantages that drive earnings growth?
- Is management allocating capital wisely, including through disciplined buybacks?
- Is the current valuation reasonable relative to the company's prospects?

Find a company where you can answer yes to all three, and you've found something worth owning.

YOUR LUNCH BREAK SUMMARY

In this chapter, you learned:

- **Three drivers create capital appreciation**: Earnings growth is the foundation, share buybacks amplify returns, and P/E multiple changes provide powerful boosts when all three align.
- **The holy grail of compounding**: Companies with high returns on capital AND long runways to reinvest create extraordinary wealth. Each dollar retained generates more dollars, which generate more dollars still. Finding both qualities in one company is rare – and powerful.
- **Buybacks require discipline**: They create value when shares trade below intrinsic value but destroy it when management overpays or uses debt to fund them.
- **Pricing power drives outsized profits**: A 10% price increase can drive a 33% profit increase. Companies that can raise prices without losing customers – like See's Candies or Netflix – possess a rare and valuable advantage.
- **Spot multiple expansion setups**: Ask three questions – is this a broken business or broken stock? Is management responding or denying? How much pessimism is already priced in? When a quality business answers right on all three, the re-rate can be powerful.

YOUR NEXT STEP

Now that you understand what drives returns, you need to evaluate who's making the decisions. Great businesses can be destroyed by bad management, while average businesses can thrive under exceptional leaders. In the next chapter, we'll explore why management quality can make or break even the best business models – and how to spot the difference before it's too late.

CHAPTER 5
IT'S ALWAYS ABOUT MANAGEMENT

SO FAR WE'VE explored what makes a quality business and what drives shareholder returns. But there's one variable that determines whether any of it materializes: the people making the decisions.

Moats don't widen themselves. Capital doesn't allocate itself. During crises, someone has to make the calls that separate survivors from casualties.

And crisis is where you really see what management is made of.

In the early days of the Covid-19 pandemic, the market was in freefall. Quality companies were getting crushed right alongside the junk.

Booking Holdings caught my attention. I'd admired this company for years for its asset-light model and powerful network effects. Now its stock had cratered from $2,000 to $1,177, a ~41% collapse. The P/E had compressed to just 18x, far below its historical 30x.

The travel industry was at a standstill.

The numbers were brutal. In Q2 2020, Booking's total travel bookings collapsed 91% year-over-year – from $25 billion to just $2.3 billion. The company posted its first quarterly loss in nearly two decades. By Q4, the bleeding continued: a $165 million net loss and $577 million in cash burned in just three months.

Wall Street analysts were writing obituaries for the entire travel sector.

My first move was checking the company's balance sheet. Could they survive extended lockdowns? But survival wasn't enough – I needed to know if leadership could turn crisis into opportunity.

Crisis reveals character. It separates managers who panic from those who position for dominance when competitors fail.

During the Q4 2020 earnings call, Booking's CEO Glenn Fogel laid out his strategy with remarkable clarity: stabilize the business, optimize operations, position for recovery.

No sugarcoating. No corporate buzzwords. Just honest assessment and decisive action.

While competitors played defense, Fogel played offense. He cut costs ruthlessly, but kept investing in technology. He negotiated better supplier terms. He prepared for the travel snapback that others thought might never come.

Warren Buffett nails it: "Only when the tide goes out do you discover who's been swimming naked." Fogel was fully dressed and ready to surf.

I bought at $1,200, then more at $1,400. By the end of 2024, that investment had returned 292%. Booking didn't just survive. It dominated the recovery.

This experience reinforced what I'd learned over and over: In extreme uncertainty, the difference between wealth creation and destruction comes down to leadership.

Fogel's clarity and decisiveness during crisis separated him from the pack. While others were trying to stay afloat, he was already positioning for the recovery. That's the difference management makes.

In this chapter, I show you how to spot leaders like Fogel – and how to identify the ones who destroy value. We explore five traits that define exceptional managers, why founder-led companies often outperform, and the red flags that signal trouble before it's too late.

THE KNIGHTS GUARDING YOUR CASTLE

Buffett has this perfect metaphor: "We not only look for a great economic castle, but we look for a great knight in charge of that castle. Because that's important. He's the one that throws the crocodiles into the moat and widens the moat over time."

Here's the uncomfortable truth – most competitive advantages are temporary. Consumer tastes shift. Technology disrupts. New competitors emerge with venture capital war chests. The moat protecting your investment today can dry up tomorrow if management isn't constantly reinforcing it.

Great managers don't just maintain moats. They obsess over widening them. They adapt before they're forced to. They strengthen their position especially when business is booming.

In his 2005 letter, Buffett explained this daily battle:

"Every day, in countless ways, the competitive position of each of our businesses grows either weaker or stronger. On a daily basis, the effects of our actions are imperceptible; cumulatively, though, their consequences are enormous. When our long-term competitive position improves as a result of these almost unnoticeable actions, we describe the phenomenon as 'widening the moat.'"

Then he drops the key insight: "We always, of course, hope to earn more money in the short-term. But when short-term and long-term conflict, widening the moat must take precedence."

That's the test. Will management sacrifice today's earnings to strengthen tomorrow's position? Most CEOs can't resist quarterly pressures. Wall Street demands immediate results. The board wants higher margins now. It takes exceptional leadership to say no – to choose long-term strength over short-term applause.

Think of it this way: the moat protects the castle, but only the knight decides whether to deepen it or let it fill with silt. Great knights spend their quiet years adding crocodiles to the moat, raising the walls, stockpiling resources. They fortify when enemies seem distant, not when they're already at the gates. By then it's too late.

The management graveyard is full of companies that had everything except the right leadership.

Kodak was synonymous with photography for over a century. When the digital revolution arrived, they clung desperately to their profitable film business instead of pivoting. By failing to adapt, they lost everything – bankruptcy in 2012.

Sears was a retail titan. But while management focused on short-term financial maneuvers, they neglected their stores and ignored e-commerce. Customer experience deteriorated while competitors evolved, until bankruptcy became inevitable in 2018.

Blockbuster was the king of video rentals. When streaming emerged, they dismissed it while Netflix redefined the entire market. Ten years later, all 9,000 stores were gone.

These weren't business failures. They were management failures.

Widening the moat shows up in improving returns on capital, like we discussed earlier, but it is only half the equation. The other half? Making sure that value accrues to shareholders on a per-share basis.

THE NORTH STAR OF VALUE CREATION

Management's job should be simple – maximize long-term value per share.

Most CEOs forget those last two words. Growing revenue doesn't matter if you dilute shareholders to death. Global expansion means nothing if shareholder returns plummet. Building an empire is pointless if each piece is worth less than before.

Berkshire Hathaway's owner's manual gets it right: "Our long-term economic goal is to maximize Berkshire's average annual rate of gain in intrinsic business value on a per-share basis. We do not measure the economic significance or performance of Berkshire by its size; we measure by per-share progress."

The problem? Most CEOs rise through a business due to their expertise in operations. They master supply chains, sales, manufacturing. These skills matter, but capital allocation requires different DNA.

This disconnect creates empire builders – CEOs who confuse size with value creation, making splashy acquisitions that grab headlines but destroy shareholder wealth.

Even companies owned by Warren Buffett have not been immune to this problem. In his 1996 letter, he revealed: "A far more serious problem occurs when the management of a great company gets sidetracked and neglects its wonderful base business while purchasing other businesses that are so-so or worse. Would you believe that a few decades back they were growing shrimp at Coke and exploring for oil at Gillette?"[1]

The lesson is brutal: Even the best businesses can be destroyed when management loses focus.

But focusing on per-share value doesn't mean being ruthless. The best managers understand a counterintuitive truth about value creation.

WHEN BEING GOOD IS GOOD BUSINESS

Here's what most investors miss – maximizing shareholder value doesn't mean squeezing every penny from customers and employees. It means treating everyone well.

The most successful companies create value for all stakeholders. Happy employees are productive. Satisfied customers become evangelists. Strong supplier relationships ensure quality. Healthy communities provide stable operating environments.

This isn't feel-good nonsense. It's proven economics.

John Mackey at Whole Foods built an empire on this: "Long-term profits come from having a deeper purpose, great products, satisfied customers, happy employees, great suppliers, and from taking a degree of responsibility for the community and environment we live in."

The book *Firms of Endearment* proved it with data. Companies that prioritized all stakeholders delivered 1,026% returns from 1996 to 2006. The S&P 500? Just 122%. That's an eight-fold difference.

Look at Costco under Jim Sinegal. He paid $20/hour when competitors paid $11. Provided health insurance to 85% of employees, including part-timers. Maintained legendary return policies. Built partnerships with suppliers.

Wall Street constantly attacked this "excessive generosity." Sinegal's response was perfect: "Wall Street is in the business of making money between now and next Tuesday. We're in the business of building an organization, an institution that we hope will be here 50 years from now."[2]

Costco's stock returned roughly 4,900% from its 1985 IPO through Sinegal's 2012 retirement, nearly ten times the S&P 500. In retail – where high turnover is the norm – treating employees well became Costco's secret weapon.

Treating stakeholders well isn't just ethical. It's profitable. The best managers understand this in their bones. They build businesses that create value for everyone, knowing shareholder returns will follow.

This philosophy is the foundation. But how do you identify managers who actually live it? After years of investing, I've found five core traits that separate wealth creators from wealth destroyers. You've already seen some of them in the Booking story. Later in this chapter, I'll show you how the same framework led me to trim my Lululemon position after its Q3 2025 earnings, when management lost its way.

Here's what I look for:

1. Transparency and Accountability
2. Capital Allocation Mastery
3. Strong Opinions, Loosely Held
4. The Capacity to Suffer
5. Skin in the Game

Let's look through each of these five traits in turn below.

HOW TO SPOT EXCEPTIONAL LEADERSHIP

Exceptional leadership leaves a trail of evidence. You can spot it in proxy statements, shareholder letters, earnings calls, and even Glassdoor reviews.

Pay attention to how management communicates. Do they answer questions directly? Own their mistakes? Or hide behind corporate jargon and deflection?

Here are the five core traits that define managers capable of creating exceptional long-term shareholder value (plus one powerful bonus).

1. Transparency and accountability

Several indicators reveal whether management truly serves shareholder interests. First and foremost, evaluate whether the CEO's communications are open and honest, or if they appear sanitized by public relations teams and legal departments.

Warren Buffett and Jeff Bezos exemplify excellence in shareholder communication, consistently discussing their businesses' performance with remarkable candor.

Buffett approaches his annual letters with a specific reader in mind – his sister, Bertie. While intelligent and financially savvy, she isn't a financial expert steeped in accounting or economics. His goal is to anticipate her questions and provide honest answers. This results in letters that are candid, insightful, and accessible.

By stripping away unnecessary jargon and complexity, Buffett creates communications that genuinely help shareholders understand the business. It's a model all CEOs should follow.

Jeff Bezos's famous 1997 letter – which he appended to every subsequent letter – remains a masterclass in transparent communication. It clearly outlined his vision and strategy for Amazon, explaining why market leadership was crucial for creating shareholder value:

"We believe that a fundamental measure of our success will be the shareholder value we create over the long term. This value will be a direct result of our ability to extend and solidify our current market leadership position. Market leadership can translate directly to higher revenue, higher profitability, greater capital velocity, and correspondingly stronger returns on invested capital."

This transparency helped shareholders understand Amazon's strategy and remain committed during its early, unprofitable years. More importantly, Bezos made it clear that the company's fundamental measure of success would be long-term shareholder value creation.

Owning mistakes

While we want competent management, mistakes are inevitable in business. What matters is how leaders respond when things go wrong. The best managers own their mistakes rather than hiding them.

In his 2007 letter to shareholders, Buffett acknowledged his error in judging Dexter Shoe Company's economic moat when he acquired it in 1993 for $433 million. The business later shut down completely.

But Buffett went further, highlighting that his biggest mistake wasn't the $433 million purchase price – it was using Berkshire Hathaway stock as currency. Those shares had ballooned to $3.5 billion by 2007 and continued compounding thereafter. This costly lesson made him hesitant to use Berkshire shares for acquisitions ever again, preferring cash instead.

Similarly, Jeff Bezos acknowledged the Fire Phone as "a massive failed experiment" in his 2018 shareholder letter. He explained that as a company grows, everything needs to scale – including the size of its failed experiments. If the magnitude of failures isn't growing, the company isn't inventing at a scale that can meaningfully impact results.

This level of candor builds trust with shareholders. During crises and challenges, shareholders need to understand the rationale behind mistakes – whether they resulted from calculated risks or errors that won't be repeated.

Communication style

For companies that host earnings calls, pay special attention to management's behavior during Q&A sessions,

Do executives answer questions comprehensively, or do they focus only on positives while glossing over negatives? Do they respond directly, or do they search for acceptable answers while using filler phrases like, "I would say that…" or "I'm not sure we can comment…"?

How management communicates with key stakeholders reveals their character. We want leaders who are accountable rather than those who blame everything on macroeconomics, supply chain disruptions, changing consumer preferences, or whatever external factor happens to be the excuse du jour.

We want them to tell us straight what the problems are and, more importantly, how they plan to address them – not hide behind promotional language and deflection.

What to Look For:

- CEOs who write their own letters, not PR-polished releases.
- Specific numbers and frank discussion of problems.
- Direct answers to analysts' questions, not deflection.
- Mistakes acknowledged with clear lessons learned.

2. Capital allocation mastery

The single best metric to evaluate a CEO's capital allocation skills is the increase in a company's per-share value over time.

In his book *The Outsiders*, William Thorndike shared: "You really only need to know three things to evaluate a CEO's greatness: the compound annual return to shareholders during his or her tenure and the return over the same period for peer companies and for the broader market (usually measured by the S&P 500)."

If a CEO has been running a company for decades, a look at the long-term stock price chart should suffice. Consider the value creation by companies such as Berkshire Hathaway under Warren Buffett or Teledyne under Henry Singleton – you'll find that immense share price appreciation over the long-term reflects a series of excellent capital allocation decisions.

The Five Capital Allocation Options

Most CEOs are terrible at capital allocation. They rise through operations – running factories, managing sales, optimizing supply chains. Then suddenly they're managing hundreds of millions to billions in capital. Different skill set entirely.

At its core, capital allocation is deciding what to do with excess cash. Every CEO has the same five options:

1. Reinvest in the Business

Management should only reinvest capital when the ROIC exceeds the cost of capital. Otherwise, value gets destroyed rather than created. The problem? Empire-building CEOs often invest in low-return projects that don't meet the hurdle rate. They'd rather run a larger company than enhance shareholder value.

When returns don't justify reinvestment, good CEOs return cash to shareholders. But that requires admitting the business has limits. Empire builders can't do that – they'd rather destroy value than shrink.

2. Hold Cash

Maintaining cash reserves enhances business resilience, providing a buffer against economic downturns and funding for opportunistic investments. However, this approach can go to extremes.

Apple's massive cash hoard – which at one point exceeded $250 billion – illustrates this dilemma. While providing stability, excessive cash drastically reduces a company's return on invested capital due to the bloated balance sheet. When businesses generate more cash than they can productively deploy, they should return that capital to shareholders.

According to *The Warren Buffett Way* by Robert Hagstrom, "In Buffett's mind, the only reasonable and responsible course for companies that have a growing pile of cash that cannot be reinvested at above-average rates is to return that money to the shareholders."

Exceptional capital allocators maintain sufficient cash for resilience while avoiding the drag of excessive reserves that earn minimal returns.

3. Pay Dividends

Dividends make sense when you can't reinvest profitably and shares are too expensive to buy back. But initiating dividends creates a trap – investors expect them forever, regardless of business conditions.

Disney exemplifies this perfectly. For over 40 years, they faithfully increased dividends, creating unbreakable expectations. When they acquired Fox for $71 billion and launched Disney+, they desperately needed capital to pay down debt and fund the streaming wars. The smart move was suspending dividends to strengthen the balance sheet and invest in their digital future.

Instead, they kept paying. By Q2 2020, total debt had ballooned to $55.4 billion with $365 million in interest expenses that quarter alone. They prioritized dividend expectations over financial flexibility, handicapping their ability to compete.

Only when the pandemic shuttered parks did they finally suspend dividends – forced by crisis rather than strategy. The lesson? Dividend commitments can trap management into poor capital allocation even when the business desperately needs that cash elsewhere.

4. Repurchase Shares

As Buffett emphasizes, share repurchases should only occur after management has: ensured the company has enough funds to maintain competitive position, verified there's nowhere else to reinvest at attractive returns, and confirmed the company's stock is selling below intrinsic value.

When executed under these conditions, buybacks increase per-share value for remaining shareholders. However, many companies repurchase shares regardless of valuation, often buying high and destroying value. Others repurchase shares while simultaneously issuing new ones for executive compensation, negating the benefit to shareholders.

AutoZone demonstrates disciplined buybacks – reducing shares by 88% over 25 years, turning 10% annual profit growth into 20% earnings per share growth. The company could execute this aggressive strategy because of its unique business model: strong free cash flow generation, minimal capital investment needs, and negative working capital.

Contrast this with Starbucks from Chapter 3 – borrowing money to buy back shares while the business deteriorated. When Covid hit and their share price plummeted, they had to suspend buybacks despite the aggressive drop in the company's share price because they needed to preserve liquidity.

5. Make Acquisitions

Few CEOs excel at acquisitions. The landscape is littered with value-destroying deals motivated more by empire-building than shareholder returns.

As David Packard, co-founder of Hewlett-Packard, wisely noted: "While acquisitions are often useful in expanding a company's technologies and gaining a quick entry into new markets, they are not without their problems. Chief among these is the difficulty in blending two cultures, operating philosophies, and management styles."

Facebook's Instagram purchase for $1 billion looked insane in 2012. Thirteen employees, zero revenue. But Zuckerberg saw what others missed – a platform perfectly positioned for mobile, with a culture worth preserving. He exercised patience, waiting over a year before introducing ads. In 2024 alone, Instagram is estimated to have generated close to $67 billion in revenue.

Contrast with Starbucks' serial acquisition failures. In 2012, they acquired La Boulange, a small Bay Area bakery chain, for $100 million to elevate their food offerings. The reality? Customers panned the new pastries. Running 23 cafés proved a "distraction" for management. Just three years later, Starbucks shuttered every La Boulange location.

Then there's Lululemon buying Mirror for $500 million during the pandemic. Home fitness seemed perfect! But they failed to recognize it was a temporary trend. More fundamentally, they couldn't blend Mirror's technology culture with their retail DNA. By 2023, they had written off nearly the entire investment.

The pattern is clear: successful acquisitions enhance and extend a company's core competencies, while failed ones often represent desperate attempts to enter unfamiliar territories. Integration approach matters tremendously.

These five options – reinvest, hold cash, pay dividends, buy back stock, make acquisitions – are the complete toolkit. Great capital allocators don't just excel at one. They master all five, adapting their approach based on market conditions and opportunities.

The master allocator: Henry Singleton

Henry Singleton, longtime CEO of Teledyne from 1960 to 1986, exemplifies masterful capital allocation across all dimensions.

When Teledyne's stock traded at steep valuations in the 1960s, Singleton used the high-priced stock as currency for more than 130 acquisitions. When valuations plummeted in the 1970s, he completely reversed course – between 1972 and 1984, he reduced the share count by more than 90%.

Same CEO, same company, opposite strategy. He adapted based on price and opportunity, not formula.

The results speak for themselves. As William Thorndike documented in *The Outsiders*, a dollar invested with Singleton in 1963 was worth $180 by 1990 – a 20.4% annual compound return over nearly three decades. That same dollar in the S&P 500 would have been worth just $15. Singleton outperformed the index by over 12 times. In John Train's book *The Money Masters*, Warren Buffett stated he believes "Henry Singleton has the best operating and capital-deployment record in American business."

Singleton's genius wasn't following a rigid formula – it was reading the market and choosing the right tool at the right time.

What to look for:

- Consistent ROIC above cost of capital over multiple years.
- Buybacks concentrated when valuation is cheap.
- Debt levels that leave flexibility for downturns.
- Clear explanations of capital allocation decisions in shareholder letters.
- Track record of walking away from expensive acquisitions.

3. Strong opinions, loosely held

Capital allocation skill is crucial, but markets change. Technology disrupts. Consumer preferences shift overnight. The best CEOs combine conviction with adaptability – they have strong opinions but hold them loosely.

Strong opinions create clarity. They align thousands of employees. They enable fast decisions. But those opinions must yield to new evidence. Without conviction, companies drift. Without flexibility, they become obsolete.

Reed Hastings at Netflix mastered this balance.

For years, Hastings was adamant about keeping advertising off Netflix. This wasn't just strategy – it was identity. He regularly touted this as a core competitive advantage:

"We think with our model that we'll actually get to a larger revenue, larger profits, larger market cap because we don't have exposure to something we're strategically disadvantaged at, which is online advertising against those Big Three – Facebook, Google and Amazon."[3]

Every earnings call, every interview, same message: Netflix would never have ads. Subscribers loved it. The brand promise was clear.

Then Q1 2022 hit like a sledgehammer.

Netflix reported its first subscriber loss in over a decade – down 200,000 to 221.6 million. The stock plummeted 35% in a single day. Pandemic restrictions were lifting, Disney+, HBO Max, and others were attacking Netflix's dominance, inflation was crushing discretionary spending. The perfect storm.

During that same devastating earnings call, Hastings did something remarkable. He completely reversed his position:

"Those who have followed Netflix know that I've been against the complexity of advertising and a big fan of the simplicity of subscription. But as much as I'm a fan of that, I'm a bigger fan of consumer choice."

No hedging. No corporate doublespeak. Just a clear acknowledgment that the world had changed and Netflix needed to change with it. Within months, Netflix launched a cheaper ad-supported tier – the very thing Hastings had sworn they'd never do.

The results vindicated his flexibility. By November 2024, the ad tier had reached 70 million global users.[4] By Q4 2024, total subscribers crossed 300 million. Disney+, the second-biggest streamer, had just 124 million.

This is what great CEOs do. They hold strong convictions but recognize when facts change. As Buffett likes to quote: "When the facts change, I change my mind. What do you do, sir?"

Contrast this with CEOs who treat their strategies like religious doctrine.

They'd rather go down with the ship than admit they were wrong. Their ego becomes more important than shareholder value.

We want management that defends their vision against noise, but is nimble enough to pivot when facing real change.

What to look for:

- Strategy pivots explained clearly, not buried in footnotes.
- CEOs who take responsibility without blaming external factors.
- Major changes announced with conviction, not hedged with corporate speak.
- Track record of successful adaptations, not just one lucky pivot.

4. The capacity to suffer

Tom Russo of Gardner Russo & Quinn popularized this term – "capacity to suffer" – and it perfectly captures a rare management trait: the ability to endure short-term pain for long-term gain.

Most CEOs can't do this. Wall Street demands quarterly results. Analysts want guidance beaten. The pressure to optimize today's numbers is relentless. But the best investments often require years of losses before profits materialize.

Amazon in its early days exemplifies this "capacity to suffer."

Many investors and Wall Street analysts criticized the firm for its lack of profitability even as revenue scaled, wondering if Amazon was simply a money pit. The debate became especially pronounced as operating margins declined from around 3% in the early 2010s to a razor-thin 0.2% in 2014. Critics said Amazon would never make money. Supporters said Bezos was playing a different game. The truth was hiding in plain sight – on the income statement.

This apparent profitability issue existed because Amazon was investing heavily through the income statement, pouring capital into R&D.

The reported operating margin – profit as a percentage of revenue – hovered below 6% for years. But add back R&D spending, and the picture changes dramatically.

In 2014, Amazon spent $9.2 billion on R&D. Its reported operating margin was a razor-thin 0.2%. But adjusting for R&D investments, the margin was actually 10.6%.

Figure 4.1 shows this pattern across a full decade of "suffering" – and the eventual payoff. From 2013 to 2021, reported margins barely budged above 6%, while R&D-adjusted margins climbed steadily toward 18%. The gap between the two lines represents Amazon's reinvestment in its future.

Then came the reward. By 2024, reported operating margins finally broke 10% – and the adjusted margin hit nearly 25%. Amazon now generates roughly 25 cents of pre-R&D operating profit for every dollar of revenue, up from 10 cents a decade earlier.

Figure 4.1: Amazon's hidden profitability (2013–2024)

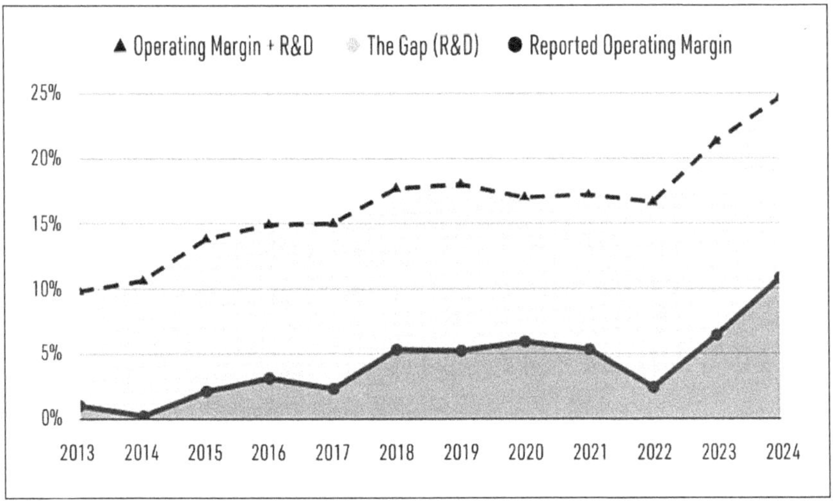

Source: Author's calculation.

Bezos was building tomorrow's profit streams through today's income statement. AWS, Prime, advertising were all new product innovations funded by "losses" that were actually investments.

As Tom Russo explains:

> The 'capacity to suffer' is key because often the initial spending to build on these great brands in new markets has no initial return. Many companies will try to invest smoothly over time with no burden on currently reported net income, but the problem is that when you are trying to invest in a new market, smooth investment spending really doesn't give you enough power to make an impression. You end up letting in a lot of competition that will drive down future margins.

Bezos understood this principle in his bones. While competitors smoothed investments to protect quarterly earnings, he went all-in.

Most CEOs would have caved. They would have cut R&D to show profits. Pleased Wall Street. Gotten their bonuses. And destroyed Amazon's future.

But Bezos had already told everyone his plan in his legendary 1997 letter:

> When forced to choose between optimizing the appearance of our GAAP accounting and maximizing the present value of future cash flows, we'll take the cash flows.

In plain English: Bezos would rather build real value than make the financial statements look pretty.

This is music to a long-term investor's ears. A CEO who won't buckle under short-term pressure. Who won't massage numbers to please analysts. Who focuses on sustainable value creation even when it makes him look bad today.

The payoff was extraordinary. Those R&D investments created AWS and Amazon's advertising business – massive profit engines. By 2024, AWS was generating $100+ billion annually while advertising approached $50 billion. Amazon's GAAP operating margins shot up to nearly 11% that same year, despite continued heavy investments in logistics and AI data centers.

The capacity to suffer is about having the courage and credibility to invest for the long term when Wall Street demands profits now.

What to look for:

- Investment that builds future moats instead of shoring up profitability for the short term.
- Management focused on three- to five-year outcomes, not just the next quarter.
- CEOs who explicitly choose long-term value over short-term optics.
- Consistent messaging about long-term strategy despite stock volatility.

5. Skin in the game

Charlie Munger said it best: "Show me the incentive and I will show you the outcome."

When executives own meaningful stakes in their businesses, they think like owners. When they're just collecting salaries and options, they think like employees. The difference shows up in every decision.

I mean owning actual shares bought with their own money – where if the stock drops 50%, their net worth drops 50%. Real skin in the game. Not stock options that only capture the upside.

What's "Meaningful" Ownership?

It depends on company size and executive wealth.

For mega-caps, even 1–3% ownership represents serious commitment. For smaller companies or founder-led businesses, I want to see 10%+. But the percentage matters less than what it represents of the executive's net worth.

When a CEO has 50%+ of their net worth in company stock, every decision affects their family's future. That concentrates the mind wonderfully.

Finding this information is easier than you'd think. Company proxy statements list exactly how many shares each executive owns – look for the "beneficial ownership" table. You can find these on the company's investor relations page or the SEC's EDGAR database. For tracking when insiders buy or sell, Form 4 filings on EDGAR show every transaction – executives must report trades within two business days.

Jeff Bezos held a double-digit percentage stake in Amazon throughout his tenure as CEO, representing the vast majority of his net worth. Every decision that hurt Amazon hurt him personally.

Warren Buffett has kept 99% of his net worth in Berkshire Hathaway throughout his tenure. No hedging. No diversification. Complete alignment.

Contrast this with professional CEOs who cash out options the moment they vest. Who own more real estate than company stock. Who diversify into venture capital while running your company. Where's the alignment?

Reading insider transactions

Peter Lynch nailed it: "Insiders [people who manage or run a business] might sell their shares for any number of reasons, but they buy them for only one: they think the price will rise."

Watch for:

Cluster buying: When multiple insiders buy simultaneously, they're seeing something the market isn't. This isn't one optimistic executive – it's collective confidence.

Crisis buying: Purchases during stock weakness or after bad news demonstrate real conviction. Anyone can buy when things are rosy.

Size matters: Token purchases of tens of thousands mean little to executives making millions. Sometimes it may be false signaling. Look for significant commitments of personal capital – purchases that represent meaningful percentages of their compensation or net worth.

What to look for:

- Insider buying during weakness, not just option exercises.
- CEOs with bulk of their net worth in company stock.
- Multiple executives buying simultaneously (cluster buying).
- Purchases representing meaningful portions of executive compensation.

WHEN TRUST ERODES

I owned Lululemon because I believed in the brand and in former CEO Calvin McDonald. When he became CEO in 2018, revenue was $2.6 billion. By 2023, it reached $9.6 billion – nearly quadrupling in five years. This was a proven track record of successfully turning around and scaling the business.

So when US sales started slowing in early 2024, I gave him the benefit of the doubt. Problems happen. What matters is whether management correctly identifies the root cause.

Here's what McDonald said on the Q1 2024 earnings call:

> In our women's business, we had some missed opportunities really, in our color palette, in particular in some of key categories such as our legging business, where we didn't have enough color, newness.

The word "color" appeared 20 times in that call. The prescription was clear: more colors, more newness, faster product cycles. They even gave specific targets – increasing new styles from 23% to 35% of their assortment.

Reasonable diagnosis. Concrete action plan. I was satisfied.

Then I watched the next four quarters unfold.

By Q2 2025, after a full year of executing on this strategy, McDonald admitted something troubling:

> While the guest is responding well to many of our new styles, they are not reacting as we had anticipated to the updated seasonal colors we brought into our core assortment.

A year of colors and sizes. A year of "newness." And the customers weren't buying it.

What they actually wanted was innovation – the technical fabrics, the quality, the things that made Lululemon *Lululemon*. But I didn't hear a single word about technical innovation on that earnings call. Instead, McDonald talked about "going faster" and "chasing trends." About reducing development cycles from 18–24 months to 12–14 months.

They were trying to out-Zara Zara instead of out-Lululemon the competition.

This is like Ferrari deciding to compete with Toyota on production speed. You don't win by abandoning what makes you special.

Meanwhile, the company's most loyal customers – their highest spenders – were pulling back. As McDonald admitted: "The opportunity is with the high-value guests. They're over-indexing on new styles and retention remains strong, but the opportunity is they're spending less with us."

Your best customers are telling you something about your product. These aren't price-sensitive shoppers looking for deals. When they stop buying, it's a signal.

What to watch for:

- **The explanation keeps changing**. First it was colors. Then it was newness. Then it was product life cycles running too long. When management cycles through explanations, they're guessing – and don't have a good grasp of the issues.
- **The timeline keeps shifting**. Fixes were promised by early 2025. Then 2026. Moving goalposts often signal a misunderstood problem.
- **They stop talking about what made them special**. When a premium brand starts discussing "speed" instead of "quality," question whether they still understand their own moat.

The lesson is simple: management evaluation isn't a one-time exercise. You assess the team when you buy, but you keep watching as conditions evolve.

I bought Lululemon partly because I trusted McDonald's judgment. That trust was earned through years of results. But trust isn't permanent. When the evidence changes – when explanations keep shifting, when timelines slip, when strategy drifts from core strengths – your assessment needs to change too.

Even great managers can lose their way. Success breeds overconfidence. Growth becomes an addiction. The same ambition that built the business can destroy it if left unchecked. Here's how to spot when good management goes bad.

THE MANAGEMENT RED FLAGS

The Under Armour collapse

Under Armour was a Wall Street darling at its peak, posting 26 consecutive quarters of 20%-plus sales growth. Investors were willing to pay an eye-watering 60+ forward P/E multiple for what appeared to be a serious threat to incumbents Nike and Adidas.

Management couldn't start an earnings call without trumpeting this growth streak.

"We are a growth company. And with our 26th consecutive quarter of 20%-plus revenue growth, we continue to demonstrate our ability to drive a bigger and better company quarter-after-quarter," he proclaimed during the Q3 2016 call.

Under Armour's CEO repeatedly positioned Under Armour as a "great American brand" transforming into a "great global company."

But trees don't grow to the sky.

Behind this promotional narrative lurked something far more troubling.

According to the SEC, Under Armour was pulling forward as much as $408 million in orders from future quarters to meet analysts' revenue targets. The SEC alleged this practice lasted from Q3 2015 through Q4 2016, with the company offering substantial sales incentives to wholesale customers:[5]

- Significant discounts,
- Extended payment terms,
- Other special arrangements to pull forward revenue.

The house of cards eventually collapsed.

This revelation came about through an SEC investigation, followed by a shareholder lawsuit alleging that the company filed materially false and misleading information while hiding this sales acceleration practice.

Under Armour announced missed estimates, and revenue growth shrank to single digits. The share price plummeted from approximately $52 in 2015 to just $7 as recently as March 2025. Following the episode, revenue growth averaged low single digits over the next few years, a far cry from the 20%-plus growth that had defined the company's rise.

The promotion trap: when hype replaces substance

When management consistently describes ordinary business activities in superlative terms – using phrases like "revolutionary," "game-changing," or "unprecedented" – it often masks a lack of substance.

The best leaders let results speak for themselves. Those most eager to hype their achievements typically deliver the least impressive outcomes.

The overpromising often starts innocently – a CEO trying to inspire confidence. But once you promise the sky, anything less looks like failure. So they promise the stars. Then the moon. Each quarter demands bigger promises to maintain the narrative. There's no graceful exit from this escalation – only eventual disappointment when reality catches up.

Be wary of aggressively promotional CEOs who seem obsessed with their stock price rather than their business fundamentals. When executives make promises they can't keep, they may resort to perverse methods to "meet the numbers."

And as Under Armour discovered, tactics like heavily discounting products to pull forward revenue can lead to permanent brand damage.

Four red flags to watch for

1. Executives who dodge straightforward questions.
2. CEOs who reframe questions to highlight irrelevant positives instead of answering directly.
3. Management teams obsessed with short-term stock performance.
4. Consistent use of hyperbolic language to describe ordinary business activities.

These patterns don't always lead to disaster. But across decades of corporate history – from Enron to Wirecard to WeWork – a promotional mindset that prioritizes perception over performance – is often the first step down a dangerous path that leads to destroyed shareholder value and, sometimes, outright fraud.

When management is selling you a dream, make sure you're not buying a nightmare.

THE KNIGHTS MAKE ALL THE DIFFERENCE

The next time you evaluate an investment opportunity, look beyond the financial statements.

The numbers tell only part of the story – management tells the rest.

Study management communications, examine their capital allocation history, and assess whether they think like owners.

This extra due diligence will sometimes mean passing on businesses with attractive financials but questionable leadership. But in the long run, it will protect you from value destruction and connect you with the rare companies where exceptional management compounds your capital for decades.

Remember: even the strongest moats won't protect shareholder capital if the knights aren't vigilant, adaptable, and fully aligned with your long-term interests.

The traits we've explored give you a complete framework for evaluating any management team.

As my experience with Booking Holdings during the pandemic proved, the true test of management comes during crisis. Anyone can look competent when the tide is rising. But exceptional managers – the kind worth partnering with for decades – reveal themselves when facing adversity.

These are the leaders who make all the difference between mediocre returns or exceptional wealth creation over time.

It's always about management.

YOUR LUNCH BREAK SUMMARY

- **Crisis reveals management's true character**: The best CEOs turn market chaos into competitive advantage while others panic.
- **Wide moats erode without great management**: Even the strongest competitive advantages are temporary if leadership isn't constantly reinforcing them.
- **Five traits separate exceptional leaders**: Transparency, capital allocation skill, adaptability, long-term thinking despite short-term pain, and meaningful personal ownership.
- **Continuous evaluation**: Trust is earned through results, but conditions change. When explanations keep shifting, timelines slip, or strategy drifts from core strengths, reassess whether the team is still right for the job.
- **Overpromising is a dangerous red flag**: When management spends more time selling the story than building the business, destruction follows.

YOUR NEXT STEP

Now that you understand moats, value drivers, and management quality, you're ready for the practical work of investing. The next four chapters will take you through the complete investment process: finding opportunities, valuing them, buying with discipline, and knowing when (rarely) to sell.

PART II

FINDING YOUR WINNERS

CHAPTER 6
FINDING YOUR FIRST STEADY COMPOUNDERS

YOU NOW KNOW what makes a business exceptional – a durable moat, a long runway to reinvest at high returns, and management that nurtures both. Those three qualities, working together, are what I call a steady compounder. Finding all three in one company is rare. But when you do, and you hold for years, the results can be extraordinary.

This chapter shows you how to find them – hiding in plain sight, in businesses you already know from daily life. By the end, you'll have a shortlist of three companies worth researching further.

But here's the catch. You can only spot these qualities in businesses you genuinely understand. Identifying moats requires understanding competitive dynamics. Evaluating runways requires understanding industry growth. Assessing management requires knowing what good looks like in that specific business. Outside your understanding, you're guessing.

This is why your circle of competence matters so much. It's not just about avoiding mistakes – it's about having the insight to recognize steady compounders when you encounter them. Within your circle, you can see what Wall Street analysts studying spreadsheets might miss.

Let me show you why this discipline matters, even for legends.

Picture this. Sun Valley, Idaho, July 1999. The most exclusive gathering of media and tech titans on the planet. The NASDAQ had risen 20% to 2,638 since the year began. Tech fortunes were being minted daily. Everyone knew the future belonged to the internet.

Then Warren Buffett took the stage as closing speaker.[1]

Many had been whispering that the oracle had lost his touch. Berkshire Hathaway's stock had declined while tech stocks soared in recent years. He'd missed the greatest wealth creation opportunity in history by avoiding internet stocks.

Then Buffett delivered a lesson that would prove prophetic.

He started with history. At one point, America had at least 2,000 car companies – an industry that transformed how humans lived. By the 1990s? Three US car companies survived. And as Buffett noted, they were "themselves no lollapaloozas for investors."

Then came airlines. Between 1919 and 1939, about 200 companies emerged. The industry shrank the world, creating immense value for society. The aggregate profit for investors? Zero.

Buffett even joked, "If I had been at Kitty Hawk, I would have been farsighted enough to shoot Orville down."

The audience sat in stone-cold silence. No laughs. Just uncomfortable shifting in seats.

His message was blunt: Picking winners in transformative industries is nearly impossible. The graveyard is littered with companies that had great stories, but delivered terrible returns.

This is why Buffett stuck to his circle of competence – businesses he could actually understand and predict. While everyone chased internet companies, he bought Dairy Queen.

As he explained, "The key to investing is not assessing how much an industry is going to affect society, or how much it will grow, but rather determining the competitive advantage of any given company and, above all, the durability of that advantage."

Then came his prediction. While investors expected 13–22% annual returns according to recent polls, Buffett forecast the next 17 years would deliver just 6%. To an audience drunk on tech gains, this seemed absurd.

The speech landed with a thud. Complete silence.

Three months later, *Barron's* published its December 1999 cover: "What's Wrong, Warren?" The article began: "After more than 30 years of unrivaled investment success, Warren Buffett may be losing his magic touch."[2]

Then everything changed.

The NASDAQ peaked at 5,048 in March 2000 before crashing 77% to 1,134 by October 4, 2002.[3] Those who had dismissed Buffett's discipline saw their fortunes evaporate. Meanwhile, Buffett built wealth through candy, furniture, and insurance while others chased the next hot thing.

From 1965 to 2024, Berkshire Hathaway delivered 19.9% annual returns compared to the S&P 500's 10.4%. A thousand dollars invested with Buffett in 1965 would have grown to $55 million by 2024. That same thousand in the S&P 500? Just $391,000.[4]

He built this fortune by staying within his circle – insurance, consumer brands, utilities. The discipline to say "that's not my game" made all the difference.

But here's the encouraging part: You don't need Buffett's genius to succeed. You just need to know your own boundaries. In fact, as a regular person with real-world experience as a customer and employee, you likely understand certain businesses better than Wall Street analysts who've never used the products they analyze.

WHEN EVEN LEGENDS CRACK

You might think, "Sure, but that's Buffett. Regular investors couldn't resist that pressure."

Let me tell you about Stanley Druckenmiller.

Druckenmiller is one of the greatest investors who ever lived – 30% annual returns over 30 years while managing money for George Soros. No losing years.

Here's what happened to him during the dot-com bubble, in his own words:[5]

"In February 1999, I shorted internet stocks with $200 million. By mid-March, I was down $600 million on that $200 million short. I was down 15% on the year. I'd never had a down year, and I thought, well, I'm finished."

He knew tech was overvalued. That's why he shorted it. But watching colleagues mint money while he bled capital? The psychological pressure became unbearable.

"Around March, I could feel it coming. I just – I had to play. I couldn't help myself. Three times that week I picked up the phone and put it down, telling myself: Don't do it. Don't do it."

But he did.

"I think I missed the top by an hour. I bought $6 billion worth of tech stocks, and in six weeks I had left Soros and I had lost $3 billion in that one play."

His reflection is the most important part:

"You asked me what I learned. I didn't learn anything. I already knew that I wasn't supposed to do that. I was just an emotional basket case and couldn't help myself."

Think about that. One of the greatest investors ever, fully aware he was making a mistake, still couldn't resist.

The difference between Buffett and Druckenmiller in 1999 wasn't analytical skill. Both saw the bubble clearly. The difference was that Buffett had spent decades building an investment philosophy centered on staying within his circle of competence – and he had the discipline to stick to it even when the world called him a fossil.

Your circle of competence is your fortress against costly mistakes. Yes, watching others profit outside your circle is painful – even legends crack under that pressure. Buffett made billions in candy and insurance while "missing" the tech boom. Druckenmiller lost $3 billion in six weeks chasing what he didn't understand.

The discipline to say "that's not my game" isn't just important – it's everything.

THE PERMISSION TO SAY "I DON'T KNOW"

Here's what most people get wrong about investing: They think they need to understand everything. Every sector. Every trend. Every opportunity.

That's backwards.

Your circle of competence is simply the stuff you actually do understand. Not hope you understand. Not pretend to understand. Actually understand. Where you can predict with reasonable confidence how a business will perform over time.

As Buffett wrote in 1996: "You don't have to be an expert on every company, or even many. You only have to be able to evaluate companies within your circle of competence. The size of that circle is not very important; knowing its boundaries, however, is vital."

He takes this so seriously that he keeps an actual box on his desk labeled "Too Hard." When an investment is too complex or outside his understanding, he physically puts it in the Too Hard box and moves on. No ego. No FOMO. Just discipline.

As Buffett describes it: "Charlie says we have three boxes: In, Out, and Too Hard. You don't have to do everything well. At the Olympics, if you run the 100 meters well, you don't have to do the shot put."

You don't need to understand crypto, biotech, semiconductors, and banking all at once. You just need genuine understanding of a few businesses.

The world will constantly tempt you to venture beyond your competence. New sectors will boom. Friends will brag about gains in businesses you don't understand. The financial media will make you feel stupid for "missing" the next big thing.

Your edge isn't catching every opportunity – it's having the discipline to wait for the ones you truly comprehend.

UNDERSTANDING YOUR REAL EDGE

Your circle of competence isn't just about what you understand – it's about where you have an actual advantage over other investors.

In October 2006, legendary investor Bill Miller, who beat the S&P 500 for 15 consecutive years running at Legg Mason Value Trust, shared a framework that transformed how I think about investing opportunities. He expanded on Buffett's circle of competence with a crucial insight: you need not just understanding, but a genuine competitive advantage.[6]

Miller identified three types of advantages in markets:

1. Informational advantage
2. Analytical advantage
3. Behavioral advantage

Informational advantage is knowing something material that others don't. It's the easiest to exploit, but the hardest to find legally. The Securities and Exchange Commission (SEC) makes sure of that – regulations require public disclosure of material information, and there are stiff penalties for insider trading. Unless you're doing primary research that uncovers something genuinely unknown, this edge is mostly a mirage.

Analytical advantage comes from taking the same public information everyone has but processing it differently. Miller's 2006 Amazon call perfectly illustrates this. With the stock at $1.60 and operating margins at just 3.6%, he wrote: "The market appears to be pricing Amazon.com as though its current operating margins in the low single digits are a permanent feature of its business model, as they are of bookseller Barnes & Noble. We think that is wrong and that Amazon's margins will soon begin a steady climb toward and perhaps into double digits."

Double digits seemed absurd for a retailer. But Miller saw what the market missed – Amazon's low margins weren't a permanent feature of its business model but a temporary phase that would give way to steady expansion. By 2024, Amazon's operating margins hit 10.8% – the double digits Miller predicted – and the stock reached $219 – a 137-fold increase.[7]

Behavioral advantage is the most interesting – and most durable. As

Miller explained: "Such results are likely to be systematically exploitable and not able to be arbitraged away as they become more widely known. That is because they represent broad findings about how large groups of people are likely to behave under well-defined circumstances. Until large numbers of people are able to alter their psychology (don't hold your breath), there is money to be made."

Think about that. Even when everyone knows about behavioral biases, most people still can't overcome them. Knowing you shouldn't panic-sell during a crash doesn't stop millions from doing exactly that. The fear is too powerful. The pressure is too intense.

This is why the steady compounding approach works. We're not trying to gain informational advantages by finding hidden data – that's nearly impossible legally and not sustainable anyway.

But we absolutely can develop analytical advantages, just as Miller did with Amazon. When you combine long-term thinking with deep understanding of businesses within your circle of competence, you see things others miss. Miller didn't have special information about Amazon. He simply understood that the market was analyzing it through the wrong lens – as a retailer rather than a technology platform. By thinking in years rather than quarters, he could see margins expanding while others fixated on current profitability.

This long-term perspective is itself an analytical advantage. When you evaluate a business based on where it will be in five or 10 years, rather than next quarter's earnings, you're already processing information differently than most market participants.

And here's the beautiful part: this analytical edge compounds with behavioral advantage. The patience to hold through volatility. The discipline to buy during pessimism. The conviction to sit still while others trade frantically. These behavioral advantages don't get competed away because human nature doesn't change. Even when everyone knows they should think long-term, most still can't resist short-term pressures.

Your real edge comes from combining both – the analytical advantage of long-term thinking within your circle of competence, and the behavioral advantage of patience and discipline. You don't need to be smarter than everyone. You just need to think differently about time horizons and have the temperament to act on those insights.

That's an advantage you can build on. And unlike informational edges that disappear once discovered, these advantages actually strengthen over time as you deepen your understanding and reinforce your discipline.

Now let's get practical about identifying opportunities within your circle of competence.

THE FIVE QUESTIONS THAT DEFINE YOUR CIRCLE

How do you know what's actually in your circle of competence?

Before you spend a single hour researching a company, ask these five questions. These questions build the conviction that matters when markets test you. During turbulent times, when the stock market is down 40% and headlines scream disaster, your understanding keeps you grounded. Real conviction can't be borrowed from others – it comes from knowing exactly what you own.

First, the simplicity test.

1. Can I explain how this business makes money in one sentence?

If you can't describe the business model simply, you don't understand it well enough to invest. Netflix makes money when customers pay monthly subscriptions to stream unlimited content. Visa takes a small percentage of every transaction processed through its network. Simple. Clear. Straightforward.

If you struggle to understand how they make money, the deeper analysis won't help. You need that foundation first – everything else builds on understanding the basic business model.

Second, the customer test.

2. Why do customers choose this over competitors?

This is about value proposition. What specific problem does it solve better? Costco saves families money through bulk buying at wholesale prices. Apple provides premium devices that work seamlessly together in an ecosystem.

You should be able to grasp why someone picks this business over competitors. Bonus point if you're able to figure out why they'll be able to do this for a long time. If you can't see why this is better than alternatives, move on.

Third, the moat test.

3. Could a reasonably capitalized competitor disrupt this business?

This is Buffett's durability filter. He once said: "If you gave me $100 billion and told me to take away the soft drink leadership of Coca-Cola in the world, I'd give it back to you and say it can't be done."

Some moats are that wide. Could a competitor with resources build Amazon's logistics network and selection today? The time, capital, and expertise required make it nearly impossible. But that hot new app everyone's downloading? A well-funded competitor could probably replicate it in months.

Fourth, the predictability test:

4. Can I reasonably predict what this business looks like in five years?

Think general direction, not precise numbers. Will people still want to stream entertainment? Netflix remains relevant. Will businesses still need payment processing? Visa's model endures. Will companies still need cloud storage? Microsoft's Azure keeps growing. Can you reasonably see this business model working in five years? If not, it's outside your circle.

Fifth, the runway test:

5. Why can this business grow for a really long time?

What's the runway? Mercado Libre can expand across Latin America's growing e-commerce market for decades. Shopify has endless small businesses to help establish online presence. But what about that fashionable drinks chain with lines out the door? Where's its growth in a decade?

If any answer is unclear, it's outside your circle. No shame in that. Buffett missed Amazon, but made billions on insurance. The size of your circle doesn't matter – respecting its boundaries does.

These five questions are your first filter. They save you from wasting hours analyzing businesses you'll never truly understand.

Take Palantir, a brilliant company with massive government contracts and impressive growth. Many investors are excited about it, and for good reason. But when I try to explain how they make money in one sentence, I stumble – they provide data analytics and software that helps organizations integrate information, or maybe it's decision-making platforms, or AI-powered something. I'm already lost.

When I ask why customers choose them, I know it has something to do with handling complex classified data that others can't, but I couldn't explain their forward-deployed engineers or ontology system without looking up on Google what those terms mean. Could competitors disrupt them? I have no idea what makes their technology special compared to Databricks or Snowflake. The five-year picture? Government contracts probably continue, but beyond that I'm guessing.

This doesn't make Palantir a bad investment – it might be incredible. But it's outside my circle of competence, so it goes in the "Too Hard" pile. That takes humility, admitting that a popular, fast-growing stock is beyond your understanding. Remember, it's not about having a large circle of competence. Buffett's circle excluded most of technology for 50 years and he built one of history's great fortunes. What matters is knowing where your boundaries are and having the discipline to respect them.

The best part? You already know dozens of businesses that could pass this test. They're hiding in plain sight – in your wallet, your daily routine, your monthly subscriptions.

START WHERE YOU ALREADY ARE

The hardest part about finding investments isn't a lack of opportunities. It's knowing where to look. Most investors start by reading financial news or screening for metrics. You have a better starting point: the businesses where you're already a customer.

This isn't about investing in every company you buy from. That would be misguided. It's about recognizing which businesses deserve deeper investigation based on your firsthand experience.

THE CREDIT CARD STATEMENT EXERCISE

Pull up your last three months of credit card statements and list every recurring charge.

Now ask yourself: Which companies have raised prices but you still buy from them without seriously considering alternatives?

When I did this exercise, two subscriptions jumped out: Google One and YouTube Premium.

Google One has become the backbone of my work. All my stock research, book drafts, and business documents live on Google Drive. The tools – Sheets, Docs, Slides – are completely free and I prefer them over Microsoft's alternatives. But I pay for Google One because I need the storage. When my laptop died last year, I bought a new one and was working again in minutes – everything was already there, automatically backed up. When Google raised prices, I grumbled for exactly three seconds before paying. That peace of mind is worth multiples of the monthly fee.

YouTube Premium was another revelation. Want to watch Berkshire's annual meetings with Buffett and Munger? YouTube. Need to learn the latest AI tools? YouTube. Want to learn cooking, investing, or woodworking? YouTube has experts teaching everything. The small monthly fee to skip ads isn't just convenience – it's buying back my time. Five seconds here, 30 seconds there. When you're learning from dozens of videos monthly, those interruptions add up.

That willingness to pay despite price increases – and to recommend them to others – suggests something worth investigating. These aren't stock tips. They're starting points for research.

YOUR PROFESSIONAL EDGE

Your job gives you insights Wall Street analysts would pay thousands to uncover. You see which businesses have their hooks in deep and which are hanging by a thread.

During the pandemic, I watched university professors get forced onto Microsoft Teams. Within months, all communication, classes, and collaboration happened on one platform. Once integrated into the academic workflow, switching became unthinkable. That's sticky recurring revenue the kind that shows up in financials quarters later, but that insiders see happening in real-time.

I witnessed the same pattern with SAP at a large corporation. Everyone complained about the interface, the cost, the complexity. But when management floated the idea of switching to save money, the IT team nearly revolted. After years of customization, SAP had become the company's central nervous system. Ripping it out would paralyze operations.

Those complaints revealed the moat's depth. Sometimes the most powerful moats are revealed through pain. The fact that switching would "paralyze operations" tells you everything about the competitive position. Still, given the choice, I prefer to invest in companies customers love over those they're locked into.

The insights aren't limited to tech. A nurse sees which medical device companies doctors actually trust versus tolerate. A retail worker knows which brands customers ask for by name versus settle for. A teacher watches which educational software actually engages students versus just checks boxes. Every profession offers these windows into competitive dynamics.

Consider what you observe at work:

- Which vendors does everyone complain about, but never replace?
- What software would cause chaos if management tried to switch?

- Which suppliers consistently deliver while others create excuses?

You're seeing competitive dynamics that won't show up in financial statements for quarters or years. That's your edge.

THE LIFE EXPERIENCE FILTER

Your daily routines reveal business quality in ways financial statements can't capture. But you need to distinguish between habit and genuine competitive advantage.

I shop at the same supermarket every week. Does that make it a good investment? Not necessarily. I go there because it's two blocks away. If a competitor opened closer, I'd switch tomorrow. Geographic convenience isn't a moat.

But consider Costco. Members drive past five other grocery stores to shop there. They pay an annual fee just for the privilege. When membership prices increase, renewal rates barely budge. That behavior suggests something defensible.

The key difference? One is settling for what's nearby. The other is genuine preference worth paying for. Look for businesses where customers go out of their way, not just settle for what's convenient.

What recurring expenses deliver value multiples above their cost? Which businesses would genuinely hurt to lose? Which companies do you recommend without being asked? Those are your research starting points.

THE INVESTOR'S LENS

Once you start investing this way, you'll never be the same shopper again.

Every purchase becomes a question. Why am I paying for this when alternatives exist? What would make me switch? Could a competitor easily steal me away – and if not, why not?

When I buy something at a premium, I catch myself thinking about margins. When I choose a service despite cheaper options, I'm seeing a moat in action. When I notice a subscription I'd genuinely miss if it disappeared, that's pricing power revealing itself.

The lens works in reverse too. When I board a plane, I think about the capital locked into maintaining that aircraft – upgrades every few years, payments that continue whether seats are full or empty. When a crisis like SARS or Covid-19 grounds travel, airlines still pay for planes sitting idle. What a brutal business. Then I think about the platform where I booked that flight and hotel – Booking.com owns no planes, no hotels, yet captures a slice of every transaction. Asset-light, highly profitable, and resilient when travel recovers. Same trip, completely different economics.

This is why it's tough to find good investments through stock screeners. Everyone runs the same filters. Any edge that existed gets arbitraged away. More importantly, the best compounders rarely screen well. They look expensive precisely because the market recognizes some of their quality – just not all of it. Your edge isn't finding what screens cheaply. It's understanding something the market hasn't fully priced in yet.

That understanding comes from observation. And this isn't an exercise you complete once and file away. It's a lens you carry everywhere.

Watch how people around you spend. The friend who won't switch streaming services despite complaining about price increases. The colleague who says the company would "never" change their CRM. That's data. Every dollar people spend tells you something about competitive dynamics.

The patterns are everywhere once you start looking. A coffee chain where customers wait in long lines despite the café next door sitting empty. A software tool your company adopted three years ago that's now impossible to rip out. A brand your friends recommend without being asked.

These observations connect directly to what we covered in Chapter 3. You're seeing moats in the wild – switching costs, brand loyalty, network effects. Not in a textbook. In real life.

But here's the important caveat: your daily observations reveal moats most clearly. Runway and management are harder to spot from the checkout line. Those require deeper research. What you're doing now is finding starting points – businesses that pass the first filter of genuine competitive advantage, observed firsthand. That's valuable. But it's the start of your research, not the end.

Keep it simple. A notes app on your phone works fine. When you notice something interesting, jot down the company, what you observed, and what question it raises.

Here's an example.

Costco: Membership fees went up $5 in September 2024. Most members renewed without hesitation – paid memberships grew from 76 million to 81 million over the following year. Note to self: Strong pricing power because the membership delivers obvious value. Plus international expansion still has room to run.

That's it. No elaborate spreadsheet. No formal template. Just capture the observation before you forget it.

Over time, your list grows naturally. You're not forcing yourself to find 20 companies in one sitting. You're collecting observations as life presents them. Some will fizzle under deeper research. Others will become genuine opportunities.

Aim for quality, not quantity. A list of five companies you genuinely understand beats 20 you're stretching to include.

YOUR TWO FILTERS

Not every company you observe deserves deeper research. Before committing hours to annual reports and earnings calls, run each candidate through two filters.

Filter 1: Do I actually understand this business?

This is the five questions test from earlier:

1. Can I explain how this business makes money in one sentence?
2. Why do customers choose this over competitors?
3. Could a competitor disrupt this business?
4. Can I predict what this looks like in five years?
5. Why can this business grow for a long time?

If any answer is unclear, it's outside your circle. No shame in that. Move on.

Filter 2: Does it show steady compounder traits?

This is where you apply what you learned in earlier chapters:

- Does it have a strong or widening moat? (Chapter 3)
- Does it have runway to reinvest at high returns? (Chapter 4)
- Is management building long-term value? (Chapter 5)

Your daily observations reveal moats most clearly. Runway and management require you to dig deeper – reading annual reports, listening to earnings calls, studying capital allocation history. But you're not starting blind. You already understand the business from lived experience.

Companies that pass both filters – understanding AND quality – become your shortlist.

PICK YOUR TOP THREE

From what remains, choose three companies for deeper research.

Why three? It's few enough to research properly, but enough to find at least one genuine opportunity.

What if you can't find three? Don't force it. One company you genuinely understand beats three you're stretching to include. If nothing qualifies today, keep observing. Your circle expands over time as your career changes, your interests shift, and you encounter new businesses. The right opportunities will emerge.

Don't be in a rush. Your edge is patience and understanding, not speed.

In the meantime, read widely – especially early in your investing journey. Find investors whose thinking resonates with you. I break down businesses regularly on my blog at *SteadyCompounding.com* – it's a good place to start. The more you study quality businesses, the sharper your lens becomes.

What if you find three candidates, but deeper research disqualifies all of them? That's the process working. You haven't failed – you've avoided mistakes. Return to your observations. Keep the lens active. New candidates will surface.

The goal isn't to always have three stocks to buy. It's to be ready when a genuine opportunity appears within your circle of competence.

THE DISCIPLINE THAT MATTERS

Every great investor started exactly where you are now – with curiosity about the businesses around them and the humility to admit what they don't understand.

Peter Lynch found some of his best investments at the mall with his family. Buffett discovered GEICO as a student under Benjamin Graham's mentorship, Coca-Cola as a consumer, Nebraska Furniture Mart as a local shopper. They didn't need sophisticated screens or insider information. They needed eyes to observe and discipline to stay within their understanding.

The world will constantly tempt you to venture beyond your competence. New sectors will boom. Friends will chase gains in businesses neither of you understand. The financial media will make you feel foolish for "missing" opportunities.

This is when you remember Sun Valley. Remember Druckenmiller's $3 billion confession. Remember that Buffett built one of history's great fortunes by understanding furniture stores and candy companies while others chased complexity.

Everyone will be pushing you toward the next big thing. Financial media screaming about hot stocks. Social media overflowing with "10x opportunities." Your group chat celebrating overnight gains. But your job is to tune out the noise. Your edge is having the discipline to say "no" to most opportunities so you can say "yes" when it counts.

The steady compounding path isn't about being brilliant. It's about being honest about what you know, patient with what you don't, and disciplined enough to tell the difference.

So go build your list. Because your shortlist is where the real work begins – annual reports, earnings calls, verifying whether the moat is as strong as you observed, assessing management, mapping out the runway. But one question is probably already nagging you: *How do I know if the price is right?*

That's the next chapter. Finding a great business is only half the equation. Even the best company in the world becomes a terrible investment at the wrong price.

LUNCH BREAK SUMMARY

- A steady compounder combines three qualities: a strong or widening moat, a long runway to reinvest at high returns, and management that nurtures both.
- Your circle of competence isn't a limitation – it's your edge. You can only identify steady compounders within businesses you genuinely understand.
- Your edge comes from observing moats, switching costs, and pricing power in daily life – insights no filter can capture.
- Run every candidate through two filters: Do I actually understand this business? Does it show steady compounder traits?
- Your edge is in companies you genuinely understand, not the breadth of your list. Quality insights over quantity.

YOUR NEXT STEP

You've identified businesses within your circle of competence that show signs of being steady compounders. Now comes the question you're probably already asking: How do I know if the price is right?

In Chapter 7, I'll show you valuation techniques you can master over lunch – no complex spreadsheets required. Because finding a great business is only half the equation. Even the best company in the world becomes a terrible investment at the wrong price.

CHAPTER 7
VALUATION

MOST INVESTORS START with valuation, plugging numbers into formulas before understanding what they're actually valuing. That's backwards. You can't value what you don't understand – which is why we spent the previous chapters building those foundations first.

Valuation is one of the most popular topics readers ask me about on *SteadyCompounding.com*. I understand the anxiety – nobody wants to overpay. Yet after years of watching investors agonize over whether a stock trades at 18x or 22x earnings while ignoring the quality of the business, I've learned something crucial.

There's no magic calculator that spits out the "right" price. That's why 10 analysts studying the same company come up with 10 different target prices. We all have slightly different assessments of the business quality, growth prospects, and competitive position. Those judgments translate into the math, which drives the valuation.

Think about it: How can you estimate future cash flows if you don't understand the moat? How can you pick the right multiple if you can't assess management? How can you project growth without knowing the business model?

That's why we spent the previous chapters building these foundations. Valuation isn't the starting point – it's the final step that brings everything together.

Most people will spend hours shopping around for flights, hotels, or a new fridge to get the best value, but won't spend 30 minutes figuring out what a stock is actually worth. In this chapter, I show you the techniques I use to value great businesses – techniques that let you assess whether an opportunity is overvalued or undervalued over your lunch break.

If a business is fragile, subject to disruption, or dependent on a handful of customers, I don't even bother with valuation. The future is too uncertain. I either move on to the next idea or demand such a massive margin of safety – paying so far below my estimate of intrinsic value that I'm protected even if I'm wrong – that the opportunity rarely makes sense.

But for quality businesses? That's where this framework shines. Let me show you how it works.

So what is a business actually worth?

Buffett crystallized it perfectly in his shareholder letters:

"Intrinsic value can be defined simply: It is the discounted value of the cash that can be taken out of a business during its remaining life."

Two parts here deserve our attention:

1. Discounted value.
2. Cash that can be taken out of a business.

Let's tackle the second part first – it's more intuitive.

When I make an investment, I expect the business to generate returns over time. As a shareholder, I'm an owner. Every dollar the business generates is mine, whether paid as dividends, used for buybacks, or reinvested for growth.

Simple enough, right?

Now for the trickier part: discounted value.

THE TIME VALUE OF MONEY (OR WHY YOUR DOLLAR IS MELTING)

Here's the painful truth about money: A dollar today is worth more than a dollar tomorrow.

This is the entire foundation of valuation.

You might be old enough to remember that a Big Mac in the US cost \$0.65 in the 1970s. Today it's over \$6. That's inflation eating away at purchasing power. Your dollar is literally melting.

Would you rather have \$1,000 today or \$1,000 next year? Today, obviously. You could invest it, earn interest, or just enjoy the certainty of having it now. The further into the future, the bigger the discount. That's why when we talk about future cash from a business, we need to discount it back to today's value.

Let me show you the math (don't worry, it's simpler than it looks).

Say inflation is 2% annually, \$100 received in five years' time is worth only \$90 today. Here's how: $\$100 \div (1.02)^5 = \$90.57$

That notation $(1.02)^5$ means 1.02 multiplied by itself five times. That's it. You've just learned discounted cash flow.

But wait – should we really use inflation as our discount rate?

That would be too generous. I also need to think about opportunity cost – what else could I do with this money? After all, why invest in a business returning 2% when I could get that from a savings account?

Buffett typically uses the long-term US Treasury rate as his baseline. But even that became problematic after 2008 when rates plummeted near zero.

Here's what Munger revealed about their thinking:

> We're guessing at our future opportunity cost. Warren is guessing that he'll have the opportunity to put capital out at high rates of return, so he's not willing to put it out at less than 10% now. But if we knew interest rates would stay at 1%, we'd change. Our hurdles reflect our estimate of future opportunity costs.

And here's the key insight from Buffett himself:

> That's the figure we quit on. We don't want to buy equities where our real expectancy is below 10%. That's true whether short rates are 6% or whether short rates are 1%.

FINDING YOUR HURDLE RATE

I've adopted the same 10% hurdle rate. Why?

Look at the S&P 500's historical returns – roughly 10% annually over decades. That's my opportunity cost. Every investment competes against simply buying an index fund. If I can't beat 10%, why bother with the extra work and risk of picking individual stocks?

The 10% rule keeps me disciplined.

Now here's where it gets tricky.

Buffett talks about cash "that can be taken out of a business during its remaining life."

Can any of us really project a business's entire life? Unless you have a crystal ball, forecasting beyond three to five years is guesswork. I struggle to predict what I'll have for lunch next week, let alone where a business will be in a decade.

What's the solution?

We estimate what we could sell the business for at the end of our forecast period – the "terminal value" – think of it as the exit price. We assign a multiple to the cash flow it generates, just like selling a house based on neighborhood comparables.

How do we pick the right multiple?

The same way you'd price your house – look at what similar properties sell for. When selling your home, you check recent sales in your neighborhood. With stocks, you examine what comparable businesses trade for.

This terminal value often represents the bulk of a company's worth, especially for high-quality, growing businesses. In fact, for the best businesses, it can represent 80–90% of the total value.

THE RENTAL PROPERTY THAT EXPLAINS EVERYTHING

Forget stocks for a moment. Let's talk about something we all intuitively understand: rental properties. The same logic applies whether you're buying an apartment building or shares of Netflix. Both generate cash flows we can analyze.

Let's start with Rental Property A.

Imagine you're buying Rental Property A that generates $10,000 a year in rent. You plan to hold it for five years, then sell for $200,000 (20x the annual rent). Your hurdle rate is 10%.

That 10% hurdle rate becomes our discount factor. For Year 1, we divide by 1.10. For Year 2, we multiply again: 1.10 × 1.10 = 1.21. Each year the divisor grows by another 10%, reaching 1.61 by Year 5. The further out the cash flow, the more it shrinks.

Here's what each year's cash flow is worth in today's dollars:

Year	Cash Flow From	Amount	Divide By	Present Value
1	Rental income	$10,000	1.10	$9,091
2	Rental income	$10,000	1.21	$8,264
3	Rental income	$10,000	1.33	$7,519
4	Rental income	$10,000	1.46	$6,849
5	Rental income	$10,000	1.61	$6,211
5	Sale proceeds	$200,000	1.61	$124,224
Total				$162,158

That $162,158 is the intrinsic value of Rental Property A. It's what I'd pay today to earn my required 10% return.

But here's where it gets interesting.

What if, instead of flat rent, you could increase it by 15% annually? Maybe it's in a prime location with growing demand. Or it's a well-furnished apartment that commands premium rent. These are the same traits that make a steady compounder: quality assets that can raise prices consistently.

Let me introduce Rental Property B.

Same starting rent of $10,000, but this time it grows 15% every year. And because this property demonstrates consistent growth and superior quality, buyers will pay a premium. Instead of 20x rent, it commands 30x. This is exactly how high-quality businesses work: growth prospects translate into higher multiples.

First, let's see the rental income grow:

Year	Rental Income
1	$10,000
2	$11,500
3	$13,225
4	$15,209
5	$17,490

The sale price jumps to $524,700 (30x the Year five rent of $17,490).

Now let's discount these growing cash flows:

Year	Cash Flow From	Amount	Divide By	Present Value
1	Rental income	$10,000	1.10	$9,091
2	Rental income	$11,500	1.21	$9,504
3	Rental income	$13,225	1.33	$9,944
4	Rental income	$15,209	1.46	$10,417
5	Rental income	$17,490	1.61	$10,863
5	Sale proceeds	$524,700	1.61	$325,901
Total				**$375,720**

With cash flows growing at 15% annually and the terminal multiple rising from 20x to 30x, Rental Property B is worth 132% more than Rental Property A.

Let that sink in.

This is why growth is such a critical component of value. You get a double benefit: higher annual cash flows and a much higher terminal value. It's like having twin engines propelling your returns.

The beloved Costco, for example, has traded at a median of 34x forward earnings from 2015 to 2025. Hermès at 44x over the same period. Quality businesses that grow consistently often command high multiples.

This is the magic of Steady Compounders. The market recognizes predictable growth backed by strong economic moats and pays accordingly.

WHERE DOES THE VALUE REALLY COME FROM?

You may have noticed something in the Property A and Property B tables: a large chunk of the intrinsic value comes from the terminal value. And the difference between Property A and Property B is striking.

Let's break down exactly where the value comes from.

Rental property A:

Year	Cash Flow From	Present Value	% of Total
1	Rental income	$9,091	5.61%
2	Rental income	$8,264	5.10%
3	Rental income	$7,519	4.64%
4	Rental income	$6,849	4.22%
5	Rental income	$6,211	3.83%
5	Sale proceeds	$124,224	76.61%
Total		**$162,158**	**100%**

Even for a flat-rent property, the terminal value accounts for 77% of the total intrinsic value. The rental income from years one through five? Just 23%.

Rental property B:

Year	Cash Flow From	Present Value	% of Total
1	Rental income	$9,091	2.42%
2	Rental income	$9,504	2.53%
3	Rental income	$9,944	2.65%
4	Rental income	$10,417	2.77%
5	Rental income	$10,863	2.89%
5	Sale proceeds	$325,901	86.74%
Total		$375,720	100%

Look at the numbers above. For the growth property, 87% of the intrinsic value comes from the terminal value. The first five years of rental income contribute just 13%.

Now pay special attention to the first three years. Collectively, they contribute only ~8% of Property B's intrinsic value.

This is true for high-quality businesses generally. The combination of consistent growth and a premium multiple means the vast majority of intrinsic value is tied to the future, not the present.

You can see this pattern between Property A and Property B. For the slower grower, 23% of the value comes from the first five years of rental income. For the faster grower, it's just 13%. The rest comes from the terminal value. For declining businesses, this becomes even more pronounced. Most of the value of a declining business sits in the near-term cash flows, with little coming from the terminal value.

Rule of thumb: The faster a company is expected to grow, the more of its value lies in the distant future. This is why temporary problems in quality businesses often create opportunities – the near-term matters less than most investors think.

But here's the flip side. If 87% of value is tied to terminal value, you need to be right about the long term. What determines that terminal value? The durability of the moat. The length of the growth runway. Management's ability to reinvest wisely. This is why we spent so much time on those topics in earlier chapters. Get the qualitative analysis wrong, and your valuation falls apart.

THE OPPORTUNITY IN CHAOS

Here's the principle in action: when a quality business faces a temporary setback, the market tends to overreact. Investors fixate on near-term problems while forgetting where the value actually lies.

This only applies to high-quality businesses that will survive and thrive. For a weak or declining business, a two-year earnings hit might represent 20% or more of its intrinsic value. The math only works in your favor when the business has the moat, management, and balance sheet to weather the storm.

Here's how this plays out in practice.

Chipotle: When food safety became a crisis

In late 2015, Chipotle faced every restaurant's nightmare: an E. coli outbreak that spread across multiple states, followed by a norovirus incident that drew national media attention. Comparable sales dropped 30% in December 2015 alone.

The stock crashed 37%, from around $15 to $9.50 (split-adjusted). Net income collapsed 95%, from $476 million in 2015 to just $23 million in 2016.

Wall Street turned brutal. Deutsche Bank analyst Brett Levy questioned "whether Chipotle will ever regain its lost luster."[1] CNN reported "Wall Street is not convinced that Chipotle will ever be what it once was."[2] By late 2017, the narrative had only worsened: "The recovery from the E. coli crisis is essentially dead. Unbelievably, Chipotle is exiting 2017 in worse shape than it entered it."[3]

This is exactly the kind of moment where our framework becomes valuable.

Yes, the damage was severe. But even if Chipotle's sales were impaired for two full years, would that justify a 37% drop in intrinsic value? Based on what we learned about where value comes from, the math didn't add up.

The real question was whether the damage was temporary. And here, we had precedents. McDonald's had weathered multiple food safety scares: the European mad cow crisis in 2000–2001, a US mad cow case in 2003, and the "pink slime" controversy in 2012. Each time, the stock took a hit. Each time, customers eventually returned.

Chipotle had built a powerful brand with loyal customers. Management responded aggressively, implementing what they called an "industry-leading food safety program," including DNA-based testing of produce and meats, enhanced food tracing systems, and new preparation protocols. The costs were real, adding roughly 2% to food and labor expenses. But these were fixes to regain trust, not signs of a broken business model.

The recovery took time, but it came. Revenue dropped from $4.5 billion in 2015 to $3.9 billion in 2016. By 2017, it had recovered to $4.48 billion. By 2024, it reached $11.3 billion, compounding at approximately 14% annually from the trough.

The stock followed, rising from $7.50 to $60.30 between 2016 and 2024, roughly 30% annualized. Part of that was the fundamental recovery. But a larger part was a violent re-rating of multiples as investors recognized the business wasn't broken after all.

The crisis was real. The permanent damage to intrinsic value was not.

Alphabet: When AI was supposed to kill search

In early 2025, the narrative was clear: Google Search was dead, ChatGPT and Perplexity were eating its lunch, and tech commentators declared they'd stopped using Google entirely.

The stock crashed to $143 in March, trading at just 14.7x forward earnings – the kind of multiple you'd assign to a business in permanent decline.

I published "Why It's Premature to Cancel Google Search" on March 3, 2025.[4] The pushback was intense, and my inbox filled with arguments about Google's demise.

But the narrative didn't match the numbers. Quarter after quarter throughout 2024 and early 2025, management kept emphasizing that search ad revenue was still growing, even with AI Overview. Google Cloud was accelerating and YouTube remained dominant. The doom narrative made it seem like ad revenue was collapsing when the opposite was true.

Wall Street hates uncertainty, and investors were pricing in a future that hadn't materialized while ignoring a present that showed otherwise. As the stock declined, the negativity intensified: narrative follows price.

I kept coming back to the framework. Even if AI disrupted some portion of search queries, would that justify pricing Google like a dying business? The company still had infrastructure advantages built over two decades, and its competitors were burning cash with no clear path to profitability. Unlike a food safety crisis, this wasn't even confirmed damage; it was fear of future damage.

When Alphabet reported Q3 2025 results in November, it was their first-ever $100 billion quarter. Search revenue grew 15% year-over-year, an acceleration from 12% the prior quarter. The AI features everyone said would destroy search economics? They were monetizing at the same rates as traditional search while creating billions of net new queries.

The stock hit $300 by late 2025, trading at 28x forward earnings. Same company, completely different narrative.

At 15x forward earnings, the market had priced in disaster; at 28x, it priced in dominance. The intrinsic value of the business hadn't doubled in eight months. The perception had.

MARKET CRASHES: WHEN EVERYTHING GOES ON SALE

Sometimes the temporary problem isn't company-specific. It's everything at once.

During the pandemic crash of March 2020, the market dropped more than 30%. Consumer-facing businesses like Starbucks saw their outlets shut down worldwide, and the stock fell 40%, from $97 to $58.

Here's what Bill Ackman, who manages roughly $18 billion at Pershing Square, wrote to his investors during the pandemic selloff:[5]

> The revenues and earnings for the majority of businesses over the next year or so will be extremely poor, and in some cases disastrous, but for companies with strong balance sheets, dominant market positions, and which do not need access to capital, the virus will likely only disrupt the next 12 to 24 months of cash flows. In a discounted cash flow valuation of a company, the loss or disruption of the first, and

possibly second, year of cash flows, does not generally destroy more than 5% to 10% of the value of the business.

This is exactly what we saw earlier. The first two years? Just 5–10% of intrinsic value. Yet stocks had dropped 30–60%. The math was clear. The market overreacted.

Ackman loaded up on Starbucks during this period, and the stock shot back above $100 within a year. I was buying too, because this framework led me to the same conclusion.

Broad market drawdowns like this are my favorite hunting ground. The analysis is almost simpler – I don't need to untangle company-specific problems like food safety scandals or AI disruption fears. Everything just goes on sale at once.

Whether it's a broad crash or a company-specific crisis, the framework remains the same. I ask myself two questions.

THE TWO QUESTIONS THAT MATTER

1. Will this permanently impair the business's earning power?

For Chipotle, would customers permanently avoid the brand? For Alphabet, would advertisers abandon search? For Starbucks, would people stop drinking coffee after the pandemic? In each case, the answer was no.

2. Can the business survive the storm?

This is where balance sheets matter. A company with high debt and thin margins might not make it through a prolonged crisis, no matter how temporary the underlying problem. But a business with a strong balance sheet, dominant market position, and no need for external capital can weather almost anything.

If the company goes bankrupt, there are no future cash flows to discount.

The value is zero. That's why I only apply this framework to businesses I'm confident will survive.

THE LUNCH BREAK VALUATION

Now that you understand where value comes from and why temporary problems create opportunities, let's talk about the math itself. How quickly can you actually run this analysis?

Munger once teased Buffett: "Warren often talks about these discounted cash flows, but I've never seen him do one." Buffett cheekily replied, "There are some things you only do in private."

The truth is, the less math that's required, the better the opportunity. Or as Buffett himself put it, "If the value of a company doesn't just scream out at you, it's too close."

We don't always need a spreadsheet to know if a company is overvalued or undervalued; it's usually glaringly obvious and we should be able to estimate a company's worth on the back of an envelope.

The beauty of back-of-the-envelope valuation is that it forces you to articulate your assumptions clearly. When you can't hide behind complex models, you have to think deeply about the business – its growth prospects, margins, and competitive position. This process of stepping back and asking "Are these assumptions reasonable?" is often more valuable than the calculation itself.

Let's use a hypothetical example, called "CordCutter TV," which is a profitable streaming company that has earned $30 billion in revenue in the past 12 months. Operating leverage is also playing out at the company; as the company grows, it becomes more profitable. It achieved 15% net income margins in the last 12 months.

Let's assess the value in six easy steps.

THE 6-STEP BACK-OF-ENVELOPE VALUATION:

1. Project five-year revenue.
2. Estimate future margins.
3. Forecast share count.
4. Calculate Year five EPS.
5. Apply appropriate multiple.
6. Compare expected returns to your hurdle rate.

Now let's walk through each step.

Step 1: Revenue growth forecast

CordCutter TV has grown revenue at over 20% annualized over the past three years. Although the company is huge and it's the market leader, the trend of cord cutting from linear TV to connected TV is still underway and the company has demonstrated success in growing internationally.

Some of the growth levers that the company has at its disposal are: a growing number of subscribers, raising prices, and perhaps introducing new revenue engines from advertisements, or perhaps even gaming.

While there's plenty to be optimistic about, I usually like to err on the conservative side of things – after all, nothing ever really grows to the sky, and size is like an anchor to growth rates over time. There are certainly exemptions, where a company is able to grow at a more than 20% growth rate over two decades, but again, I don't like to count on the odds of that repeating for the next five years, and it's more prudent if our investment doesn't require the heaven and stars for it to make sense.

So in this case, I'm going to assume a 12% annualized growth rate over the next five years.

Year five Revenue Forecast: \$30 billion x $(1.12)^5$ = \$53 billion

Step 2: Net margin projections

Next I think about future profitability. As a company scales, margins typically rise due to operating leverage – and this is one of the things I look for in a steady compounder. This is because, if you think about it, whether the number of subscribers grows by one million or 10 million, content spending doesn't scale proportionally. CordCutter TV's content budget ranged between $12 and $17 billion between 2020 and 2024, regardless of subscriber count. More subscribers, same content costs, higher margins.

Over the past three years, the company has expanded operating margins from 10% to 18%. And during this period, management has communicated confidence that operating margins can continue to expand at 3% a year due to the predictability of recurring subscription revenue and visibility of future content expenses. Similarly, further down the income statement, net profit margins expanded from 7% to 11%.

For our model, let's assume CordCutter TV's net income margins expand to 20% at year five.

So, based on step one, with the revenue for year five forecasted at $53 billion…

Year five Net Income Forecast: $53 billion x 20% = $10.6 billion

Step 3: Share count projections

Everything will be measured on a per share basis. Why? Because as an investor, you own shares, not the entire company. If a company doubles its earnings but also doubles its share count, you haven't gained anything – your slice of the pie stays the same size.

If the company has been diluting shareholders by issuing shares as stock-based compensation or to raise capital in the stock market, then it'll have a negative impact on earnings per share. On the opposite spectrum, if they buy back shares, it'll have a positive impact.

In our case, while CordCutter TV has been diluting shares by roughly 1% annually, that was because they were earlier in the S curve and had to spend to take market share. Now, because of operating leverage, we can expect profitability and cash flow margins to widen at an accelerating pace, and as such we probably can expect them to either hold the share count steady, or reduce shares through buybacks over the next five years.

In this example, let's assume they reduce their share count by 0.5% through buybacks every year. Currently, they have roughly 455 million diluted shares outstanding.

Year five Diluted Shares Outstanding Forecast: 455 million x (0.995)^5 = 444 million

Step 4: Year five earnings per share (EPS) calculation

Alright, now that we've done most of the heavy lifting, it's time to compute the EPS by dividing the net income forecast by the diluted shares outstanding forecast.

Year five EPS: $10.6 billion ÷ 444 million = $23.87

Step 5: P/E multiple

But wait – what multiple should we use?

My Rule-of-Thumb Multiple Framework:

- Lousy Business: 10x (commodity-like, no moat).
- Average Business: 20x (S&P 500 quality, some moat).
- Outstanding Business: 30x+ (wide moat, consistent growth).

Why these numbers? A lousy business deserves a low multiple because its future is uncertain – you're not willing to pay much for earnings that might not materialize. An outstanding business commands a premium because its earnings are predictable and growing. The market pays up for certainty.

For high-quality businesses, it's not uncommon to see them trade at P/E multiples above 30×. I'm going to apply a 25× terminal multiple to CordCutter TV's year five EPS. I do think it's an outstanding business, but I'd rather underestimate than overestimate. If the multiple expands to 30x, that's upside I didn't pay for.

Year five Expected Share Price: $23.87 × 25 = $596.75

Step 6: Expected returns

Now for the moment of truth – if CordCutter TV is currently $356 per share, is it a good investment today?

Given:

- Current Share Price: $356
- Year five Expected Share Price: $596.75
- Time Horizon: five years

Total Return Calculation: ($596.75 - $356) ÷ $356 = 67.6%

This means that you're looking at a total return of 67.6% return over five years. But I like to look at the annualized returns, so let's go one step further.

To convert total return to annual return, we use this formula:

Annual Return = (Ending Value ÷ Beginning Value) to the power of (1/Years) - 1

Don't worry about the notation – we're just figuring out what annual return gets us from $356 to $596.75 over five years. The math gives us:

Expected Annualized Return Calculation: 10.9%

So we're looking at roughly an 11% annualized return over the next five years.

IS THIS ATTRACTIVE?

Remember our 10% hurdle rate from earlier? At 11% expected returns, CordCutter TV barely clears the bar. I generally like to compare opportunities to the S&P 500's historical returns of 8% to 10%.

So 11% barely beats it, and I'd much prefer 15%.

But 10% is my minimum threshold. Besides, my assumptions for forecasts generally lean on the conservative side, and for high-quality businesses, time is our friend and can usually fix the problem of slightly paying up with a long time horizon.

By now, you might have guessed.

CordCutter TV is Netflix!

This is the same process you can run on any business in your watchlist. The numbers change, but the six steps don't.

Here's how this played out with my actual investment. I'll walk you through the math that gave me conviction to keep buying while the share price dropped from $340 to $175.

I was analyzing the streaming giant in early April 2022, right after Wall Street abandoned it. The stock had crashed from $690 to around $390 – a brutal 43% haircut – after a weak Q4, 2021 guidance spooked investors in January.*

I placed my first order around $340. Then Netflix reported its first subscriber loss in a decade. Over the following weeks, the stock nosedived to a low of roughly $175. It was a gut punch.

My stomach churned as I watched my position crater 50% in two weeks. Even after a decade of investing, that sinking feeling of "Did I miss something crucial?" never fully goes away.

But I had my research, thesis and conviction written down. This is exactly when your journal works its magic.

With the share price at new lows at $175, the expected annualized returns went from 11% to a tantalizing 28%.

Expected Annualized Return (CAGR) Calculation: ($596.75 ÷ $175)^(1/5) - 1 = 27.8%

But here's what's even more interesting. I averaged UP, buying another tranche of shares as the share price recovered to $250, even though this price of $250 was over 40% higher than my second purchase at $175. Watch why that still made mathematical sense:

Expected Annualized Return from $250: ($596.75 ÷ $250)^(1/5) - 1 = 19.0%

Even at $250 – 40% higher than the bottom – the expected return was still 19% annually. This is why you don't need to catch the bottom. You just need a reasonable estimate of what the business is worth and the discipline to buy when the price is well below it.

When we think of ourselves as business owners, we should welcome

* All Netflix share prices in this book reflect pre-split values. Netflix completed a 10-for-1 stock split in November 2025. To compare with today's stock charts, divide by 10.

opportunities like these to deploy our second or even third tranche. The share price had risen, but the expected returns were still excellent.

Fast forward to July 2025, just over three years later. Netflix's share price had soared past $1,300. When the company did a 10-for-1 stock split in November 2025, each share worth around $1,200 became ten shares worth around $120 each. The temporary problem had become a distant memory. But here's what makes this framework so powerful – it forced me to ground my assumptions in business reality.

You might be wondering: How did I come up with that 12% revenue growth and 20% margin assumption? Were these just wild guesses?

Here's exactly how I tied the numbers to Netflix's actual business.

MAKING SURE YOUR NUMBERS MAKE SENSE

When thinking about forecasting revenue in step 1, the numbers should roughly make sense from a business perspective.

Let's look at what Netflix must achieve to grow revenue from $29.5 billion to $53 billion.

In 2021, Netflix had on average roughly 211 million subscribers with streaming revenue of $29.5 billion.[6] That works out to $140 per subscriber annually.

Netflix can grow revenue two ways: more subscribers and higher prices.

I estimated subscribers would grow from 211 million to 311 million by 2026 – capturing roughly a third of the 800–900 million addressable households. That's about 8% annual growth. Reasonable, given the company's global expansion potential.

For pricing, I estimated Netflix would raise prices by about 4% annually, from $140 to $170 per subscriber. It's reasonable to assume it'll roughly match inflation over five years, considering the entertainment value delivered relative to disposable income.

By 2026: 311 million subscribers × $170 per subscriber = $53 billion in revenue.

This is how you tie your forecast to the business – it has to make sense operationally.

As I sit here in 2025, three years have passed, so let's see how the forecast compared to reality.

Netflix Metrics	**2021 Actual**	**2026 Forecast**	**2024 Actual**
Average paid members	211 million	311 million	278 million
Revenue	$29.7 billion	$53 billion	$39 billion
Revenue per member	$141	$170	$140
Growth Rates (Annualized):			
Subscriber growth	-	8% projected	10% actual (2021-24)
Pricing growth	-	4% projected	0% actual (2021-24)
Revenue growth	-	12% projected	10% actual (2021-24)

From $29.7 billion to $39 billion in streaming revenue[7] – that's a 10% annualized growth rate. Close to my 12% forecast.

The composition was different than expected though. Membership growth exceeded expectations while pricing stayed flat instead of growing.

This was largely due to the introduction of the advertisement tier (along with password crackdown), which brought in price-sensitive customers. As the ad tier scales in the future, I expect ad revenue will more than compensate for lower subscription prices.

This investment has done well since I first published the Netflix stock report on *SteadyCompounding.com*. Part driven by business performance, part by multiple expansion. As I'm writing this in mid-2025, Netflix trades at a forward PE multiple of 44x. Pretty nuts, but that's what markets do – swing from extreme pessimism to extreme optimism.

The future rarely unfolds as we expect. As the saying goes, "When you plan, God laughs." Netflix proved this perfectly – membership grew faster than expected while pricing grew slower, yet the investment still worked because the direction was right even if the precise path wasn't.

This is why I keep my projections simple. Many analysts build elaborate models projecting subscribers by region, revenue per user by geography, and every operational expense line item. They get lost in the weeds and miss the forest.

As Curtis Jensen wisely put it: "A DCF is like the Hubble telescope – turn it a fraction of an inch and you're in a different galaxy." The more complex your model, the more ways it can spectacularly miss reality.

When it comes to forecasting, it's better to be roughly right than precisely wrong.

What matters is understanding the business dynamics: Netflix had pricing power, global growth potential, and operating leverage. The exact path was uncertain, but the direction was clear.

The Netflix story shows valuation in action. But you might be wondering – where do I actually find these numbers?

WHERE TO FIND THE NUMBERS

Believe it or not, I used to write letters to companies asking them to mail me their annual reports. Physical copies. In the post.

I'd wait weeks for a thick envelope to arrive, then spend hours flipping through pages looking for the numbers I needed.

Today, what used to take weeks now takes minutes. Earnings calls, transcripts, management interviews are all available instantly.

There are both paid and free options for accessing this data. If you're just starting out, I recommend the free route: go straight to the source materials and get your hands dirty. Even today, while I use several paid tools, when it's time to go deep on a company, I still pull up the original filings. There's no substitute for reading the source.

Here are the documents that matter.

The 10-K (annual report)

This is the company's comprehensive annual filing with the SEC (the US Securities and Exchange Commission, the government body that regulates public markets). Think of it as the company's full report card for the year.

Why it matters: The 10-K gives you the complete picture. You'll find the financial metrics we covered in earlier chapters: revenue, net income, margins, share count. You'll also find the business description, competitive landscape, and risk factors. For our six-step framework, this is your primary source.

The 10-K also contains segmental information that doesn't appear in headlines. For example, Meta breaks down its Family of Apps performance: Daily Active Users (DAU), Monthly Active Users (MAU), and Average Revenue Per User (ARPU). These details help you understand what's actually driving the business.

The 10-Q (quarterly report)

Same idea as the 10-K, but filed every quarter. It's shorter and covers just the past three months.

Why it matters: The 10-Q helps you track whether your thesis is playing out. If you're analyzing a company mid-year, the latest 10-Q shows you where things stand. Same segmental data, updated quarterly.

Earnings transcripts

Every quarter, management hosts a call with analysts to discuss results. The transcript captures their prepared remarks and the Q&A session that follows.

Why it matters: This is where you hear management explain strategy, address concerns, and answer tough questions. You'll notice when a CEO sounds confident versus defensive, or when they dodge a question entirely. For assessing management quality, transcripts are invaluable.

The proxy statement (DEF 14A)

This filing covers corporate governance: executive compensation, insider ownership, and board structure.

Why it matters: It answers a critical question. Is management aligned with shareholders? You'll see how much executives are paid, how much stock they own, and whether incentives reward long-term performance or short-term metrics. This ties directly to the skin in the game framework from Chapter 4.

WHERE TO FIND THEM

Start with the company's investor relations page. Just search Google for "[company name] investor relations" and you'll find annual reports, quarterly filings, transcripts, and proxy statements.

If something's missing, head to sec.gov/edgar. This is the SEC's public database. Every filing from every US public company lives here, free to access.

For transcripts, investor relations pages sometimes only include prepared remarks without the Q&A. A quick search like "Netflix Q3 2025 transcript" usually surfaces the full version.

A NOTE ON TOOLS

Paid platforms can speed things up once you're comfortable with the basics. Since these tools change constantly, I keep an updated list at lunchbreakinvestor.com/tools, covering both free and paid options. You'll also find a financial data tracking template and a guide on using AI to extract data for you. Lunch break investing is about working smarter, not harder, so we can spend time on things we love.

Now that you know where to find the numbers, let's tackle the two judgment calls that trip up most investors.

THE ART OF CHOOSING THE RIGHT MULTIPLE

When deciding the multiple to apply to the year five EPS, I like to look at a few things before deciding:

1. What has the company historically traded at?
2. What its competitors in the same industry are trading at.
3. What businesses with similar quality trade at in mature stages.

But here's the challenge – for growth companies with depressed earnings, historical multiples are meaningless. Competitors might all be losing money. And finding truly comparable mature businesses can be tricky. That's why I also use a simple framework to anchor my thinking.

You've already seen my rule-of-thumb framework in Step 5:

- **Commodity Business**: 10x (no moat, no differentiation).
- **Average Business**: 20x (S&P 500 quality, some moat).
- **Outstanding Business**: 30x+ (wide moat, consistent growth).

These aren't precise numbers. They're mental anchors. But where do they come from?

The commodity business multiple of 10x comes from a Morgan Stanley study on commodity P/E multiples from 1961–2020, finding an average of roughly 10x for businesses creating no value above their cost of capital.[8]

The average multiple of 20x is based on the S&P 500's 10-year average PE of roughly 20x. During this period, the S&P 500 grew market cap weighted revenue at roughly 5% annualized, with earnings growing around 8% annualized.

Outstanding businesses often trade above 30x, with examples being companies like Mastercard, Hermès and Costco. These businesses generally grow earnings consistently in the low-to-mid teens, with wide economic moats.

For Netflix, I couldn't rely on historical multiples because its earnings were artificially depressed from heavy content investment. Its competitors were losing money chasing growth, so they were not useful as a comparison. So I focused on point three – looking at what similar quality subscription businesses trade at once they mature. That's how I landed on 25x for my conservative case, even though outstanding businesses often trade higher.

Sometimes the market gets so pessimistic that quality businesses trade at commodity multiples. That was exactly the case with Meta at $88 in late 2022. Even if you assumed Meta was nothing more than a commodity business – which was absurd given their three billion users and network effects – and slapped a measly 10x multiple on normalized earnings, the returns still looked tantalizing. When quality trades at commodity prices, you swing hard.

The key is using both approaches together. The three considerations give you market context. The multiple framework keeps you grounded. Combined, they help you avoid both extremes – paying fantasy valuations for growth stories at one end of the scale, or missing quality businesses because they look "expensive" relative to the market at the other end of the scale.

Choosing the right multiple requires judgment, combining your assessment of the moat, growth prospects, and competitive position. This is why investing is as much art as science. You're not just plugging numbers into a formula – you're making educated guesses about the future.

Once you've decided on a multiple (Step 5), you face another choice that trips up many investors: should you use earnings or free cash flow (Step 4)?

EARNINGS VERSUS CASH FLOW: KEEP IT SIMPLE

If you've tried reading financial reports, you've probably seen analysts use a barrage of multiples – price to earnings multiple, free cash flow multiple, operating earnings (i.e., EBIT) multiple, EBITDA multiple, and many more.

Now if you were to speak to a DCF absolutist, or a finance professor, they will probably burst a vessel when they hear this. But in most instances, when we're looking at quality businesses, just use earnings. It's simpler, and the difference won't matter for your analysis.

Let me explain why.

The difference between earnings and cash flow

Net income is your accounting profit. Revenue minus expenses, following accounting rules. Operating cash flow (OCF) is the actual cash that came in from running the business.

They differ because of timing. You might record a sale before the customer pays, or record an expense before you write the check. Net income captures what you earned on paper. OCF captures what landed in the bank.

You'll find both in the 10-K: net income on the income statement, operating cash flow on the cash flow statement.

Why quality businesses make this easy

Quality businesses often have great working capital dynamics. Customers pay quickly. Suppliers get paid slowly. Cash arrives before it leaves.

Think about it: if customers pay you upfront and you don't need much inventory, your cash flow naturally tracks your earnings. There's no gap between "earned on paper" and "cash in hand."

This is why I use a simple litmus test: compare operating cash flow against net income. For high-quality businesses, OCF should be at least 80% of net income. If it passes, just use earnings.

Meta: A digital business

Let's take a look at Meta from 2022 to 2024:

In billions	2022	2023	2024
OCF	$50.5	$71.1	$91.3
Net income	$23.2	$39.1	$62.4
OCF/Net income	218%	182%	146%

Meta passes with flying colors, earning far more in cash than it reports in net income. Customers pay upfront for ad placements. As a tech company, it has minimal inventory. The cash comes in before it even recognizes the revenue. That's a beautiful business model.

Apple: Even with physical products

Now let's look at Apple, which sells physical goods:

In billions	2022	2023	2024
OCF	$122.2	$110.5	$118.3
Net income	$99.8	$97	$93.7
OCF/Net income	122%	114%	126%

Apple isn't as strong as Meta because it has inventory, but it is still best-in-class with a ratio consistently above 110%. It collects cash from customers in under 30 days while paying suppliers around 100 days later, creating a substantial cash float. Even with physical products, its cash generation is exceptional.

The bottom line

When you're looking at high-quality businesses, their earnings mirror their cash flow pretty closely, or in some cases, underestimate it slightly. Which is fine, because we don't need to work to the closest decimal point.

For the vast majority of steady compounders, earnings work just fine for Step four of our framework. If a business passes the 80% test, use earnings. If it doesn't, consider looking elsewhere. Weak cash conversion usually signals complexity you don't need.

THINK IN RANGES, NOT ABSOLUTES

Don't think about valuation as something fixed – a single number carved in stone. Think in terms of three scenarios: bear case, base case, and bull case.

Repeat the six-step process for the bear case. In the worst-case scenario, what would my returns be? Am I willing to accept that? What's the likelihood of this happening?

Similarly, repeat it for the bull case. Under the most optimistic (but still reasonably possible) assumptions, what would my returns look like? If it isn't attractive even on this rosy lens, put it aside in your waitlist and look at it again when Mr. Market decides to throw a fit and send the share price down.

This is crucial because intrinsic value changes as the business evolves, sometimes for the better, sometimes for the worse. If the company finds success with new revenue avenues, like Netflix with advertisement revenue, perhaps it warrants a revision upwards. Or if artificial intelligence is able to reduce operating expenses, increasing its profitability, perhaps that too.

Or it may go the other direction. Competitive pressures kick in and the company can't raise prices. Then perhaps we need to adjust intrinsic value downwards. The point is, we have to be ready to update our estimates if the facts change.

I typically find my base case lands somewhere around 15% expected returns for a quality business I want to own. My bear case might show 8–10% returns – still acceptable but not exciting. My bull case might show 25%+ returns if things go better than expected.

With so many quality businesses in the market, why settle for mediocre returns? If my base case doesn't show at least 10% returns, I move on to better opportunities.

This range thinking protects you from false precision. You're not pretending to know exactly what will happen. You're mapping out the reasonable possibilities and making sure the odds are stacked in your favor.

CONCLUSION

You now have everything you need to value any business over your lunch break. Not with complex models or specialized software, but with simple math and clear thinking. The same framework that helped me recognize opportunity in Netflix's drawdown can work for any quality business.

The goal of valuation isn't false precision – it's understanding whether you're paying a reasonable price for the quality and growth you're buying. When you can't justify the returns even with optimistic assumptions, you walk away. When the math shows compelling returns even with conservative assumptions, you've found something worth owning.

Remember what we learned: the bulk of a quality business's intrinsic value comes from the long term. This is why temporary problems create such powerful opportunities – the market obsesses over next quarter while you're thinking about next decade.

Combine this valuation framework with what you've learned in previous chapters – identifying moats, evaluating management, recognizing buying opportunities – and you have a complete system for building wealth through steady compounding.

The math is simple. The judgment calls require practice. But now you have the tools to make those calls with confidence.

LUNCH BREAK SUMMARY

- **Most value lives in the distant future**: For quality businesses, the bulk of intrinsic value comes from year five and beyond – that's why temporary problems create opportunities.
- **Simple beats complex**: Back-of-envelope math that's roughly right beats precise models that miss the big picture.
- **Growth gets double credit**: Growing businesses benefit twice – higher future cash flows AND higher terminal multiples.
- **Quality at commodity prices wins big**: When great businesses trade at multiples typically reserved for mediocre ones, you've found gold.
- **Think in ranges, not absolutes**: Bear, base, and bull scenarios protect you from false precision while stacking the odds in your favor.

YOUR NEXT STEP

Pick one company from your watchlist. Run the six-step valuation with bear, base, and bull scenarios. Don't aim for perfection – just get comfortable with the process. In Chapter 8, we'll explore buying strategies – how to build positions patiently when you find great businesses at reasonable prices.

PART III

THE MECHANICS

CHAPTER 8
BUYING STRATEGIES

I REMEMBER WHEN I first bought shares in 2008.

I had roughly $2,500 in investible funds and my entire due diligence process consisted of one question.

"Auntie, what stock should I buy?"

I've come a long way since then.

The stock she recommended was Cambridge Industrial Trust (CIT), a Singapore company that owned industrial warehouses, collected rent from tenants, and paid it out as dividends. The thesis was simple: at $0.40 per share, it seemed cheap. Now that you've come this far in the book, I hope you immediately grasp how flawed my thinking was.

Industrial properties have terrible pricing power. They're extremely cyclical. I was clueless about asset quality. I only thought about dividends, ignoring total shareholder returns.

And just because the share price is under a dollar doesn't mean it's cheap.

But here's what really happened after I bought it.

I couldn't stop checking the price.

Several times a day.

Remember, this was 2008 – no brokerage apps. Every time I wanted to check, I had to turn on my laptop, connect to Wi-Fi, and key in my username and password like a savage.

Most of my savings were in one position: CIT.

When the share price went up and my portfolio increased by even $50, I felt like a genius. On red days, anxiety crept in. It was like a drug. I kept checking prices that swung daily, even though the business didn't change from Tuesday to Wednesday.

All that monitoring. All that emotional energy.

Five weeks later, I sold for a grand total profit of $100.

Then I repeated the cycle. Buy, monitor obsessively, sell for a quick profit that didn't move the needle.

It was exhausting. It wasn't sustainable. And it certainly wasn't the path to financial freedom.

But dipping my toes in at a young age led me to a crucial insight. Some lessons can't be taught – they must be experienced. From this early mistake, I learned not just about investing, but about myself. About how I behaved when real money was at risk.

Most importantly, I learned that successful buying isn't about timing the market perfectly or monitoring prices obsessively. It's about having a framework that manages both risk and psychology – and understanding why the market keeps serving up the same opportunities over and over.

The goal of investing is freedom, not staring at screens. Let me share the buying framework I've developed over the years – one that actually lets you sleep at night, frees up your time, and compounds your wealth.

Now that you can identify great businesses and value them properly, let's tackle the psychological challenge of actually pulling the trigger.

But first, you need to understand what you're up against.

THE THREE TRAPS THAT KEEP YOU FROM PULLING THE TRIGGER

Every investor faces three psychological traps that sabotage smart buying decisions.

The first trap is analysis paralysis.

You've done your research. Found a quality business. The valuation looks reasonable. Yet your finger hovers over the "buy" button.

What if it drops tomorrow? What if you're missing something?

What if, what if, what if?

I've seen investors spend months "preparing" to invest, never actually pulling the trigger. They read one more analyst report, check one more data point, listen to one more earnings call.

As Nassim Taleb wrote in *The Black Swan*, "The more information you give someone, the more hypotheses they will formulate along the way, and the worse-off they will be. They see more random noise and mistake it for information."

More research feels productive. But past a certain point, we're sabotaging ourselves.

The second trap is anchoring to past prices.

"I'll wait for it to drop back to $50 like it was last month."

But markets don't care about your reference points. Netflix at $300 after proving its ad tier works might be cheaper than Netflix at $200 when everyone thought it was dying.

Stock prices are just numbers. Value is what matters.

The third trap sits on the opposite end of the spectrum – FOMO.

Fear of missing out.

Your colleague made 50% on some hot stock. Your barber is talking about a "sure thing." The cabbie is giving stock tips. You see prices running up daily and that voice screams "buy NOW before it's too late!"

This is how people end up chasing momentum in businesses they don't understand. They buy the story, not the business. They buy the price action, not the value.

All three traps have one thing in common: they're emotional reactions, not rational decisions.

The antidote isn't more analysis or better timing. It's clarity about what you're actually buying. And clarity comes from a surprisingly simple test.

THE CRAYON TEST

Peter Lynch said it best: "If you can't explain to an 11-year-old in two minutes or less why you own a stock, you shouldn't own it."

I call this the crayon test.

This isn't about dumbing things down – it's about true understanding. Complex jargon often masks fuzzy thinking.

But here's what most people miss about these quotes. Lynch and Feynman aren't just talking about simplicity. They're talking about the act of explanation itself.

Writing is thinking.

When you write down your investment thesis – actually put pen to paper or fingers to keyboard – something magical happens. The fuzzy becomes clear. The complex becomes simple.

Or sometimes, you realize you don't understand it at all.

But here's the deeper reason writing matters, something most investors never grasp: your brain is constantly rewriting history.

Every time you remember why you bought a stock, your brain doesn't retrieve a recording – it reconstructs a story. And that story changes based on what has happened since. Stock went up? Your brain conveniently remembers how confident you were, how obvious the opportunity was. Stock went down? Suddenly you "remember" having doubts all along.

As Gautam Baid wrote in *The Joys of Compounding*, "A significant part of human memories is mostly fiction." Our brains are meaning-making machines, constantly filling in gaps with whatever seems plausible now, not what we actually thought then.

This is why even brilliant investors make the same mistakes repeatedly. Without written records, they literally can't remember what they were thinking when they bought a company. The brain has already revised the story to fit the outcome.

Your written thesis becomes your defense against your own brain. When Netflix drops 70% and every headline screams disaster, you can't trust your memory of why you bought. But you can trust what you wrote. Those words capture what you actually understood before the noise, before the drawdown, before your brain started its revisionist history.

Writing down your investment case isn't about creating lengthy reports – a single page, written over one lunch break, captures everything that matters. But that page becomes your anchor when markets test you and your own mind plays tricks.

What exactly should you write? Three critical components will crystallize your thinking and prepare you for the volatility ahead.

First: Your investment thesis in one paragraph

This is where everything clicks together. Write one paragraph that explains how the business makes money, what stops competitors from stealing those profits, where future growth will come from, and why you trust management to deliver.

Take Netflix. Here's my thesis, condensed from what I published on April 13, 2022:

> Netflix charges a monthly fee for your subscription and you get to watch unlimited TV shows and movies… Netflix's ability to spread the fixed costs of content, markets, and technology across a much larger subscriber base than any of its competitors is continually reinforced through superior customer service, a powerful recommendation engine, and an amazing, habit-forming product… Netflix as the dominant player can set the bar for competitive content high enough, such that the smaller players will have to keep burning cash to survive while it makes a good living… Throughout Netflix's history, management has demonstrated a willingness to innovate, move fast and correct their actions when required.

If you can't write a clear paragraph about your investment thesis, you're not ready to buy. Keep researching.

When Netflix dropped 70% two weeks after I published that thesis, I pulled up what I'd written. The fundamentals I'd documented – scale advantages, competitive position, management's ability to adapt – remained intact. The stock price was noise. The business was signal. That document gave me confidence to add to my position when it drew down aggressively. Not because I was fearless, but because I understood its value.

Second: Your expected returns

Before pulling the trigger, ask yourself: What returns can I reasonably expect from today's price?

This isn't about precise calculations – we covered the detailed valuation framework in the previous chapter. It's about a sanity check. Are you expecting 10% annual returns based on steady growth and reasonable assumptions? That might work. But if you need the company to grow at 40% annually for a decade, or the market to value the company like the next Apple, you're betting on miracles.

The best business in the world becomes a terrible investment at the wrong price. Know what you're signing up for before you buy.

Third: The premortem

Before you buy a stock, visualize that a year has passed from the date of your purchase and that you have lost money on your investment, even in a steady market.

Now, write down on a piece of paper what went wrong in the future.

This prospective hindsight technique forces you to think beyond your bullish thesis. It opens your mind to the full range of outcomes – not just the ones you want to see. What could actually break this investment? Regulatory changes? Competitive threats? Execution failures?

These risks may not become deal-breakers, but identifying them prepares you for the volatility ahead. You'll know which drops are temporary panic and which might signal real problems.

The premortem is particularly powerful because it combats our natural optimism bias.

If we are mentally prepared for the worst-case scenario and have a contingency plan ready to cope with it, we will be far less susceptible to overreacting and making costly mistakes under sudden stressful conditions.

These three components – your thesis, your expected returns, and your premortem – work together like a three-legged stool. Remove any leg and you'll fall on your face when markets get rough.

Your written thesis is your battlefield preparation.

I keep a simple document for every position I own – and equally important, for companies on my watchlist. When opportunity strikes, I'm ready.

For myself, I keep a record of my watchlist on *SteadyCompounding.com*. This forces me to think through my analysis before I need to act.

But here's the unexpected benefit of writing publicly: other investors challenge my blind spots, share perspectives I missed, and force me to defend my thinking. These discussions always make my thesis more robust. Write before you buy. Not after. Not during. Before.

There's a saying in the stock market: narrative always follows price movement. If it goes up, the business is invincible and it can grow rapidly for a long time. If it goes down, competitive pressures are intense and it is facing disruption.

Your written words from the past won't lie to you. They're your anchor when the market is screaming and your emotions are shot.

That simple act – putting thoughts to paper before putting money at risk – will save you from more mistakes than any other investment practice I know. More importantly, it will give you conviction when opportunity appears and everyone else is paralyzed by fear.

THREE SITUATIONS THAT CREATE OPPORTUNITY

With your thesis written and your conviction tested, the question becomes: when do you act?

Buying is part art and part science.

I prefer buying when I can see at least 15% annualized returns for three to five years. That's the science part. The art is recognizing when Mr. Market serves up those opportunities.

Over the years, I've found three situations that consistently create attractive entry points. Let's look at each of these in turn.

1. Misunderstood pivots

This is when companies make strategic changes that strengthen their business, but which Wall Street initially hates.

Adobe's shift to subscriptions is the textbook example.[1] When they announced in 2011 they were moving from selling boxed software to cloud-based subscriptions, Wall Street freaked out. Think about it – Adobe was asking customers who'd been buying Creative Suite every few years for up to $2,600 to instead pay monthly forever. The immediate hit to revenue was obvious. The long-term brilliance wasn't.

Dan Cohen, then vice president of corporate strategy, later explained: "In November 2011, we announced our intentions to Wall Street – it was a full day of briefings, with financial analysts focused on communicating the strategy, ramifications, and financial expectations… We decided to shift $200 million in operating expenses toward these high-growth opportunities. After we announced our plans, the stock price dropped by 6%."

Patient investors who understood the strategic brilliance saw something different.

Predictable recurring revenue instead of lumpy sales. Lower entry price expanding the addressable market to students and hobbyists. Continuous updates creating stickier customers. And piracy – which had plagued Adobe for years – became nearly impossible with cloud verification.

The pain came first. When Adobe launched Creative Cloud on April 23, 2012, transitioning Creative Suite to a subscription model, the financial impact was brutal. Net income plummeted 65% the following year as the company absorbed the transition costs. But by April 2016, the market caught on and Adobe's stock had nearly tripled from that 2012 launch date.[2] The subscription model transformed Adobe from a one-time software seller into a recurring revenue powerhouse – exactly what patient investors saw coming while Wall Street obsessed over quarterly earnings.

2. Temporary setbacks

These are fixable problems the market treats as permanent death sentences.

Here's what most Wall Street analysts get wrong: they expect businesses to grow in a perfect straight line. Quarter after quarter of smooth, predictable growth. That only happens in fairy tales.

The truth is far more nuanced. Even the best businesses face setbacks – supply chain disruptions, competitive pressures, execution mistakes. Growth is lumpy. Great businesses still move in an upward direction despite the lumpiness.

The problem? Wall Street can't see beyond one or two quarters. When a champion stumbles, analysts assume they'll never get up again. That's when our edge as patient investors kicks in.

Netflix in 2022 was the perfect temporary setback. A first drop in subscriber numbers in a decade sent the stock from $690 to $175. The narrative was brutal – competition from Disney+, password sharing killing growth, the ad-free model was a sign of desperation.

But had the fundamentals really changed? I'll show you exactly how I navigated this opportunity – and why I kept buying while everyone else sold – later in this chapter.

3. Broad market drawdowns

This is when quality gets thrown out with the bathwater during panic selling.

March 2020 showed this perfectly. When Covid hit, markets didn't discriminate. Everything got destroyed. Booking Holdings – the highest-quality travel aggregator with a fortress balance sheet – saw its share price fall from $2,000 to $1,177.

Yes, travel stopped. Booking owned no planes and no hotels though. They could cut marketing spend to zero and wait. With $7 billion in cash, they had the resources to survive and grab market share from weaker competitors.

Those who recognized quality in the chaos made 300%+ returns in under four years.

Think 2008 financial crisis, the pandemic meltdown, or the inflation fears of 2022. These are defining moments for investors. Wealth transfers in a significant way from those who panic to those who keep their shit together.

During these moments, I don't chase optically "cheap" stocks. I focus exclusively on the highest-quality businesses at reasonable prices. These companies weather storms with strong balance sheets, recover fastest when sentiment improves, and compound wealth for decades after.

Now, these three scenarios are where I focus most of my buying energy. But here's what most investors miss: these opportunities exist because of a predictable pattern of human psychology. Understanding this pattern – what I call the sentiment cycle – transforms these scary moments into systematic opportunities. Figure 8.1 shows how this cycle unfolds.

THE SENTIMENT CYCLE: WHY OPPORTUNITIES KEEP APPEARING

I've observed this pattern repeatedly throughout my investing journey. It explains why quality businesses become mispriced and why most investors do exactly the wrong thing at the wrong time.

Here's how it unfolds.

First, negative news emerges. Maybe it's a missed earnings target, a competitive threat, or a strategic pivot Wall Street doesn't understand. Initial selling pressure begins, typically driving the stock down 20%.

Then Wall Street piles on. Analysts downgrade their ratings, institutional investors start selling to protect their quarterly numbers. The stock drops another 15%.

Finally, panic spreads. Retail investors capitulate, financial media runs doom-and-gloom headlines, and social media amplifies the fear. Another 15% disappears.

By now, a quality business might be down 50% or more. This is when value investors start accumulating. They recognize that while the stock price has been cut in half, the business value hasn't.

The company continues executing its plan. Maybe the strategic pivot starts working, the competitive threat proves overblown, or the missed quarter was just a blip. Fundamentals drive recovery to fair value.

Eventually, sentiment overshoots in the other direction. The same investors who fled at the bottom chase the stock higher, often pushing it beyond intrinsic value. Quality businesses cycle through predictable phases of pessimism and optimism. The darkest moments – when panic spreads – are often the best buying opportunities.

Figure 8.1: The sentiment cycle

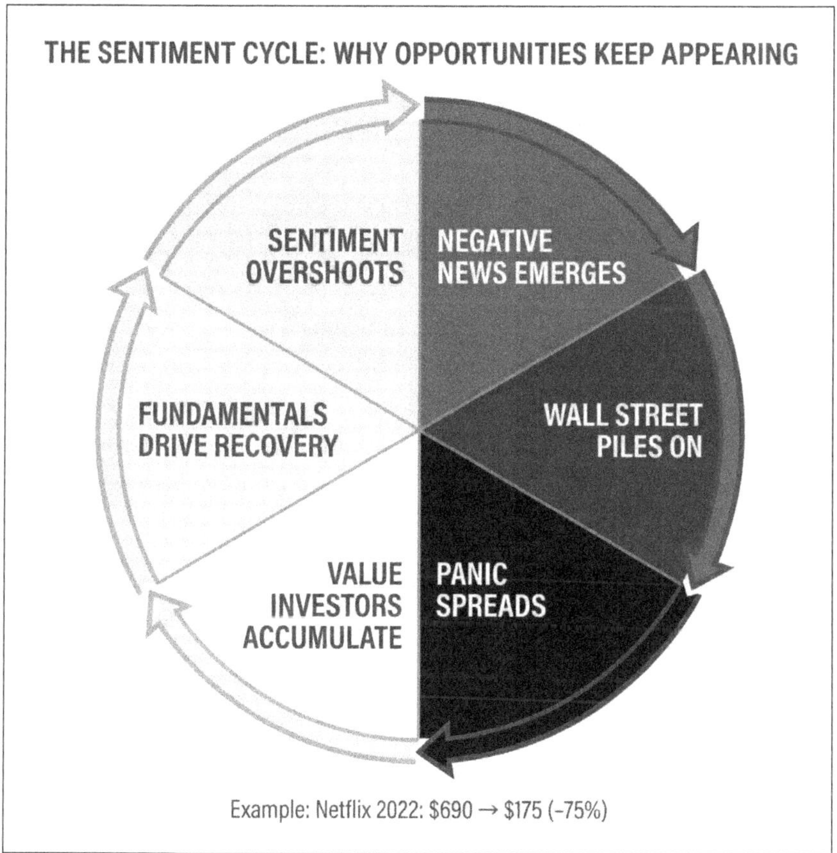

Source: Created by Thomas Chua.

Netflix in 2022 followed this exact pattern. When subscriber growth slowed, the stock cratered from $690 to $175 – a 75% decline. But did Netflix's earnings power and long-term fundamentals deteriorate by 75%? Of course not.

WHY THESE PATTERNS PERSIST

These opportunities keep appearing because of these three psychological forces:

Institutional constraints. Fund managers can't afford to be wrong and alone. Being wrong in a crowd is survivable; being wrong alone ends careers. So they sell when everyone else sells, even when they know better.

Time horizon mismatch. Most investors think in quarters. We think in years. They panic about next month's earnings. We focus on the next three to five years of cash flows. This mismatch is our edge.

Availability bias. Human brains overweight recent events. A bad quarter becomes a broken business in investors' minds. They extrapolate the present into the future, forgetting that business cycles are just that – cycles.

The beautiful part? These forces are structural. They're not going away. Fund managers will always face career risk. Quarterly pressures will persist. Human psychology hasn't changed in millennia.

This means patient investors with conviction will always have opportunities.

Now that you understand both when opportunities appear and why the market creates them, let's talk about how to act. Because finding the opportunity is just the first step. How you build your position matters just as much as what you buy.

THE THREE-DATE RULE

Once you've identified an opportunity, resist the urge to go all-in immediately.

I build positions in tranches – typically three purchases over several months, usually starting with 1–3% of my portfolio for the first tranche, then potentially adding similar amounts if the thesis strengthens. I do this for two reasons.

First, psychological resilience. Buying in tranches means you can watch a position drop 30% without panic. You've only committed a modest amount while you learn how the business handles adversity. If your thesis was wrong, you've limited the damage. If you were right, you have dry powder to add at better prices.

Second, letting the business prove itself. Quarters pass. Management delivers what they promised – or they don't. The moat widens – or shows cracks. Your conviction should grow from evidence, not hope.

Think of it like dating. Your first investment is a first date. You're interested but not committed; if you see any red flags, you're out. The second purchase is getting serious – you've seen enough good traits to want to deepen the relationship. The third investment – there's proven compatibility.

Let me show you exactly how this played out with Netflix – the temporary setback I mentioned above.

Case study: Buying Netflix while everyone sold

I first invested in Netflix in April 2022. The weak Q4 2021 earnings announced in January had caused the stock to tumble from its peak of $690 to around $390, and it had continued drifting lower. I took my position at around $340. The pandemic streaming boom was coming to an end, and investor sentiment was already souring. That was my first tranche – my first date with the stock.

Little did I know, when Netflix reported Q1 2022 results two weeks later, the stock would ultimately lose nearly half its value from where I'd bought it. The streaming giant reported a loss of 200,000 customers against their forecast of gaining 2.5 million. The first decline in a decade. Management forecast Q2 would see another two million customer loss.

Ever since starting *SteadyCompounding.com*, I've made most of my investment theses public, and it's been surprisingly valuable. Other investors challenge my blind spots, share insights I missed, and force me to defend my thinking. That day I wrote:

"In the near term, growth may be challenged as countries ease lockdowns and inflation erodes consumer spending power. In the long run, linear TV will continue to decline as streaming services gain market share.

First order effect: Because of macroeconomic factors and a challenging competitive environment, Netflix is likely to experience declining growth or churn in the near future.

Second order effect: If Netflix, who has the largest content library and is already profitable and cash flow positive, would suffer in this environment, then the other smaller players would suffer and bleed even more."

The stock ultimately bottomed at $162.71 – enough to scare away most investors. All sorts of doomsday narratives emerged. Disney was supposedly disrupting Netflix's dominance. Competition would destroy Netflix's economics forever. But my assessment hadn't changed. In fact, the odds for Netflix had improved at these prices. I deployed my second tranche at around $175.

By August 2022, Netflix had recovered to around $250, though headlines still screamed doom. "Disney+ overtakes Netflix in just 2.5 years!" But these surface-level analysts were missing something crucial.

I dug deeper and wrote on my blog:

> May I bring your attention to the Average Monthly Revenue Per Paid Subscriber for Disney+ Hotstar: a grand total of $1.20. And Disney+ Hotstar accounts for 58.4 million out of 152.1 million Disney+ subscribers. Meanwhile, Netflix's average monthly revenue in Asia Pacific is $8.83 per month.
>
> Disney's subscriber count is also misleading. Households who subscribe to bundle offerings (Hulu Live TV + SVOD, Disney+ and ESPN+) are counted as THREE unique subscribers. These bundles cost just $13.99 but count as three subscribers. Netflix's Standard plan costs $15.49 and counts as one subscriber.
>
> Hot takes like 'Disney+ overtaking Netflix in record time' capture attention, but they're not good for your investing health. Always look under the hood.

After this analysis confirmed my thesis, I took my third tranche at around $250. Notice something important: I was averaging UP from my second purchase at $175. The stock had risen 43% from my second purchase, but my conviction had grown even more.

Most investors would have either sold for the quick 43% gain or waited for a pullback. I did neither. The Netflix I was buying at $250 – with subscriber bleeding stopped, password sharing being addressed, and the ad tier launching – was fundamentally stronger than the one I'd bought at $175.

The tranche approach transformed a 75% drawdown from terrifying to manageable. Each purchase felt reasonable because I wasn't betting everything on perfect timing. This is where most investors fail – they can't bring themselves to buy more at higher prices, even when the business has become stronger.

THE COUNTERINTUITIVE LOGIC OF AVERAGING UP

We're conditioned to think buying higher is foolish, even when the business itself has become fundamentally stronger. This reveals a fundamental misunderstanding though – we know the prices of everything but the value of nothing.

Most investors would have sold Netflix when it rose from $175 to $250 – a 43% profit in just a few months. Sure, nobody became poor by taking profits. But nobody became seriously rich that way either.

Those who sold at $250 were looking at price, not value. They missed the run all the way beyond $1,300 before the stock split in late 2025. A 43% gain feels smart until you realize how much you left on the table.

There's another group of investors who make an even costlier mistake. They sell their winners to chase stocks that look "cheap" – usually broken businesses trading at low multiples for good reason.

Peter Lynch called this "cutting your flowers and watering your weeds." We'll explore why this instinct is so destructive – and so hard to resist – in Chapter 9. For now, just notice: the tranche approach helps you *add* to winners rather than abandon them. Each purchase builds conviction rather than triggering the urge to "take profits."

Your winners are usually winning for good reasons. Stronger moats. Better execution. Expanding opportunities. These improving fundamentals often justify higher prices.

The key is to evaluate every investment decision based on forward returns from today's price, not yesterday's price.

Your cost basis is a mental anchor that sabotages good decisions. It makes you hesitate to add to winners. It makes you hold losers too long. It makes you kick yourself for not buying when you first considered it.

This anchoring makes investors think they've "missed the boat" after a big rise. But here's the truth: a stock that eventually rises 100x must first rise 10x. Even investors who bought Amazon *after* that first 10x still made 10x on their money. You don't need to catch the bottom. You need to recognize quality and hold on.

Forget what you paid. Forget what you could have paid.

Focus only on this: What returns can I expect from here?

When you find true compounders – businesses with widening moats and long runways – be willing to pay up. Your best investments often get more expensive, not cheaper. Reward your strongest holdings with more capital, not less.

But can you pay too much for quality?

WHEN GREAT COMPANIES BECOME TERRIBLE INVESTMENTS

Always remember that a great business doesn't always mean a great investment. Valuation matters.

Cisco in 1999 was the market leader in networking equipment.[3] The internet was exploding. Every company needed Cisco's products. The business was sound. The problem? It was trading at over 200 times earnings.

The company kept growing revenue and free cash flow. But it still took 25 years for the stock to come close to its all-time high again.

Not because the business failed. Because the price assumed perfection for decades.

Microsoft tells a similar story.[4] Trading above 60x earnings at its dot-com peak, it took 16 years to reclaim that high. A phenomenal business that became a terrible investment because price diverged too far from value.

These were exceptional companies where investors paid prices that required flawless execution for decades just to justify the entry point.

Today, Costco is an incredible business and everyone knows it.

Membership renewal rates above 90%. They treat employees and customers exceptionally well. The Kirkland brand has become a phenomenon in its own right.

With a forward earnings multiple of 55 times in early 2025, however, the math for decent future returns for investors in Costco's shares gets tougher. Revenue grows at mid-single digits. Earnings grow at high single digits to low teens. At this valuation, you need everything to go right. Continued expansion without saturation. Membership fee increases without pushback. E-commerce growth acceleration. No margin pressure from competition.

Could Costco pull it off? Absolutely. This is one of the best-run companies in history. But when you're paying 55x earnings for a retailer with these growth rates, you're betting on continued flawless execution with little room for disappointment.

The lesson is to understand what you're signing up for. When excellent businesses trade at valuations that require perfection, at least acknowledge the bar you're setting. Know whether you're investing based on probable outcomes or hoping for the best-case scenario.

Understanding the sentiment cycle helps you recognize when fear has pushed prices too far below value. But it also warns you when euphoria has pushed them too far above it. The cycle swings both ways.

Remember: Our goal isn't to own great businesses at any price. It's to own them at prices that give us good odds for attractive returns even if reality is messier than our projections.

MY EVOLUTION AS AN INVESTOR

Sixteen years have passed since I nervously bought those first shares of Cambridge Industrial Trust.

That young investor who checked prices multiple times a day, who sold after five weeks for a $100 profit, would barely recognize my approach today. Yet I'm grateful for his mistakes. They taught me what no book or mentor could – that successful buying isn't about outsmarting the market or timing entries perfectly.

It's about building a system that acknowledges how your mind actually works under pressure.

The framework I've shared – from the Crayon Test to buying in tranches to knowing when opportunity appears – came from multiple market cycles, countless mistakes, and one goal: to let you compound wealth without losing sleep.

Because here's what I've learned: To succeed as investors, we don't need to catch every opportunity or time every bottom. We need a repeatable process that compounds wealth while we live our lives.

That anxious 18-year-old refreshing prices on his laptop didn't understand the magic ingredient. It wasn't perfect timing or constant portfolio activity.

It was time.

Time for great businesses to compound. Time for competitive advantages to widen. Time for reinvested earnings to create more earnings. Time for the market to recognize what you saw early.

And the key to this, apart from starting early, is to survive the market with a strategy that's sustainable and will let you succeed in the long run. Not through heroic acts or perfect timing, but through a framework you can actually follow when markets test you.

The market doesn't award style points for difficulty. There's no extra credit for complex strategies, frantic trading, or checking prices every hour. In fact, the opposite is true – investing rewards the simple, patient approach. The obvious quality businesses bought at sensible prices and held for years.

My best investments today require the least maintenance. I check on them quarterly, reading earnings reports and annual letters. Between those checkpoints? I live my life. I write. I spend time with people I care about. The businesses compound while I'm not watching.

I've learned that great businesses don't need my constant supervision. Once you've done your analysis, written your thesis, and bought at a reasonable price, the hardest thing to do is often nothing at all.

LUNCH BREAK SUMMARY

- **Written conviction beats borrowed opinions**: Your brain rewrites history after the fact – only written analysis captures what you actually understood before the noise and drawdowns.
- **Three traps sabotage buying decisions**: Analysis paralysis costs you years of compounding; anchoring to past prices ignores value changes; and FOMO makes you chase stories instead of businesses.
- **Patient accumulation follows predictable patterns**: Misunderstood pivots, temporary setbacks, and broad market panics consistently create opportunities for those with clarity and conviction.
- **Building positions in tranches beats timing**: Start small to test your thesis, add as the business proves itself, and average up when fundamentals strengthen – even at higher prices.
- **Great businesses at any price still lose**: Cisco and Microsoft took decades to recover from extreme valuations – understand what returns you're signing up for before you buy.

YOUR NEXT STEP

You now have everything you need to start buying like a patient accumulator.

You understand the three psychological traps that sabotage smart decisions. You know how to write a thesis that creates conviction before you need it. You can spot the three situations that consistently create opportunity. You understand why buying in tranches beats going all-in. You even know why averaging up often makes more sense than averaging down.

Once you've done your buying well, the next challenge isn't finding the next great idea. It's the hardest thing of all: sitting still and doing absolutely nothing while your investments compound.

In the next chapter, we'll explore when that patience should end – the selling decision. Because while buying great businesses at reasonable prices is crucial, knowing when to let go (or more often, when not to) can be equally important for long-term success.

But that's tomorrow's lesson. Today's lesson is simpler: Your journey to building lasting wealth starts with that first written word.

CHAPTER 9
SELLING STRATEGIES

"All of humanity's problems stem from man's inability to sit quietly in a room alone."

–Blaise Pascal

EVER SINCE I started sharing my investment journey on *SteadyCompounding.com*, friends regularly ask what I'm doing with my positions – especially when they see something up 30% or doubled, tripled, even quadrupled.

"Nothing," I tell them.

The silence that follows is always awkward. They look at me like I'm an alien. Most people believe activity equals returns in the stock market. The idea of doing nothing when you're sitting on gains drives them nuts.

I had a friend who copied my Netflix investment in 2022. When it bounced 20% from his purchase price, he sold triumphantly. The gains paid for a nice dinner where he told me all about his "brilliant timing."

I did nothing. Just held my shares.

Netflix eventually ran past $1,300 – roughly five times what he paid. I can't help reminding him every time we meet. He sighs, but good friends tease each other. **More importantly, I'm trying to impress upon him a crucial lesson: real money isn't made in the trading. It's made in the waiting.**

Because here's the thing: he saw a ticker that had gone up 20%. I saw a business that was successfully launching its ad tier, cracking down on password sharing, and returning to growth. He saw a profit to capture. I saw a company still executing its turnaround.

The difference wasn't only patience – it was perspective. He thought doing something meant making progress. I knew that after finding a great business at a good price, the hardest part wasn't the buying or selling – it was the sitting still.

This is the costliest mistake most investors make. Not buying the wrong stocks. It's selling the right ones too early.

This chapter is about the hardest skill in investing: knowing when *not* to act.

I've referenced this challenge throughout the book – the danger of selling winners, the instinct to "take profits," the Peter Lynch warning about cutting flowers. Now we'll confront it directly. Because understanding this intellectually and executing it emotionally are completely different things.

Remember the Bessembinder research I introduced in Chapter 2 – the finding that just 4% of stocks created all the market's excess returns? Now it's time to understand what that means for how you actually invest.

Because this isn't just an interesting statistic. It's the reason selling your winners is so catastrophic. It's why patience matters more than intelligence. And it's why the entire philosophy of this book – finding quality and holding on – isn't just one approach among many. It's the only approach that aligns with how wealth actually gets created.

Let me show you the full picture.

THE PARADOX OF WINNERS

Hendrik Bessembinder studied roughly 28,600 public companies in America from 1926 to 2024.[1] His findings reveal an uncomfortable truth.

Roughly six out of every 10 stocks failed to beat Treasury bills – the baseline Bessembinder uses for measuring true wealth creation. The majority of stocks would have left you worse off than parking money in government bonds. They destroyed $10.1 trillion in value. Roughly one in 10 stocks lost essentially everything.

But here's the shocking part: Bessembinder found that just 2% of companies created 90% of all stock market wealth above Treasury bill returns, as shown in Figure 9.1. The top performers alone – including Apple, Microsoft, NVIDIA, Alphabet, Amazon, and ExxonMobil – added trillions in value, while the majority of stocks actually destroyed wealth relative to simply holding government bonds.

Figure 9.1: Where stock market wealth actually comes from

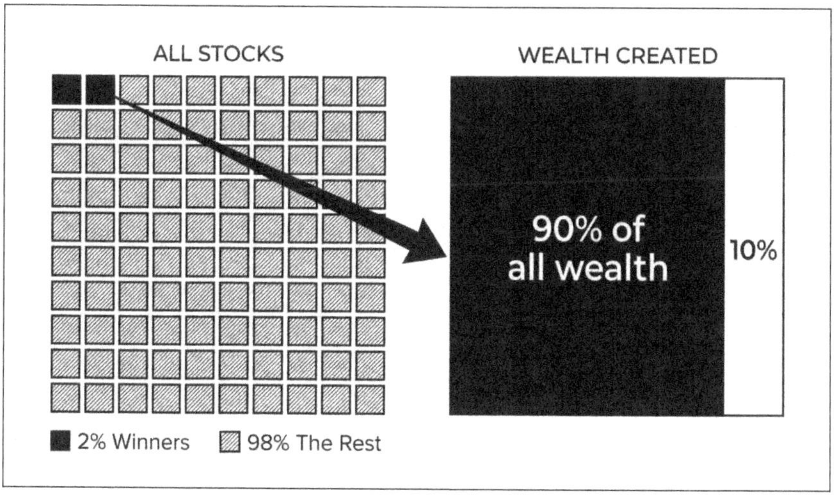

Source: Data from Bessembinder study, 1926–2024.

Of roughly 28,600 US stocks studied from 1926 to 2024, just 2% created 90% of all wealth above Treasury bill returns. The other 98% either destroyed value or barely mattered.

This creates a paradox that challenges every serious investor.

If only a tiny fraction of stocks generate massive wealth, then holding onto these rare winners becomes absolutely crucial. Miss them, or sell them too early, and you've destroyed your chances of meaningful returns. Yet these same winners are often the most volatile stocks in the market, making them psychologically torturous to own.

The human mind abhors uncertainty. When stocks plunge 50%, 70%, or even 90%, we desperately search for explanations. We create narratives to justify the price movement. The business model must be broken. Competition is catching up. Management has lost its edge.

We become amateur detectives, finding clues that confirm what the stock price is already telling us. The stock is down, therefore something must be wrong.

But holding the winners through their darkest moments is exactly what separates life-changing returns from mediocrity.

AMAZON: A $2.1 TRILLION TORTURE TEST

Take Amazon. Its lifetime wealth creation reached $2.1 trillion from its 1997 IPO to 2024. One of Bessembinder's top six wealth creators.

Yet Amazon shares dropped 95% from December 1999 to October 2001.[2] Ninety-five percent.

A $10,000 investment would have shrunk to $500. Magazine covers called it "Amazon.bomb." Analysts questioned whether the company would survive. Every rational bone in your body would have screamed to sell before it hit zero.

Even if you bought Amazon early and knew the long-term potential, could you have held through that? Through watching 95% of your investment evaporate while the media mocked your judgment?

The torture didn't end there. Amazon has experienced four separate drawdowns exceeding 50%. Each decline brought perfectly reasonable explanations about why this "overvalued" company was finally facing reality. During many periods, it traded at valuations that seemed insane.

Most investors who bought Amazon early sold during one of these collapses. They took their "sensible" profits or cut their "reasonable" losses. Few held through the full journey. That's why so few captured that $2.1 trillion in wealth creation.

Anne Scheiber held through wars and crashes for 50 years. Ronald Read never sold during any recession. Grace Groner watched her Abbott Labs shares swing wildly for decades. They had one thing in common – they did nothing when everyone else panicked. And that nothing made them rich.

The average maximum drawdown for Bessembinder's top six companies was 80%. The best wealth creators in history required shareholders to pay an enormous price – not in dollars, but in volatility.

THE MONSTER THAT MADE MILLIONAIRES

Monster Beverage tells an even more compressed story. It became a 100-bagger in just 10 years – turning $10,000 into $1 million.

But as Chris Mayer documents in *100 Baggers*, the journey was brutal. The stock fell more than 25% on at least 10 different occasions during that run. Three times it lost over 40% of its value in a single month.[3]

Each decline came with compelling narratives. Energy drinks were a fad. Competition would destroy margins. Health concerns would end the category. The reasons to sell always sounded intelligent.

The investors who made 100 times their money understood what they owned. They saw past the scary headlines and quarterly noise because they knew the business fundamentals. Most importantly, they had the discipline to sit still when everyone else was screaming run.

Figure 9.2: 10-year returns and max drawdowns (10 years to July 2025)

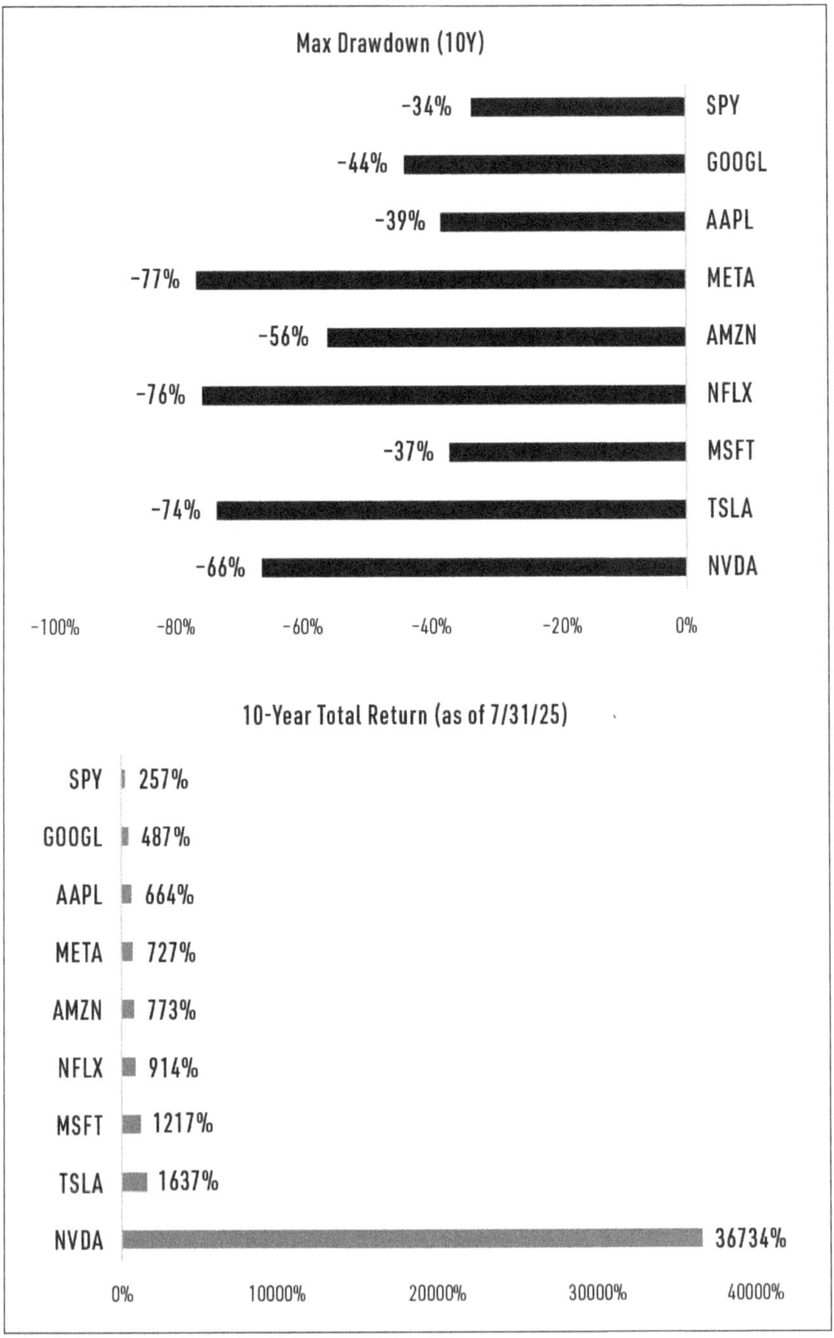

Source: Bilello, Creative Planning.

THE POWER OF SITTING STILL

This is why the best investors lean toward portfolio inactivity – minimal buying, and minimum selling when we've done our buying right. It's the cornerstone of the Steady Compounding philosophy. We continue reading quarterly reports, studying the business, learning about competitors. The inactivity is in our trading, not our thinking. We own great businesses across long periods while staying intellectually engaged with their progress.

Look at the masters and their seemingly boring holdings. Warren Buffett held Coca-Cola since 1988. Tom Russo has owned Mastercard since its 2006 IPO. Terry Smith has held Microsoft for over a decade. These multi-baggers grew because these investors held on despite bad news and periods when valuations looked stretched.

As Chris Mayer explains: "Even the fastest 100-baggers in our study needed about five years to get there. A more likely journey will take 20–25 years. ... You need to find a way to defeat your own worst instincts – the impatience, the need for 'action'."

Twenty-five years. In a world obsessed with quarterly earnings, this timeline feels like a lifetime. Yet it's the price of admission to life-changing returns.

Martin Whitman learned this through 50 years of painful repetition: "I've had a lot of experience holding stocks for three years, doubled, and sold it for somebody else, for whom it tripled in the next six months."[4]

Even Terry Smith, one of today's best investors, admits his mistakes. He sold Domino's Pizza when its valuation seemed justifiable only if rapid growth continued, which he doubted. The stock kept rising. He wrote that they sold "with some regret and trepidation. Regret since it is undoubtedly a fine business... Trepidation since selling shares in good companies is something we are justifiably reluctant to do."

Pulak Prasad of Nalanda Capital takes this philosophy to its logical extreme: "The rule for selling a great business is simple: Don't. You. Dare."

This seems radical. Even reckless. I know the irony of a chapter on selling strategies that emphasizes not selling. But picking up the wrong sell signal – panicking during a drawdown – is the costliest mistake most investors make.

THE MATH OF WINNERS VERSUS LOSERS

You might wonder: Won't this bias toward inactivity cause you to hold losers?

Yes. But here's the vital truth about investing: winners more than compensate for losers.

The maximum you can lose is 100%. There's no limit to what you can gain. One Amazon or Monster Beverage pays for every loser in your portfolio many times over.

Peter Lynch understood this asymmetry: "You have to let the big ones make up for your mistakes. In this business, if you're good, you're right six times out of 10. You're never going to be right nine times out of 10."

He also noted: "If you're lucky enough to have one golden egg in your portfolio, it may not matter if you have a couple of rotten ones in there with it."

The math is clear. In a game where your losses are capped but your gains are not, letting winners run matters more than avoiding every loser.

But knowing this intellectually and acting on it during a crisis are completely different things. Our own psychology becomes the enemy.

OUR WORST ENEMY: OURSELVES

Investors are often their own worst enemy. They act when they shouldn't and fail to act when they should.

In today's world, information bombards us constantly through mainstream media and social media. These platforms battle for our attention, and the easiest, fastest way to capture it is with pessimism.

Our brains evolved to prioritize negative information because it often signaled threats that needed immediate attention for survival. Early humans who were more attuned to potential dangers were more likely to survive and pass on their genes, embedding this negativity bias in our biology.

In financial markets, this bias works against us by making most people sell at the first sign of bad news, without considering second and third-order effects.

The most damaging aspect of negativity bias? The best purchases are usually made during moments of maximum pessimism – whether during the 2008 financial crisis or the pandemic drawdown of 2020. Yet that's precisely when our psychology screams loudest to sell.

THE META MELTDOWN

Take Meta as a case study of how pessimism destroys returns.

In February 2022, Meta reported Q4 2021 earnings. Despite beating revenue estimates, the company faced a perfect storm of challenges that sent the stock into freefall. What followed was one of the most dramatic destructions of market value in history – over $800 billion erased as the stock plummeted from $384 to $88.

But was this collapse justified by the fundamentals? Or was the market's negativity bias creating an extraordinary opportunity?

THE FIVE HORSEMEN OF THE APOCALYPSE

By early 2022, Meta faced five simultaneous crises that created a narrative so negative that even believers started doubting.

First, Apple's iOS privacy changes were devastating. Management estimated a $10 billion revenue hit in 2022 alone. Advertisers couldn't measure ROI effectively, and targeting accuracy plummeted.

Second, TikTok was eating their lunch. Facebook's daily active users actually declined in Asia-Pacific for the first time. The video-first platform had captured the younger generation that Meta desperately needed.

Third, Reels – Meta's answer to TikTok – was cannibalizing their own revenue. Every minute users spent on Reels instead of Feed meant lower monetization. Management admitted Reels was creating a $500 million quarterly revenue headwind.

Fourth, the metaverse investments looked insane. Over $15 billion poured into Reality Labs in 2022 alone, with operating margins of negative 635%. Zuckerberg seemed to be setting money on fire while Rome burned.

Fifth, macroeconomic headwinds crushed ad spending. Their largest verticals – e-commerce and consumer packaged goods – pulled back dramatically.

The market panicked.

READING BETWEEN THE LINES

In my February 2022 report on *SteadyCompounding.com* titled "Meta Is Down 23% Post-Market, What Happened?", I wrote:

"The operating margins compression was largely a result of a temporary increase in general & administrative expenses (primarily legal related expenses which tends to be lumpy) and to a lesser extent a mild increase in R&D and marketing expenses, which is not cause for concern."

But I saw something the market missed.

While everyone focused on the problems, I dug into the actual data. Engagement wasn't dying – it was thriving. Daily active people across Meta's apps grew 6% to 2.87 billion. Monthly active people reached 3.64 billion. If TikTok was supposedly killing Meta, why were more people than ever using their apps?

More importantly, Meta had a crucial advantage in the iOS battle. As I wrote in May 2022:

"All social media platforms, with the exception of Google, will be affected by the iOS changes… Granted, they should be least affected of all the social media companies."

Why? Meta had more data than anyone except Google. If Meta with three billion users couldn't figure out targeting, imagine what would happen to Snapchat or Pinterest with a fraction of that data. This second-order thinking was crucial. The market saw Meta's problems. I saw everyone else's would be worse.

The Reels transition wasn't destruction – it was evolution. Management had successfully navigated this before with Stories cannibalizing Feed after

Snapchat's threat. By August 2022, Reels had already crossed a $1 billion annual revenue run rate. By October, it hit $3 billion. The cannibalization was temporary, the growth was permanent.

THE DARKEST HOUR

October 2022 marked peak pessimism.

Meta reported Q3 earnings showing free cash flow had collapsed to just $173 million – down from $9.7 billion in operating cash flow. They were spending $9.52 billion in capex, mostly on AI infrastructure, not just the metaverse as critics claimed.

Revenue had declined for the second straight quarter. The first time in Meta's history.

The stock touched $88. It was trading at just 8.7x forward earnings – a valuation typically reserved for dying businesses.

In my October 2022 report "Is it time to sell Meta?", I addressed the panic:

> Engagement numbers are holding well, Meta continues to execute on product development with its Family of Apps. The threat from TikTok is weaker than before and they seem to be navigating iOS changes alright for now. Their weakness was largely a result of the global economic slowdown, which also impacted their competitors.

Then in November 2022, Zuckerberg announced the "Year of Efficiency" – laying off 11,000 employees, flattening management structures, and committing to profitability over growth. This wasn't capitulation. This was adaptation. The same leader who'd successfully navigated the desktop-to-mobile transition was pivoting again.

By February 2023, results were already showing. The company announced $40 billion in additional buyback authorization. They were buying their own stock hand over fist at depressed prices – $27.9 billion in 2022 alone.

More importantly, AI investments were paying off. Reels plays hit 140 billion daily across Facebook and Instagram – up 50% in six months. The recommendation engine was winning.

Fast forward to February 2024. Meta reported Q4 2023 earnings:

- Revenue: $40.1 billion, up 25% year-over-year.
- Operating margin: 41%, nearly doubled from 20%.
- Free cash flow: $11.7 billion, up 115%.
- First-ever dividend declared.

The stock hit $475 – up 440% from the October 2022 lows.

Meta posted the largest single-day market cap gain in history – adding $196 billion in value in one day. The same company that held the record for the largest single-day loss just two years earlier.

But how many investors held through the pessimism?

Those who sold at $88 because "TikTok was winning" or "the metaverse was insane" or "Apple killed their business model" missed one of the greatest recoveries in market history.[5]

The business challenges were real. But they were temporary. The engagement, the network effects, the technical capabilities – those were permanent.

This is how negativity bias destroys returns. When sentiment is darkest, when the narrative is most compelling, when every headline screams disaster – that's often when the best investments reveal themselves.

But only if you can see through the noise to the signal underneath.

You might be thinking: fine, but if I just pick the right stocks, I won't need to endure all that pain. The next study will disabuse you of that idea.

EVEN GOD WOULD GET FIRED

Wes Gray, CEO of Alpha Architect with a PhD in finance from the University of Chicago, conducted a fascinating thought experiment. What if you had godlike foresight to pick the next five years' best-performing stocks? You'd achieve "great returns, but gut-wrenching drawdowns."

Gray built a perfect-foresight portfolio using S&P 500 data from 1927 to 2016, rebalanced every five years with the top 50 stocks. The results? Annualized returns three times the S&P 500's.

Yet despite this supernatural performance, the volatility was extreme. The worst drawdown reached 76% from 1929 to 1932. There were five separate drawdowns exceeding 30%. Even the perfect portfolio severely tests investors' resolve.[6]

The individual stock data is even more sobering. Research by Morgan Stanley's Michael Mauboussin found that top performers had median maximum drawdowns of 72%, taking nearly three years to reach bottom and over four years to recover. Even buying exactly at the low, these stocks only generated 8% in annualized returns above expectations over the next five years.

These findings reveal the impossible challenge professional investors face: even with perfect foresight, the volatility would trigger client redemptions during drawdowns. While fund managers must answer to stakeholders who withdraw at bottoms and invest at peaks, individual investors have a structural advantage – no one can force us to sell at the worst possible moment.

This freedom from stakeholder pressure is perhaps the greatest edge individual investors have in building long-term wealth.

But of course, a bias against selling doesn't mean never selling. Some situations do warrant it. Which brings us to the framework that can guide these decisions.

THE THREE REASONS TO SELL

The irony is, the better you get at buying (Chapter 7), the less you need this chapter. When you've done your homework – written your thesis, bought in tranches, truly understood the business – the best course of action is usually to do nothing.

Unless one of these three conditions arises.

1. Deterioration in business fundamentals

Real deterioration means a permanent impairment of the business model or competitive position – not just a temporary setback.

Key indicators to watch: sustained margin compression that isn't just temporary pressure; declining return on invested capital over multiple years; market share losses that appear structural rather than cyclical; weakening competitive advantages evident in key performance indicators; or management integrity issues coupled with drastic changes in capital allocation.

These aren't quarterly blips. They're fundamental shifts in the business trajectory.

Case study: Peloton – riding into the sunset

This one was a pandemic darling that many investors adored.

Founded in 2012, Peloton became a household name by combining high-end exercise equipment with a subscription-based digital fitness platform. Or as some skeptics called it more affectionately back then, a bike with an iPad.

The pandemic turbocharged demand. Market valuation soared from approximately $6.5 billion to $50 billion in early 2021. Revenue exploded 337% from $915 million in 2019 to $4 billion in 2021.

At its peak, the company was trading for 20 times trailing 12-month sales.

And it was during this period many investors believed that Peloton would reshape the world of fitness forever. How a Peloton Bike priced at $1,895 with a $39 monthly subscription was worth more than most gyms. How users saved time traveling to gyms. How celebrity instructors cultivated communities so tight that churn stayed low.

Investors bought into the Peloton growth story, and who can blame them?

Peloton was everywhere. Financial media and influencers praised this new Wall Street darling. Social media overflowed with Peloton posts. Even management shared the same enthusiasm, believing the pandemic hypergrowth would continue indefinitely.

They extrapolated. And then they bet the company on it.

Red flag #1: Pursuing growth at all costs

In 2021, the company went on a spending spree: $6.2 million for 223 acres in Ohio for a massive factory, $412 million cash to acquire Precor's manufacturing capacity, and $241 million in capital expenditures on headquarters, studios, and facilities worldwide. Total committed: over $650 million in expansion during peak pandemic chaos.

Meanwhile, inventory ballooned from $244 million in 2020 to over $1.1 billion in 2022.

All this expansion during a pandemic when supply chains were chaos and everything cost a fortune. Yet management pressed ahead, financing it all with debt.

By end of 2021, the damage was clear:

- $850 million in long-term debt.
- $9 million quarterly interest expense.
- Operating cash flow flipped from positive $376 million to negative $240 million.

This was red flag number one for investors to exit.

Management was locking investors into massive commitments – debt, leases, capital expenditures – while trading at 20x sales. Priced to perfection, any slowdown would trigger both multiple contraction and operational disaster.

When investing, we don't want businesses that put growth ahead of survival. Debt destroys flexibility during crises. It increases fragility exponentially.

Amazon was also investing aggressively during this period. But their balance sheet was rock solid. A forecasting error for Amazon meant a slap on the wrist. For Peloton? Life or death.

Red flag #2: The 12-day flip flop

Investors grew nervous about Peloton's aggressive expansion, massive debt, and negative cash flow in late 2021. Revenue growth was slowing. Perhaps demand wasn't infinite after all.

At a Q1 2022 earnings call on November 4, 2021, CFO Jill Woodworth attempted to calm investors and explicitly stated: "I think just cutting to the chase we don't see the need for any additional capital raise based on our current outlook."

She reassured investors they had $924 million in cash and marketable securities. Plus an untapped $285 million credit facility.

Just 12 days later on November 16, 2021 Peloton announced a $1.2 billion equity offering. Over 27 million shares at $46 per share.

I've never seen a company flip its stance this fast.

If there was ever a clearer red flag, this was it.

Wall Street was worried enough about cash flow for the CFO to address it during the earnings call. Twelve days later, reality contradicted those reassurances. Whatever the explanation – miscommunication, rapidly deteriorating conditions, or poor forecasting – investor trust was shattered.

Post-pandemic, reality hit like a freight train. Sharp demand slowdown. Excess inventory. Cash flow nightmares. Revenue growth collapsed.

The stock told the story. From $120 per share in July 2021 to $7–10 over the next two years. As I write this in mid-2025, it trades at $6.50.

The warning signs were all there. Overly aggressive expansion unsupported by balance sheet or cash flows. Excessive debt based on best-case scenarios. Extrapolating temporary trends as permanent. Management flip-flopping destroying confidence.

These are clear sell signals.

Case study: Lululemon – Why I trimmed my position

Peloton shows clear deterioration – warning signs that warranted a clear decision to exit. But not every sell decision is that straightforward.

In Chapter 5, I described how Lululemon's management spent a year misdiagnosing their US slowdown. They prescribed colors and newness when the real issue was that they'd stopped innovating on what actually matters – technical fabrics and quality. But the misdiagnosis wasn't just a strategic error. It was actively alienating their most valuable customers.

By Q2 2025, management acknowledged that their most valuable customers – the ones who built the brand – were pulling back. They were still loyal. They still bought when something genuinely new launched. But they'd stopped adding to their wardrobes with variations of products they already owned. Total spend was down.

These aren't price-sensitive shoppers waiting for sales. When your most loyal customers reduce their spending, they're telling you something about your product. And they were telling Lululemon directly – the brand's subreddit was filled with complaints about declining quality. Fabrics pilling faster. Seams not holding up.

The product issues kept surfacing. In summer 2024, Lululemon pulled its "Breezethrough" line weeks after launch due to fit complaints. In January 2026, they launched "Get Low" leggings that customers immediately called see-through. When you're paying $128 for leggings, you expect them to work.

The wrong direction

What worried me wasn't just the misdiagnosis. It was the proposed cure.

Instead of doubling down on what made Lululemon special – technical fabrics, innovative design, quality that justifies premium pricing – management talked about "going faster" and "chasing trends." About reducing development cycles from 18–24 months to 12–14 months.

Not one word about technical innovation in the entire earnings call.

Lululemon's moat is built on being the premium choice. Customers pay a premium because they believe they're getting something better – better fabric, better fit, better durability. The moment that perception erodes, the pricing power disappears. And once pricing power goes, the margins follow.

Management's direction risked exactly that erosion.

Transparency matters too

There was a second issue – and this one raised questions about transparency.

Lululemon had been shipping roughly two-thirds of its US e-commerce orders from Canadian distribution centers. They were taking advantage of a rule called De Minimis, which allowed duty-free shipments under $800. It was a legal way to reduce costs.

On April 2, 2025 – "Liberation Day" – President Trump signed an executive order signaling that De Minimis treatment would end once systems were in place to collect tariffs. The writing was on the wall.

Lululemon's Q1 2025 earnings call happened on June 5th – two full months later. Management said nothing about their exposure.

It wasn't until the Q2 earnings call, after the July 30th order made it official, that investors learned the impact: 220 basis points of gross margin compression, roughly $240 million. Of that, 170 basis points came specifically from the De Minimis change.

Bad news happens. What matters is how management handles it. As Buffett says: "Get it right, get it fast, get it out, get it over." Two months of silence – when a significant risk was materializing that management should have been assessing – raises questions. A company shipping two-thirds of US e-commerce orders from Canada doesn't need hindsight to recognize De Minimis exposure as material. Whether the omission was strategic or simply slow-footed, the result was the same: investors were left in the dark.

Why I trimmed – not sold

I trimmed my position by 50%.

The brand hadn't broken. Customers were frustrated, not gone. Lululemon still had $2 billion in cash, zero debt, and the highest operating margins in the industry. The moat was weakening, not destroyed.

McDonald has since announced his departure. The next chapter will be written by new leadership. If the new management team proves themselves – renewed focus on quality, transparent communication, coherent strategy – I'll hold, and possibly add if the business trends in the right direction. If they continue down the wrong path, I'll reduce exposure further.

2. Egregious overvaluation

This is the trickiest selling trigger because quality businesses often appear "overvalued" for years while continuing to compound wealth.

When thinking about valuation, remember Buffett's wisdom: "It is better to be approximately right than precisely wrong."

We don't need complicated models with 1,001 variables. Focus on understanding the business, management, and likely outcomes.

Peloton illustrates both problems at once – deterioration *and* overvaluation – which is why the sell signals were so strong. At its peak in January 2021, Peloton commanded a $49 billion market cap on just $2.4 billion in trailing revenue. That's 20 times sales – a valuation typically reserved for the fastest-growing software companies with 80%+ gross margins.

But Peloton's gross margins were 45%. After all operating expenses? Net margins of 2%. The company generated only $50 million in actual profits.

Think about that. Investors valued this company at $49 billion, yet it produced only $50 million in profits. Nearly the entire valuation rested on future promises, not current earnings.

The hope stemmed from two beliefs. First, that pandemic hypergrowth would continue indefinitely. Second, that high-margin subscription revenue would eventually transform this low-margin hardware business into a software-like profit machine.

But hope isn't analysis. You can test whether a stretched valuation makes sense before you finish your coffee. I call this the Lunch Break Sanity Check. Here's how.

Step 1: Set your hurdle. I prefer seeing 15% annually over three to five years for taking on the risk of owning individual stocks. That roughly doubles my money. So Peloton's $49 billion market cap needs to reach $99 billion in five years to justify buying in.

Step 2: Give it a generous multiple. Let's stack the deck in Peloton's favor. Assume it matures into a wildly successful company and trades at 30x earnings – a multiple reserved for great businesses. To reach a $99 billion market cap at 30x, divide $99 billion by 30. The company needs to earn $3.3 billion in net profit.

Step 3: Back into the revenue. Now, how much revenue does Peloton need to produce $3.3 billion in profit? Again, let's be generous – give them a 15% net margin, a level only the most profitable companies sustain, far better than the losses Peloton was actually reporting. At 15% margins, $3.3 billion in profit requires $22 billion in revenue.

Step 4: Check if it's realistic. Peloton had $2.4 billion in revenue. Growing to $22 billion means 56% annually for five years. On expensive exercise bikes. After lockdowns ended. Against increasing competition. And remember – we were *generous* at every step.

When the math requires near-impossible assumptions, that's your signal to walk away.

3. Better opportunities elsewhere

Sometimes selling makes sense not because anything is wrong with the company, but because your capital can work harder elsewhere.

Capital is scarce. You want your money working where it can generate the highest returns. If you discover a higher-quality idea with better future prospects, it might warrant selling to establish a position.

But beware the next shiny object syndrome.

If you've bought well, often the best investments are already in your portfolio. Write down your investment thesis before making changes. Always have something to compare against new opportunities.

A common mistake I made starting out was selling stocks with high multiples – what seemed "pricier" from a valuation standpoint.

The truth? High-quality businesses always seem expensive. And they tend to outperform despite stretched multiples.

In Chapter 4, we saw Terry Smith's striking finding – investors could have paid seemingly insane multiples for quality compounders in 1973 and still beaten the global market over the next 46 years. That data has an even more important implication for selling. If decades of compounding can overcome even a terrible entry price, imagine what you forfeit when you sell a compounder mid-stride just because the multiple looks rich. Once you exit, the compounding stops for you. The business keeps growing. You just won't be there for it.

The point isn't to overpay. It's that high-quality businesses tend to outperform even when multiples appear stretched. Unless they're egregiously overvalued, I'd rather sell based on business quality. The weakest company gets sold for new positions.

Crisis creates opportunity

Occasionally, your portfolio gets a chance to climb the quality ladder during broad market drawdowns – when markets sell indiscriminately regardless of business performance.

Take the pandemic meltdown in early 2020. The S&P 500 lost 34% in just 23 trading days – the fastest correction of this scale ever recorded.

Booking Holdings crashed from $2,000 to $1,177, a ~41% decline. The market panicked. Travel bans, flight suspensions, and lockdowns brought travel to a near-total halt. Hotels and airlines went bankrupt. Though Booking owned no hard assets, the carnage in travel sent investors fleeing.

For me, this was a window of opportunity.

The company was sitting on nearly $7 billion in cash. No planes or hotels meant no maintenance capex. As travel ground to a halt, they could turn off marketing spend – and they did. They reduced workforce to stay lean.

I trimmed some weaker positions and took a stake in Booking Holdings.

Booking emerged stronger, as strong companies do. Challenges strengthen their position as weaker players lose share. Fast forward to mid-2025: the stock trades at $5,475, up 365% from its pandemic low.

Sometimes attractive opportunities warrant trimming your portfolio to capture them. The key is upgrading quality during crisis, not chasing trends during euphoria.

CONCLUSION: THE VIRTUE OF PATIENCE

We began this chapter with Pascal's insight that humanity's problems stem from our inability to sit quietly alone.

It's the perfect metaphor for investing.

The hardest part isn't knowing when to sell. It's having the discipline to sit still when every fiber of your being screams for action. It's watching your stocks drop 50% and not panicking. It's seeing them triple and not taking profits. It's trusting the process when everyone else is losing their minds.

I know the irony of spending a chapter on selling strategies emphasizing not selling. But Bessembinder's data– the research we explored at the start of this chapter – makes the case undeniable: just 2% of stocks create 90% of wealth. The asymmetry is brutal. Selling a loser too late costs you one position. Selling a winner too early can cost you a fortune. In this winner-take-most game, letting your winners run isn't just important. It's everything.

Yes, there are times to sell. When fundamentals permanently deteriorate like Peloton. When valuations reach egregious levels. When genuinely better opportunities emerge.

But these moments are rarer than most investors think.

The default should always be inaction. Make selling the exception, not the rule. The biggest risk isn't holding a loser too long – it's selling a winner too early.

My friend who sold Netflix for a 20% gain learned this the hard way. He made enough for a nice dinner. He missed out on a life-changing return. The difference wasn't intelligence or information. It was perspective and patience.

Pascal was right. Most of our problems come from our inability to sit quietly. In investing, as in life, sometimes the most profitable thing you can do is absolutely nothing.

Real money isn't made in the trading. It's made in the waiting.

LUNCH BREAK SUMMARY

- **A handful of stocks drive most of the stock market returns** – missing or selling these rare winners early destroys your chances for meaningful returns, making the ability to identify and hold rare winners the most crucial investing skill.
- **Volatility is the price for extraordinary returns** – the best wealth creators require investors to endure multiple drawdowns exceeding 50%, testing every fiber of conviction.
- **Negativity bias destroys wealth systematically** – our evolutionary wiring makes us sell during pessimism, yet maximum pessimism creates maximum opportunity for those who see beyond the narrative.
- **Three reasons to sell** – permanent business deterioration, egregious overvaluation requiring impossible growth assumptions, or genuinely better opportunities during crisis.
- **Individual investors have a structural edge** – freedom from stakeholder pressure allows patience that professional managers can't maintain, even when they know they're right.

YOUR NEXT STEP

You now know how to find steady compounders, when to buy them, and – just as important – when to sell them (or leave them alone). But a collection of great stocks isn't automatically a great portfolio. In Chapter 10, we'll build the framework for how your positions work together – how many to own, how to size them, and how to keep the whole portfolio resilient when markets test your conviction.

CHAPTER 10

BUILDING A WINNING PORTFOLIO

FROM STOCK PICKING TO PORTFOLIO BUILDING

MOST INVESTORS PUT tremendous focus and energy into analyzing individual businesses. They master moat analysis. They evaluate management. They calculate valuations. And rightfully so – these skills are crucial.

But they miss something equally important: putting it all together in an investment portfolio.

Without a clear portfolio framework, you're left improvising. You don't know how much to buy. You hesitate when stocks drop. You panic when positions blow up. You're stuck reacting instead of executing.

Most investors don't fail because they picked one bad stock. They fail because they didn't manage risk at the portfolio level. One oversized position explodes. A moment of panic leads to selling a winner. Or they end up with 40 stocks they barely understand.

The goal is simple: Let your winners flourish while preventing losers from derailing your compounding journey.

Because in investing, you can't win the long game if you don't survive the short run. And oddly enough, by simply doing better than average over the long term, you'll end up ahead of the pack.

Remember the Howard Marks discovery from Chapter 2 – the General Mills pension fund that never ranked above the 27th percentile in any single year, yet finished in the top 4% over 14 years?

Most investors eventually self-destruct. They chase hot trends, make aggressive bets, swing too hard for short-term results. One or two bad years undo a decade of good ones.

VanBenschoten avoided those blow-ups. He stayed in the second quartile, year after year. That consistency beat almost everyone in the long run.[1]

The math of losses explains why. Look at what it takes to recover from various drawdowns:

Table 10.1: Portfolio loss vs gain needed to breakeven

Portfolio Loss	Gain Needed to Breakeven
-10%	+11%
-20%	+25%
-30%	+43%
-40%	+67%
-50%	+100%
-60%	+150%
-70%	+233%
-80%	+400%

A 50% loss requires a 100% gain just to get back to even. That's why Buffett's first rule of investing is "Don't lose money." And rule two? "Don't forget rule number one."

This isn't about avoiding all volatility. It's about avoiding permanent capital loss at the portfolio level. When we're wrong – and we will be wrong – we need those mistakes to be contained so that they don't blow up our entire journey.

That's what portfolio construction is for. We're not here to win a single year. We're here to win the next 20 years.

We want to build a portfolio where losers aren't large enough to derail your compounding journey, and winners are sizeable enough to move the needle and grow your wealth over time.

You have a massive advantage over professional managers. You don't have clients pressuring you for short-term results. You don't have to own whatever's most popular just to protect your career. That freedom is your edge.

It means you can build a portfolio based on conviction, not consensus. You can buy great businesses when they're out of favor, hold through the noise, and focus entirely on the long game. While others are forced to explain every bump in the road, you get to keep your eyes on the destination.

Use it.

HOW MANY STOCKS DO YOU ACTUALLY NEED?

Building a resilient portfolio starts with two questions: How many businesses should you own? And how much should you put in each one?

Let's start with the first.

You don't need to own 50 companies. You need 15 to 25 well-understood, resilient businesses. That number gives you enough diversification to protect against unknowns – while still being concentrated enough for each winner to matter.

As Joel Greenblatt pointed out in his book, *You Can Be a Stock Market Genius*, holding eight stocks eliminates 81% of the diversifiable risk of owning just one. Holding 32 stocks eliminates 96%.[2]

Notice the diminishing returns? Going from one to eight stocks eliminates 81% of risk. But going from eight to 32 – quadrupling your holdings – only eliminates an additional 15%. Beyond 32 stocks, you're adding almost nothing in risk reduction while multiplying the complexity of monitoring and understanding each business.

Burton Malkiel's academic research confirms this pattern. In his classic, *A Random Walk Down Wall Street*, he demonstrates that by the time a portfolio has 20 or so holdings, the incremental reductions in portfolio volatility from new holdings is very small.[3]

The math from both Greenblatt and Malkiel reaches the same conclusion: modest diversification captures most of the benefit.

But there's another problem with over-diversification that Peter Lynch captured perfectly: "Owning stocks is like having children – don't have more than you can handle."

Can you really understand 50 businesses deeply enough to have conviction during drawdowns? And it isn't just the research burden. It's also that you dilute your best ideas. If you own 50 stocks, each position is just 2% of your portfolio. Even if one of these 2% positions doubles, it barely moves the needle on the overall portfolio.

I've found that 15 to 25 stocks is the sweet spot. It's enough to protect against the unexpected, but not so many that you lose track of what you own. You can follow each company's quarterly reports, understand their competitive dynamics, and maintain conviction when markets test you.

POSITION SIZING: THE RETURNS ON HEADACHE FRAMEWORK

Now, how much should you put into each position?

I call this my "returns on headache" framework. Because in the long run, it's not just about return on investment. It's about building a portfolio you can live with – one that keeps growing without keeping you up at night.

Chapter 8 covered how to build individual positions in tranches. Here's the portfolio question: how much total capital should each position get?

For most positions, I limit my cost basis to 5% of the portfolio. It balances two realities. Big enough to matter if I'm right. Small enough to survive if I'm wrong.

But not all businesses deserve the same allocation. Your position sizes should reflect both the quality of the business and your conviction level.

For businesses with more uncertainty – fashion retailers like Lululemon whose moats depend on fickle consumer preferences, or companies in highly cyclical industries – I typically limit my allocation to 3–5% of the portfolio. These can be great investments, but their inherent unpredictability means smaller positions are prudent.

For stable compounders with proven track records – think Microsoft, Visa, or Berkshire Hathaway – the standard 5% position makes sense. These businesses have demonstrated resilience through multiple cycles.

Very occasionally, I go beyond 5%. But this is rare and deliberate.

To justify a larger allocation – say 7% to 10% – a business needs to check several boxes:

- Resilient through cycles.
- Multiple durable cash flow streams.
- Conservative balance sheet.
- Proven, aligned management.
- Valuation that offers a clear margin of safety.

During the 2020 pandemic drawdown, I went to 10% with Berkshire Hathaway. I wasn't swinging for the fences with a risky turnaround. I was leaning into one of the world's most conservatively run companies – well-capitalized, diversified across industries, flush with cash, and helmed by Warren Buffett. Berkshire was built to withstand crises, and that's exactly what I wanted in the heart of one.

I occasionally miss opportunities because I won't pay up for steep valuations. That's part of the discipline. Other times, the right size is deliberately small and I'll initiate a small starter position to track a high-quality business while waiting for Mr. Market to serve up a better opportunity.

Take Wise. Everything about the company impressed me. Transparent pricing, disciplined cost management, long-term thinking. But the valuation was steep. So I invested just 1% of my portfolio – below my usual starter position.

That position is up 70% now, but because I started so small it hasn't moved the needle for my portfolio. I'm comfortable with that outcome. The process matters more than any single position. I'd rather maintain discipline and occasionally miss opportunities than abandon my framework chasing returns.

The right position sizing isn't about concentrating into ideas with the highest upside alone. We have to account for the risks involved. Does the business have concentration risks with customers or suppliers? Are they reliant on regulatory approvals? Are valuations so steep they depend on flawless execution far into the future?

It's about identifying investments with the best risk-adjusted returns – those offering the greatest long-term reward relative to the risks you're actually taking. We can't think about returns without considering risks. What if the future doesn't unfold as we expect? We need to think about this at the portfolio level too.

During the 2022 broad market drawdown, the S&P 500 fell roughly 20% for the year and the Nasdaq dropped around 33%. Both Netflix and Meta fell more than the broader market.

I wanted to add to both – they were high-quality businesses facing temporary headwinds. But I'd already reached my 5% cost basis limit with Meta. So I put most of my fresh funds into Netflix.

That's portfolio-level thinking. Not just, "Is this stock attractive?" but, "How does this improve my overall portfolio without over-concentrating?"

A brilliant idea that keeps you up at night isn't brilliant. A great business you can hold through drawdowns – that's where wealth builds.

Good sizing protects you from both portfolio risk and emotional overreaction. It lets your best ideas work – while keeping mistakes from sinking the ship.

This "returns on headache" principle extends beyond individual positions. Your entire portfolio should generate returns without generating sleepless nights. We'll explore this philosophy more deeply in the next chapter – how wealth should enhance life, not consume it.

WHY DIVERSIFICATION ISN'T OPTIONAL

Joel Greenblatt learned one of investing's most important lessons the hard way – and it happened with one of his very first investments.

He'd found what looked like a great opportunity in Florida Cypress Gardens, a theme park. Harcourt Brace Jovanovich (HBJ), a large publisher, had announced they were acquiring it in a stock swap: shareholders would receive 0.16 shares of HBJ for each share of Cypress Gardens. With HBJ trading around $52, that valued each Cypress Gardens share at about $8.30.

But Cypress Gardens wasn't trading at $8.30. It sat at $7.50 – a discount, because deals don't always close. Greenblatt saw an opportunity: buy at $7.50, collect $8.30 worth of HBJ stock in three months. That 80-cent profit worked out to roughly 50% annualized.

A few weeks before the deal was supposed to close, Florida Cypress Gardens fell into a sinkhole. The main pavilions literally collapsed into a hole that appeared out of nowhere.

As Greenblatt later recounted: "It just tells you, things can happen that you don't anticipate, that it's not really your fault. I'd never even heard of a sinkhole before I read about this happening."

He ended up losing money when they re-cut the deal at a lower price. Not catastrophic, but enough to teach him a lesson he'd never forget.

The lesson? No matter how thorough your analysis, reality can surprise you in ways you never imagined.

Howard Marks learned this same lesson from his father's story about gambling: "I tell my father's story of the gambler who lost regularly. One day he heard about a race with only one horse in it, so he bet the rent money. Halfway around the track, the horse jumped over the fence and ran away."

Think about that. The gambler had considered everything – the horse getting sick, stumbling, running slowly. But jumping the fence? That possibility never even entered his mind.

Both stories illustrate what former Defense Secretary Donald Rumsfeld famously described: "There are known knowns. There are known unknowns. But there are also unknown unknowns – the ones we don't know we don't know."

These unknown unknowns are the most dangerous risks in investing. As financial advisor Carl Richards put it: "Risk is what's left over after you think you've thought of everything."

A global pandemic shutting down the world economy. A technological breakthrough making an entire industry obsolete overnight. Or in Greenblatt's case, a sinkhole swallowing your investment – literally.

No analysis, no matter how rigorous, can account for risks you can't even imagine.

The only protection against unknown unknowns is diversification. Not because we lack confidence in our analysis, but because we're humble enough to know we can't possibly imagine everything that could go wrong.

When you concentrate too heavily, you're not just betting on what you know. You're betting that nothing you don't know – and can't even conceive of – will matter. That's not investing. That's gambling.

This is why I limit most positions to 5% of my portfolio on a cost basis. Currently, my portfolio holds 20 stocks, as opposed to concentrating on my five best ideas. It's about having the humility to respect the existence of unknown unknowns.

The largest positions in my portfolio are those with the lowest probability of permanent capital loss – businesses so resilient that even severe shocks are unlikely to destroy them. But even then, I size to my "sleeping point" – the maximum allocation where I can still sleep soundly at night, regardless of what happens to the business. If a position grows uncomfortably large, I reassess (more on that in the maintenance section).

DIVERSIFICATION THAT ACTUALLY MATTERS

Knowing we need diversification is one thing. Knowing how to diversify effectively is another.

Now that we understand we can't predict every risk, you'd think the solution would be simple – just follow traditional diversification advice. But here's where most investors, and even many advisors, get it wrong.

Traditional financial advice will tell you to "diversify across sectors." Own some tech, some financials, some consumer goods. Spread your bets across the different sectors of the economy.

This sounds sensible. It's also deeply flawed.

The problem? Sector labels are so broad they're almost meaningless. Consider what "technology" actually encompasses. Is it subscription software like Adobe? Ad platforms like Meta? E-commerce infrastructure like Amazon? Consumer hardware like Apple?

These businesses have completely different economics, customers, and vulnerabilities. Grouping them as "tech" and thinking you're diversified is false comfort.

WHEN LABELS HIDE REALITY

When the pandemic hit in 2020, these "tech" companies had wildly different experiences:

- **Microsoft 365** saw explosive demand as the world went digital overnight.
- **Apple** faced severe supply chain challenges with factory shutdowns in China.
- **Ad platforms** like Meta and Google saw businesses slash advertising budgets during the uncertainty.
- **E-commerce** platforms experienced massive pull-forward of demand as physical retail shut down.

Same sector label. Completely different business impacts.

As I write this in 2025, we're seeing the same phenomenon in retail. Lululemon, Dollar General, and Costco are all "retail" stocks. But they're responding differently to inflation and tariff pressures.

Lululemon faces significant slowdown as consumers cut discretionary spending on premium athletic wear. Dollar General, whose core customers are lower-income, sees severe pressure as those shoppers struggle with higher prices. Meanwhile, Costco thrives – their sticky membership program and bulk pricing become more valuable when consumers seek savings.

Three retailers. Different consumer segments, different outcomes. The sector label tells you nothing.

BEYOND THE LISTING LOCATION

Geographic diversification has the same problem. Many worry their portfolio is "too US-centric" because their stocks trade on American exchanges.

But where a company lists tells you little about where it operates.

Apple trades on the NASDAQ but generates more than 50% of revenue internationally. Visa lists on the NYSE but earns close to 60% outside America. Sea Limited, despite being US-listed, generates 0% from the US – virtually all revenue comes from Southeast Asia.

A portfolio of US-listed multinationals can be more globally diversified than one mixing regional players from different countries. What matters isn't the headquarters or exchange. It's where the customers are.

WHAT REAL DIVERSIFICATION LOOKS LIKE

True diversification asks better questions:

- Where does revenue actually come from?
- What drives the business economics?
- Which external factors could impair each holding?
- How would different economic scenarios affect each business?

Howard Marks captured this perfectly: "Most investors think diversification consists of holding many different things; few understand that diversification is effective only if portfolio holdings can be counted on to respond differently to a given development in the environment."

Instead of checking sector boxes, think about economic drivers. Do you own:

- Businesses dependent on consumer discretionary spending?
- Companies that benefit from economic uncertainty?
- Enterprises with pricing power during inflation?
- Organizations resilient to technological disruption?

The goal isn't to smooth volatility. It's to ensure no single type of crisis destroys your portfolio. When you own businesses with fundamentally different drivers, your portfolio can survive whatever form the next crisis takes.

This is what real portfolio construction looks like. Not 15–25 stocks spread across arbitrary sector labels, but 15–25 businesses that respond differently to economic cycles. Some thrive during expansion, others prove their worth in recession. You're building a portfolio that can survive not just the risks you can identify, but the unknown unknowns you can't even imagine.

Now that we've built this resilient structure, the challenge becomes maintaining it without overreacting to every market move. Let's explore how to keep your portfolio on track while actually living your life.

LET IT WORK – MAINTAINING AND GROWING YOUR PORTFOLIO

You've done the hard part: built a portfolio of great businesses, sized intentionally, and diversified sensibly. Now comes the challenge most investors fail to navigate – knowing when to step back.

It's tempting to tinker. To check prices daily. To make changes just to feel productive. But often, the more you intervene, the more you interrupt the very compounding you set out to achieve.

Here's what actually matters: Let winners run unless they become dangerously large. Check quarterly earnings to ensure the thesis remains intact. Stay invested unless valuations become truly insane.

That's it. The hard part isn't knowing what to do. It's having the discipline to sit still.

THE SELF-DRIVING PORTFOLIO

Josh Tarasoff of Greenlea Lane Capital Management has a powerful framework for thinking about portfolio construction. He calls it a "self-driving portfolio."

The concept isn't about automation or never touching your investments. It's about owning businesses so strong they shoulder the work of compounding themselves. You approach each investment expecting the company to drive its own growth indefinitely while you focus on living.

Tarasoff points out the brutal math most investors face: a portfolio with 24 stocks and a two-year average holding period demands one new market-beating idea every month. Without end. And that's considered low turnover by industry standards – most managers need an even faster pace.

This necessity creates what he calls "endemic hurriedness." You can see it on investors' faces, hear it in their voices. They're always on the verge of the next great idea, always rushing, always searching.

But when you own true compounders – businesses that reinforce their own advantages year after year – the portfolio essentially runs itself. These companies don't just survive different economic conditions; they strengthen their competitive positions regardless of the business cycle. They compound through booms and busts, innovations and disruptions, while requiring minimal intervention from you.

The ideal, as Tarasoff describes it, is for the portfolio to eventually take over all the work. Not through neglect, but through owning businesses so competent that your main job becomes staying out of their way.

This creates a virtuous cycle: less time pressure improves decision quality, which strengthens the portfolio, which further reduces time pressure. The opposite – rushed decisions weakening the portfolio, increasing pressure – is what destroys most investors.

The self-driving portfolio isn't just about better returns. It's about sustainable investing – an approach you can maintain for decades without burning out from the constant pressure to find the next great idea.

WHEN (AND WHEN NOT) TO REBALANCE

Rebalancing sounds smart in theory. But in practice, it can become a way of interrupting your own compounding.

Say one of your positions starts at 5% of your portfolio and then doubles, so it's now 10% of your portfolio. What now? Do you trim it just because the weight doubled?

Not necessarily.

If the business is still performing well, the valuation remains reasonable, and your conviction is high, there may be no reason to touch it. In fact, trimming just because something has gone up is one of the fastest ways to stunt your portfolio's compounding.

We covered the psychology of selling winners in Chapter 9 – the instinct to "take profits" that destroys returns. Keep cutting your flowers and leaving the weeds, and eventually that's all you'll have – a garden full of weeds. At the portfolio level, the implication is structural: build a portfolio you can psychologically afford to leave alone.

But that doesn't mean you hold blindly either. Apart from the three reasons outlined in Chapter 9 on selling, there are moments when trimming is the right call.

As Pat Dorsey wrote in *The Five Rules for Successful Stock Investing*, when a winner grows into an outsized position, it's worth considering a trim:

> If an investment is more than 10% to 15% of your portfolio, it's time to think long and hard about trimming it down no matter how solid the company's prospects may be. (These percentages are a rough guide – you might be comfortable with more money in a single stock, or you might want to be more diversified.) It simply doesn't make sense to have too many of your eggs in one basket.

When a position runs to 15% of my portfolio, I start asking harder questions. How resilient is this business really? Could a single regulatory change cripple it? Does it depend heavily on one product, one market, one key customer? Are revenues truly diversified and recurring? Is it becoming egregiously overvalued?

For something like Berkshire Hathaway – with its diverse operations, multiple revenue streams, and fortress balance sheet – I might be comfortable letting it run larger if valuations remain reasonable. But for most businesses, concentration requires extra scrutiny.

The goal is to let your winners run while ensuring no single position carries outsized risk at the portfolio level. And that depends not just on the size of the position, but on the resilience of the business itself.

FIND YOUR PACE (ESPECIALLY IF YOU'RE JUST STARTING)

If you're new to investing, deploying capital can feel scary – and for good reason. You've worked hard to earn that money. The idea of putting it into something volatile can be overwhelming.

That's why I love a principle shared with me by Chin Hui Leong, co-founder of The Smart Investor, who learned it from Tom Engle, an investing legend in the Motley Fool community.

Tom was from humble beginnings in Louisville, Kentucky, sharing a two-bedroom house with his grandparents. He watched his parents climb out of poverty by investing, and learned at a young age to invest what money he could – and most importantly, to keep it invested. After working just nine years at a gas station, he was able to retire. Not from a windfall. Not from a high-paying job. From decades of patient, steady compounding.[4]

And this is his advice for deploying capital: **if it took you two years to save the money, take at least half that time to invest it**.

You don't need to invest all your capital in a rush. When you deploy slowly, you give yourself time to:

- Learn how businesses behave across different cycles.
- Test and refine your investment process.
- Understand how you respond emotionally when things move.

And here's what matters most: if you're still early in your journey, you're bound to make mistakes. That's part of the learning process. This approach helps ensure those early mistakes aren't too expensive.

Tying your investment pace to how long it took you to earn the money is a helpful emotional anchor. The faster you deploy relative to your income, the more pressure you'll likely feel. This framework gives you time to learn the businesses – and learn yourself.

Your job isn't to be fast. It's to be ready. You're training the muscle of long-term conviction. That takes time. Let it.

MONITORING: DON'T LET THE NOISE STEER THE SHIP

Most stock brokers are built for action. Their business models thrive on trading activity – so they design the user experience to provoke it. Flashing tickers. Charts. News alerts. Gamified mobile apps. All of it creates the illusion that you should be doing something, all the time.

It feels like progress. But it's usually just noise.

In my experience, the more frequently you act, the more likely you are to hurt your long-term returns. You don't need to be busy to be effective. You need to be consistent – and deliberate.

So set your own rhythm.

Don't check prices every day. Don't open your brokerage app out of boredom. Don't confuse a stock price moving with the business itself changing.

Just because a stock drops 8%, doesn't mean the company's performance has deteriorated. One is a quote from Mr. Market. The other is a signal from the business.

And be especially wary of loud voices in the media. Pundits and headlines often exist to provoke reactions, not to improve outcomes. They play on urgency and fear – not long-term thinking.

Instead, focus on what's real – quarterly reports, strategic updates, and competitive shifts that actually affect your holdings.

You don't need to check these every week. A quarterly rhythm works well for most investors: earnings season is your time to revisit the facts, reflect on the thesis, and scan for material changes. Once or twice a year, take a step back and ask the bigger questions: "Would I still buy this today? Has something fundamental changed in the business – or in my thinking?"

Build a portfolio that doesn't need babysitting – and learn to give it that space.

THE QUARTERLY PORTFOLIO CHECK

Every quarter, I review my portfolio as a whole. The centerpiece is what I call the **Thesis Health Check**. For each position, I revisit why I own it. The best reason to hold is the same reason you'd buy today: the business is high-quality, has a long runway, and trades at a reasonable valuation relative to its prospects.

This quarterly review ensures the businesses I own are still executing well and my investment thesis remains intact. If the fundamentals have deteriorated or the thesis has broken, it's time to reassess. Simple as that.

WHY I DON'T TRY TO TIME THE MARKET

One of the most common questions I get is: "Are you raising cash to wait for a market crash?"

My answer is always the same: No.

For me, a cash position is an outcome, not an objective. If there are fewer opportunities in the stock market, my cash levels naturally rise. If opportunities abound, cash drops. I don't wake up one day and decide I need 20% cash, then start selling stocks to get there.

Why am I so adamant about not timing the market based on economic forecasts? Because it's essentially impossible, and trying to do it is one of the costliest mistakes investors make.

Howard Marks, in his brilliant memo, "The Illusion of Knowledge," explains why economic forecasting is fundamentally flawed. Consider what you're actually trying to predict when you attempt to time the market. The

US economy has 330 million participants, with billions of daily interactions between consumers, workers, and businesses globally. To forecast where the economy is heading, you'd need to predict the behavior of all these participants – how they'll react to energy price changes, geopolitical events, or emerging technologies.[5]

As Marks explains, this would require modeling billions of nodes and interactions. But here's the crucial difference from the physical sciences: humans don't behave predictably like electrons. Marks quotes physicist Richard Feynman's brilliant observation: "Imagine how much harder physics would be if electrons had feelings." That's precisely the problem – economic participants have emotions that change unpredictably.

Even if you somehow nailed the economic forecast, you'd still need to predict market psychology. Will investors panic or stay calm? See opportunity or danger? These psychological factors are unknowable. You need both the economic forecast AND the market's reaction to be right – multiplying the difficulty exponentially.

This impossibility extends even to those who should know best. The Federal Reserve, with 400 Ph.D. economists, has what economist Gary Shilling called "a miserable record of forecasting." In 2015, Fed members projected the 2016 federal funds rate at 0.90%. The actual rate? 0.38%. These are the people who literally set the rate, yet couldn't predict their own actions.

If the world's most sophisticated forecasters can't reliably predict the economy or markets, why would individual investors bet their portfolios on market timing?

Peter Lynch put it perfectly: "Far more money has been lost by investors trying to anticipate corrections than has been lost in the corrections themselves."

The data backs him up decisively.

A study by J.P. Morgan Asset Management looked at S&P 500 returns from 2004 to 2024. Investors who stayed fully invested earned an annualized return of 10.6%. But if you missed just the 10 best days during that stretch, your return was cut in half to 5.3%.[6]

Even more striking? Seven of those 10 best days happened within two weeks of the 10 worst days. So if you pulled out during a panic and waited for clarity, you likely missed the recovery too.

That's the paradox: the days that make your portfolio are often right next to the ones that tempt you to flee.

Even perfect timing doesn't help much. Lynch ran the numbers: if you had invested at the peak of the market every single year from 1965 to 1995, your return would've been 10.6%. If you somehow timed the bottom perfectly each year, you'd have earned 11.7%. The difference? Just 1.1%. Hardly a reward worth chasing for thirty years of impossible clairvoyance.[7]

That's why I don't adjust cash levels based on market predictions. I look at the businesses I own or want to own. Are they still resilient? Reasonably valued? Are there better opportunities?

Unless valuations become truly egregious, I stay invested. Selling a great business to sit in cash, then missing a few powerful up days – that's how you destroy long-term returns.

Market timing is a fool's errand. Wealth isn't built by calling tops and bottoms – it's built by buying great businesses and staying invested long enough to let them work. The best portfolios, like bamboo, spend years looking like nothing's happening – until suddenly they don't.

FINAL THOUGHT: A PORTFOLIO THAT WORKS SO YOU DON'T HAVE TO

This chapter wasn't about creating the perfect portfolio through optimization formulas or complex rebalancing schedules.

It was about building a system that's resilient enough to grow your wealth over decades – something you can maintain with clarity, conviction, and minimal stress.

As Howard Marks showed us at the beginning, the goal isn't to generate hall of fame returns in any single year. It's to perform consistently well over the long run. That steady, above-average performance – never spectacular but never terrible – becomes exceptional given enough time.

You now have the tools: a right-sized set of holdings (15–25 stocks), a sensible sizing framework (3–10% based on quality and conviction), real diversification (by business model, not just sector), and a process to stay on course – without overreacting.

That's the whole point of this book: to help you build wealth so you can spend your time doing what you love. A great portfolio doesn't demand your attention every day. It gives you your attention back – to use on the things that matter.

The goal isn't to outperform in any single year – it's to avoid the one mistake that derails the decade.

LUNCH BREAK SUMMARY

- **Consistency beats brilliance**: The funds that avoid disasters consistently outperform those swinging for spectacular returns in the long run.
- **15–25 stocks is the sweet spot**: Most risk reduction comes from your first dozen holdings; beyond that, you're adding complexity and diluting your best ideas.
- **Unknown unknowns demand humility**: Greenblatt's investment literally fell into a sinkhole – no analysis can predict what you can't imagine, which is why even your highest conviction ideas need position limits.
- **Sector labels create false comfort**: Companies in the same "sector" often respond oppositely to the same crisis – true diversification means owning businesses with fundamentally different economic drivers, not collecting different labels.
- **Stay invested – the best days cluster around the worst**: Markets deliver most of their long-term returns in brief, violent bursts that typically follow sharp selloffs – investors who flee during panic miss the snapback that creates wealth.

YOUR NEXT STEP

You've now built a portfolio that compounds wealth without constant supervision. But what's the point of all this patient accumulation?

In the next chapter, we'll zoom out. We'll talk about what happens after the spreadsheets – how money enables freedom, what changes when you no longer need a paycheck, and how to define your own version of "enough." Because in the end, the goal isn't just financial independence. It's a life lived on your terms.

PART IV

THE LONG GAME

CHAPTER 11
BEYOND THE NUMBERS

TIME'S SILENT DEADLINE

My grandmother's kitchen always smelled like sesame oil and safety. When tempers flared at home, I'd escape to her flat. That was my safe harbor. She never asked questions, never made a fuss. Just turned on the stove and made her signature fried rice.

One egg, leftover rice, a splash of dark soy sauce. Nothing fancy, yet familiar. A predictable bowl of warmth in a world that often felt unpredictable.

As I got older and more financially secure, I told myself that once I had more time, I'd take her out more. Accompany her back to her hometown in Melaka, Malaysia. Let her enjoy a few comforts she never asked for but always deserved.

But I kept putting it off, thinking I'd have time.

After my grandfather passed, her health declined faster than I expected. She had difficulty walking. I wasn't always around, but I heard from relatives that she'd ask about me often. That's when it really sank in – if I didn't make time now, I might never get the chance.

We'd go out for meals. One of our last was Peking duck – something she loved but would never have ordered for herself.

She savored every bite. Then the bill arrived. Her eyes widened, and she scolded me in rapid Hokkien – the same tone she'd used when I was seven and wasted rice. I laughed. Some things never change. Even now, she couldn't bring herself to splurge. I just wanted her to feel cared for in the way she'd always shown it to me – through food and time together.

That meal stayed with me because it ended up being one of our last.

I never got to accompany her back to Melaka. Never carved out the time for something I always assumed I'd get to. As her body grew too weak to travel, that window quietly closed.

Not long after she passed, I came across one of Charlie Munger's final interviews. He sat there – 99 years old, worth billions, sharp as ever. Then he said something that has never left me:

"Well… I am so old and weak compared to when I was 96 that I no longer want to catch a 200-pound tuna. It's just too goddamn much work… I would have paid any amount to catch a 200-pound tuna when I was younger. I never caught one. Now, if you give me the opportunity, I would just decline."[1]

Even someone with all the money and wisdom in the world had something he couldn't buy back: time, health, and the ability to act on the things he once wanted.

We all have our 200-pound tuna – something we assume we'll get to later. A trip. A conversation. A dream we think will wait for us.

For me, it was that simple trip to Melaka with my grandmother, who never asked for anything.

But if you wait too long, it's not just the opportunity you lose. It's the strength to take it. The people to share it with. And slowly, even the desire fades – not because you stopped caring, but because the moment passed you by.

That's the thing about time – it doesn't announce its deadlines. It just closes windows, quietly.

My portfolio has survived every market crash, but it couldn't protect me from this lesson: the most expensive thing you can buy is the belief that you have more time than you do.

I think back to that 13-year-old sitting in darkness after the power was cut, watching neighbors' lights through the window. The same boy who watched his mother's wedding jewelry get pawned for gambling money.

That desperation to escape poverty drove me to build wealth. But wealth without time to use it is just numbers on a screen.

Some lessons come too late. Others arrive just in time.

LEARNING TO LIVE, NOT SURVIVE

The pen felt heavier than it should have.

I was signing my scholarship bond – four years of security in exchange for one signature. For someone from a ~~low~~ no-income family, it was the most responsible thing I could do. A full ride through university. A stable job in the public service. A way to carry my family forward.

I was – and still am – grateful.

Yet something felt off, though I couldn't quite put my finger on why, since this would take away most of my financial miseries.

Looking back, I now know why.

I wasn't just accepting a job. I was burying a dream.

Ever since my teens, I'd been obsessed with investing – reading company filings, scribbling thoughts from Warren Buffett's letters, highlighting footnotes most people skipped. It wasn't a phase. It was the one thing that made me feel most alive. But I told myself that passion had to wait.

The bond came first.

For years, I showed up. Did good work. Got promoted. Built my savings. From the outside, I was succeeding.

But success and alignment are different things.

The job itself wasn't bad. I had great colleagues, meaningful responsibilities, and plenty of opportunities to grow. But it wore me down – not in some dramatic, soul-crushing way, but through the quiet erosion of days that didn't feel like mine.

There was one afternoon I still remember clearly.

I was replying to emails under the buzz of fluorescent lights, back stiff from the office chair I'd sat in for years, when it hit me.

Not like lightning. More like recognition of something I'd always known.

I had become good at surviving a life I didn't want.

The bond was almost up. But even as it neared its end, I sensed something else holding me there. This was a stable job with clear career progression.

The irony wasn't lost on me. The same traits that once lifted me out of poverty – discipline, caution, frugality – were now holding me back. I was still behaving like the teenager who couldn't afford the power bill. Still turning down small indulgences, overthinking whether to take a cab, optimizing every choice as if ruin was one wrong step away. The scarcity script ran deeper than I'd realized. I had money in the bank but still walked 20 minutes to save on bus fare. Not because I needed to. Because I didn't know how to stop.

I had outgrown the script, but I was still performing it.

My bond was ending. I had a financial cushion. My writing at *SteadyCompounding.com* was growing. People were reaching out – fund managers, thoughtful investors, curious readers. For the first time, I felt like I was in the right room.

Yet the idea of leaving wasn't easy.

I was choosing uncertainty over stability. A solitary path over a well-paved one. A career in investing isn't exactly a safe bet – especially when you're walking away from lifetime job security.

But what helped me most was a mental model I had read about: Jeff Bezos's Regret Minimization Framework.[2] Picture yourself at 80, looking back. What would you regret?

Would I regret giving up a stable job to pursue something I loved? Maybe.

Would I regret never giving it a shot?

Absolutely.

So I called my boss and told her I was resigning.

There was no grand speech. No cinematic moment. Just a steady voice after years of quiet preparation.

That afternoon, I sat at my desk, hands slightly cold, heart calm. I opened a blank email to my colleagues and titled it simply:

Thanks Everyone!

I thanked them for the years. Shared the Bezos framework. And said something I truly believed:

Sometimes the biggest risk is not changing. Not evolving. Staying in a story you've already outgrown.

Leaving wasn't just about chasing a dream. It was about honoring what got me here – and recognizing when it was time to write a new script.

Because the values that help you survive poverty don't always know when their job is done.

And freedom isn't something you find. It's something you learn to claim.

STEADY COMPOUNDING WINS TWICE

"So what do you actually DO all day?" my former colleague asked over coffee.

The question made me smile. After 10 chapters of moats and management, valuations and portfolios, here is what really matters – what happens beyond the spreadsheets?

I could see him trying to picture it. Multiple monitors. Bloomberg Terminal. CNBC on in the background. Maybe a whiteboard covered in calculations.

"Yesterday? I read Netflix's quarterly earnings. Went for a game of basketball. Had lunch with my mum."

His expression shifted from curiosity to confusion. "But... how do you stay on top of everything? The Fed minutes? Earnings previews? The market?"

This wasn't the first time I'd had this conversation. People assume that investing well means living inside the market's every twitch. That success requires constant motion. That more activity equals better returns.

But I'd learned something different from studying the best investors. Warren Buffett's calendar is famously empty – he spends most of his time reading and thinking. As Charlie Munger put it: "A great company keeps working when you're not. A great company will eventually earn more and more while you're just sitting and doing nothing."

That's the paradox most people miss. In investing, we're paid for the quality of our decisions, not the quantity of our activity. And certainly not for how complex it looks. As I like to say: there are no style points in investing.

My portfolio wasn't filled with stories. It was filled with great businesses. Steady compounders that kept working while I wasn't.

I was spending more time thinking, writing, having slow lunches. More time being present.

I'd been buying steady compounders for years. While I was stuck in meetings, they were bringing in sales. While I slept, they were innovating. While I lived my life, they were compounding.

For a long time, I thought this was the norm – owning businesses the way Buffett described it: not as blips on a chart, but as partial ownership of real enterprises.

But the more I spoke with others, the more I realized that's not the default. Many people assume being a serious investor means staying constantly informed, constantly active. They imagine speed equals skill. Action equals edge.

Howard Marks captured this perfectly:

"Day traders considered themselves successful if they bought a stock at $10 and sold at $11, bought it back the next week at $24 and sold at $25, and bought it a week later at $39 and sold at $40.

If you can't see the flaw in this – that the trader made $3 in a stock that appreciated by $30 – you probably shouldn't read the rest of this book."[3]

All that motion. All that stress. All those taxes. For a fraction of the return.

My friend stared at his coffee. "But don't you worry you're missing something? Some opportunity?"

"I used to," I admitted. "When I first started investing, I thought constant activity meant I was doing it right. Checking prices every hour. Reading every headline. Trying to get ahead of every move."

"What changed?"

"I realized I was confusing motion with progress. The best businesses don't need my supervision. They need time. Time to execute and compound."

Since leaving my job, this truth had become even clearer. By owning steady compounders, I wasn't just building wealth. I was buying back my calendar. Every position that didn't require constant monitoring was another day I could spend however I chose.

The less I tinkered, the more I earned. The less I monitored, the more present I became. And the more stillness I allowed, the more clearly I could see what actually mattered.

It reminded me of Pascal's wisdom from centuries ago – that humanity's problems stem from our inability to sit quietly in a room alone. The same principle that makes selling too early so costly, as we explored in Chapter 9, makes patient ownership so powerful.

"So you just… do nothing?" my friend asked.

"I do what only I can do," I said. "Spend time with people I love. Write things that might help others. Review reports and think deeply about a few important decisions – instead of obsessing over many small ones that don't move the needle."

He looked skeptical but intrigued. The way most people do when they first encounter this idea.

As we parted, he asked one more question: "Doesn't it get boring?"

I thought about my grandmother's kitchen. About windows that close. About all the years I'd optimized for tomorrow while forgetting to live today.

"The opposite," I said. "It's the most interesting life I could imagine."

Because this isn't about doing nothing. It's about letting the right things compound – wealth, relationships, presence – while you focus on what can't be delegated or deferred.

The best investments are the ones that let you sleep at night and live your days.

That Tuesday morning coffee with an old colleague? Being able to play basketball while my body allows? That long lunch with my mum where we talked about everything and nothing? And of course, being able to travel whenever I want to see the world?

Those weren't the gaps between real work.

They were the point.

My friend had asked what I do all day. But the real question was what I don't have to do. I don't check prices. I don't chase trends. I don't lose sleep over positions.

That's how steady compounding wins twice.

First win: Your wealth grows while you sleep. Meta keeps innovating.

Amazon keeps expanding. Mastercard keeps processing. They don't need your help.

Second win: You get your life back. Every position that doesn't require daily attention is another day that's actually yours.

Most investing strategies promise the first win by sacrificing the second. Steady compounding delivers both.

WHAT WILL YOU COMPOUND?

Maybe you're reading this during your lunch break, stealing moments between meetings. Maybe you're asking the same question I once did: Is there a better way to build wealth than this?

The answer is yes. But it's not the path most people expect.

Learning to think like an owner – to see beyond stock prices to actual businesses, to buy with conviction instead of speculation, to hold when others panic – rewires how you see investing. And it doesn't require quitting your day job or staring at screens all day.

Your first analysis might take days. Your first investment might keep you up at night. But each report you read, each business you understand, each quarter you hold through will compound into something powerful: quiet confidence.

And with it comes freedom.

The paradox of steady compounding – buying quality businesses at reasonable prices and holding them for years while they do the work – is that it requires patience and discipline upfront so that, eventually, your money works harder than you do. Not through speculation. Not through chasing the next hot thing. But through owning pieces of great businesses and giving them time.

This is how real wealth is built – quietly, patiently, inevitably. And with that wealth comes something precious: the freedom to choose.

Because someday you'll want to say yes when it matters. Yes because you can. Yes while there's still time.

That's what we're really compounding. Not just wealth, but the power to choose.

So start where you are. Pick a business you already understand. Write one page of analysis. Put your thesis down on paper.

You now have the framework: how to spot moats, evaluate management, calculate value, and build a resilient portfolio. Everything you need to compound your capital into lasting wealth.

We all start this journey for different reasons. For me, it was escaping the constraints that poverty placed on my family. For you, it might be freedom from a demanding boss, time with family, or simply pursuing your dreams. But we all discover the same thing: the power to choose.

Now it's your turn.

How will you begin your compounding journey?

LUNCH BREAK SUMMARY

- **Time has silent deadlines**: Windows close without warning, and money can't reopen them once health, desire, or people are gone.
- **The values that help you survive don't always know when their job is done**: Recognizing when to evolve beyond the scripts that once protected you is crucial.
- **Steady compounding wins twice**: Your wealth grows while you sleep, and you get your life back – most strategies promise only one of these.
- **The best investments require the least maintenance**: Great businesses compound while you live your life – not the other way around.
- **Building wealth isn't the goal**: It's the tool that enables choice, presence, and the ability to say yes when it matters.

A NOTE FROM THE AUTHOR

Thank you for joining me on this journey. This book represents everything I wish I'd known when I started – how to build wealth while actually living your life.

If this book helped you see investing differently, I'd be grateful if you'd leave a review on Amazon. Your honest feedback helps other investors find this book.

Every week at *SteadyCompounding.com*, I explore businesses I'm watching and share what I'm learning from my own portfolio. If you'd like to continue this journey together, subscribe to my free newsletter at steadycompounding.com/subscribe or find me on Instagram and X at @steadycompound.

Here's to your compounding journey.

Thomas Chua

ACKNOWLEDGMENTS

A book has one name on the cover and many hands behind it. This one is no exception.

Craig Pearce, for shaping this book into something better than the manuscript I first sent. He pushed back where it mattered, and the book is sharper for it.

And to everyone else at Harriman House: Amy Webber for holding production together, Lucy Vincent for marketing, Ellie Tucker on the audiobook, and the typesetters, proofreaders, and many others who turn a manuscript into a book.

Robert Vinall, Eugene Ng, Gautam Baid, Clay Finck, Chin Hui Leong, and Bogumil Baranowski all read early versions and endorsed the book. Robert and Eugene also sent back notes that made the book better. Endorsements are a real ask, and I'm grateful for every one of them.

Some of the most important teachers in this book are people I've never met. Warren Buffett, Charlie Munger, and Peter Lynch have taught a generation of investors how to think about businesses. I'm part of that generation, and I hope this book carries some of what they gave me forward.

To the readers of SteadyCompounding.com. Your questions shaped what I learned to explain, what I learned to skip, and what I learned to say plainly. This book couldn't have happened without you.

To my mother, who taught me hard work, saving, and patience long before I knew about steady compounding.

Thank you.

GLOSSARY

This glossary defines key investment terms as they are used in this book. For the busy investor, these definitions provide quick reference without interrupting your reading flow.

Asset-light business. A company requiring minimal physical assets to generate revenue, typically producing high returns on capital. Software companies, platforms, and franchisors are common examples.

Balance sheet. A financial statement showing a company's assets, liabilities, and shareholders' equity at a specific point in time. The fundamental accounting equation: Assets = Liabilities + Equity.

Bull market/Bear market. A bull market features rising prices and investor optimism; a bear market sees prices fall 20% or more from recent highs. Both are normal parts of market cycles.

Buy and hold. An investment strategy of purchasing securities and holding them for years or decades, minimizing trading costs and taxes while allowing compounding to work.

CAGR (Compound Annual Growth Rate). The constant annual growth rate that would take an investment from its starting value to its ending value over a period. Useful for comparing investments with different time horizons.

Capital allocation. How management deploys company cash: reinvesting in the business, making acquisitions, paying dividends, buying back shares, or reducing debt. Perhaps the most important skill for a CEO to master.

Capital expenditures (Capex). Money spent acquiring or improving physical assets like buildings, equipment, or technology. Required to maintain and grow a business.

Cash flow statement. A financial statement tracking actual cash movements across three categories: operating activities, investing activities, and financing activities. Often more reliable than the income statement.

Circle of competence. The areas where you have genuine knowledge and expertise. Warren Buffett's principle: invest only where you can properly evaluate business quality, and honestly acknowledge the boundaries of what you understand.

Compounding. The process where investment returns generate their own returns over time, creating exponential growth. Often called 'the eighth wonder of the world' – the foundation of long-term wealth building.

Cost of capital. The minimum return a company must earn on investments to satisfy its investors. A business creates value when its returns exceed its cost of capital.

Discounted cash flow (DCF). A valuation method estimating what a business is worth by projecting future cash flows and discounting them to present value. Precise but highly sensitive to assumptions.

Diversification. Spreading investments across multiple holdings to reduce risk. True diversification means owning businesses that respond differently to economic events – not just collecting different sector labels.

Dividend. Cash payments distributed by a company to shareholders from its profits. One of three ways investors profit from stocks, alongside price appreciation and buybacks.

Dollar-cost averaging. Investing fixed amounts at regular intervals regardless of price. Reduces the risk of buying everything at a market peak.

Drawdown. The decline from a portfolio's peak value to its lowest point. A 50% drawdown requires a 100% gain just to return to breakeven – which is why avoiding large losses matters so much.

Earnings per share (EPS). A company's net profit divided by shares outstanding. The 'E' in P/E ratio – shows profit attributable to each share you own.

EBITDA. Earnings Before Interest, Taxes, Depreciation, and Amortization. A measure of operating profitability that strips out financing decisions and non-cash accounting charges.

Economic moat. A sustainable competitive advantage protecting a company's profits from competitors, like a castle moat protects against invaders. Wide moats can endure for decades; narrow moats may erode within years.

ETF (Exchange-Traded Fund). An investment fund that trades on stock exchanges like individual stocks. Can track market indices, specific sectors, or investment strategies. Combines diversification with trading flexibility.

Founder-led. A company still run by its original founder(s). Often associated with long-term thinking and aligned incentives, since founders typically hold significant equity.

Free cash flow (FCF). Cash remaining after all operating expenses and capital investments. The money truly available to shareholders – often more reliable than reported earnings.

Gross profit. Revenue minus the direct cost of goods sold. Shows profitability before operating expenses. Higher gross margins often indicate pricing power.

Hurdle rate. The minimum return an investment must offer to be worth pursuing. Your personal benchmark – typically 10–15% annually for stock investments.

Income statement. A financial statement showing revenue, expenses, and profit over a period (quarter or year). Also called the Profit & Loss statement or P&L.

Index fund. A mutual fund or ETF that tracks a market index like the S&P 500 by holding all or most of its components. Offers broad diversification at low cost with no stock-picking required.

Insider buying. When executives or board members purchase company shares with their own money on the open market. Often a bullish signal – these insiders know the business better than anyone.

Intrinsic value. The 'true' worth of a business based on its future cash flows, independent of current market price. A stock is undervalued when price is below intrinsic value.

Loss aversion. The psychological tendency to feel losses more painfully than equivalent gains feel good. Can lead investors to hold losers too long or sell winners too early.

Margin of safety. The gap between your estimate of intrinsic value and the price you pay. A larger margin provides protection against errors in your analysis.

Market capitalization. A company's total market value: share price multiplied by shares outstanding. Commonly categorized as large-cap (over $10 billion), mid-cap, or small-cap.

Mr. Market. Benjamin Graham's allegory: imagine the stock market as an emotional business partner who offers daily to buy or sell shares at varying prices. You choose whether to transact – never let his moods dictate your decisions.

Multi-bagger. An investment returning multiple times your initial capital. A '10-bagger' returns 10x your money. Term coined by Peter Lynch.

Multiple expansion / contraction. When investors become willing to pay more (expansion) or less (contraction) per dollar of earnings. Improving growth prospects typically drive expansion; uncertainty drives contraction.

Net income. The 'bottom line' profit after all expenses, interest, and taxes have been paid. What shareholders ultimately own.

Net margin. Net income divided by revenue – the percentage of each sales dollar that becomes profit after all expenses.

Network effects. When a product becomes more valuable as more people use it. Facebook grows more useful with each new user; Visa becomes more valuable as more merchants accept it.

Operating cash flow. Cash generated from core business operations before capital investments. Found on the cash flow statement – the starting point for calculating free cash flow.

Operating margin. Operating income divided by revenue – shows what percentage of sales becomes profit from core business operations, before interest and taxes.

Opportunity cost. The returns you give up by choosing one investment over another. Sometimes selling a good company to buy a better one makes sense.

P/E ratio (Price-to-Earnings). Stock price divided by earnings per share. Shows how much investors pay for each dollar of annual profit. A P/E of 20 means paying $20 for every $1 of earnings.

Forward P/E. P/E ratio calculated using next year's estimated earnings rather than trailing results. More relevant for growing companies whose future earnings will exceed the past.

Permanent impairment. When a business's competitive position is destroyed and unlikely to recover – as opposed to a temporary stock price decline. A valid reason to sell.

Position sizing. Determining how much of your portfolio to allocate to a single investment. Balances potential return against concentration risk.

Pricing power. The ability to raise prices without losing significant customers. One of the clearest signs of competitive advantage and brand strength.

REIT (Real Estate Investment Trust). A company that owns income-producing real estate and must distribute at least 90% of taxable income as dividends. Provides real estate exposure through stock ownership.

Revenue. Total money received from selling goods or services before any expenses. The 'top line' of the income statement – where everything starts.

ROIC (Return on Invested Capital). A measure of how efficiently a company uses capital to generate profits. Higher ROIC typically indicates stronger competitive advantage. Calculated as operating profit after tax divided by invested capital.

Runway. The potential for future growth – how much room a company has to expand before saturating its market. Longer runway means more years of compounding ahead.

S-curve. The typical growth pattern of a business: slow initial adoption, rapid acceleration, then maturity and slowing. Helps identify where a company sits in its lifecycle.

Share buyback. When a company uses cash to repurchase its own shares, reducing shares outstanding and increasing each remaining share's ownership percentage of the business.

Skin in the game. When management has significant personal wealth invested in company stock, aligning their interests with shareholders. Executives who own shares think like owners.

Steady compounder. A high-quality business that can compound wealth over decades through durable competitive advantages, strong management, and consistent returns on capital. The central investment philosophy of this book.

Switching costs. The time, money, effort, or data loss that makes it painful for customers to switch to a competitor. High switching costs create customer 'stickiness' and protect profits.

TAM (Total Addressable Market). The total potential revenue if a company captured 100% of its target market. Indicates growth ceiling and remaining opportunity.

Thesis break. When your fundamental reasons for owning a company are no longer valid. Signals it's time to sell, regardless of current price or unrealized loss.

Tranche. Building a position through multiple purchases over time rather than investing all at once. Reduces timing risk and allows averaging into a position.

Valuation. The process of estimating what a business is worth. Compares the price you pay to the value you receive – the foundation of intelligent investing.

Volatility. The degree of price fluctuation in a stock or market. For long-term investors, volatility creates buying opportunities rather than just risk.

Working capital. Current assets minus current liabilities. Measures short-term financial health. Negative working capital can actually be a competitive advantage for companies like Amazon and Costco that collect payment before paying suppliers.

REFERENCES

CHAPTER 1

1. James K. Glassman, "An Old Lady's Lesson: Patience Usually Pays," *The Washington Post* (December 17, 1995), www.washingtonpost.com.

2. Anna Prior, "Ronald Read's $8 million estate," *The Wall Street Journal* (March 19, 2015), www.wsj.com.

3. Associated Press, "Gladys Holm's $18 million bequest," *The Washington Post* (July 31, 1997), www.washingtonpost.com.

4. "Grace Groner's Abbott Labs investment," *Business Insider* (March 5, 2010), www.businessinsider.com.

CHAPTER 2

1. Yefei Lu, "Warren Buffett's partnership returns 1957–1968," *Columbia University Press* (2016), www.degruyterbrill.com.

2. "Peter Lynch's performance and work habits" PBS Frontline, www.pbs.org/wgbh/pages/frontline/shows/betting/pros/lynch.html.

3. Barbara Kiviat, "Warren Buffett's family life and work habits," *Time* (September 23, 2008).

4. Howard S. Marks, "Howard Marks' pension fund study," Oaktree Capital memo, www.oaktreecapital.com/docs/default-source/memos/1990-10-12-the-route-to-performance.pdf?sfvrsn=33bc0f65_2.

5. Andrew Bary, "Buffett Shows Value of Working Past 65. That's When He Really Got Rich," *Barron's* (August 12, 2025), www.barrons.com.

6. Schroders, "Short-term investors have faced significant risks of losing money, longer-term investors have not," Analysis based on rolling periods for US stock market using data from Robert Shiller. Data January 1871-March 2020, www.schroders.com; Note: From 1926 to present, US stock market data refers to the S&P 500 index. Before 1926, it refers to the Cowles Commission Index, a widely-accepted proxy for the US stock market reconstructed by economist Alfred Cowles using historical stock prices, dividends, and earnings data. Source: www.econ.yale.edu/~shiller/data.htm.

7. Hendrik Bessembinder, "Do Stocks Outperform Treasury Bills?" *Journal of Financial Economics* (September 2018).

CHAPTER 3

1. Tim Koller, Marc Goedhart, and David Wessels, *Valuation: Measuring and Managing the Value of Companies* (McKinsey & Company Inc., 2020).

2. Michael Mauboussin, "Measuring the Moat," Credit Suisse, 2013.

3. Warren Buffett, "Berkshire Hathaway 2007 Letter to Shareholders" (February 2008), www.berkshirehathaway.com/letters/2007ltr.pdf.

4. Howard Schultz details investor rejections in his book, *Pour Your Heart Into It: How Starbucks Built a Company One Cup at a Time* (Hachette Books, 1997).

5. Visa's payment volume and revenue figures, "Visa Fiscal 2024 Annual Report" s29.q4cdn.com/385744025/files/doc_downloads/2024/Visa-Fiscal-2024-Annual-Report.pdf.

6. Backlinko, "TikTok global user growth statistics," backlinko.com/tiktok-users.

7. "SAP claims 77% of world's transaction revenue touches their systems," SAP Press Release, (December 16, 2020), news.sap.com/sea/2020/12/digital-transformation-imperative-for-business/.

8. Intuitive Surgical recurring revenue percentage. Intuitive Surgical 2024 Annual Report, isrg.intuitive.com/static-files/500ff989-ad91-4b32-a59e-f94a34d75997.

9. Netflix content spending 2016-2024. Statista, compiled from Netflix and Media Play News data (March 2025),www.statista.com/statistics/964789/netflix-content-spend-worldwide/.

10. Gillette's 70% US razor market share. CNBC, "Startups shook up the sleepy razor market" (September 2018), www.cnbc.com/2018/09/26/startups-shook-up-the-sleepy-razor-market-whats-next.html.

11. Nike Inc., "Q2 2025 Earnings Call Transcript" (December 19, 2024), s1.q4cdn.com/806093406/files/doc_financials/2025/q2/NIKE-Inc-Q2FY25-OFFICIAL-Transcript_-FINAL.pdf.

CHAPTER 4

1. Meta Q1 2022 Earnings Call Transcript. Meta Platforms, Inc. s21.q4cdn.com/399680738/files/doc_financials/2022/q1/Meta-Q1-2022-Earnings-Call-Transcript.pdf.

2. Meta Q4 2022 Press Release. Meta Platforms, Inc. s21.q4cdn.com/399680738/files/doc_financials/2022/q4/Meta-12.31.2022-Exhibit-99.1-FINAL.pdf.

3. The "spawners" framework was introduced by value investor Mohnish Pabrai in a lecture at Peking University's Guanghua School of Management (December 3, 2020), www.youtube.com/watch?v=pUiwBs_N5cE.

4. Jason Andrew, "Buffett's sweetest acquisition: A financial teardown of See's Candies," SBO Financial (April 17, 2024), sbo.financial/blog/financial-teardowns/sees-candies-a-financial-teardown/.

5. "Here is the full transcript of billionaire investor Warren Buffett's interview with CNBC," CNBC Interview (February 27, 2017), www.cnbc.com/2017/02/27/billionaire-investor-warren-buffett-speaks-with-cnbcs-becky-quick-on-squawk-box.html.

6. Terry Smith on extreme valuations overcome by quality. Fund Insiders Forum presentation (October 20, 2020),www.youtube.com/watch?v=oHRgxqpYDoE.

CHAPTER 5

1. Buffett's observation about Coke and Gillette. Berkshire Hathaway 1996 Annual Letter (February 28, 1997), www.berkshirehathaway.com/letters/1996.html.

2. Alan B. Goldberg and Bill Ritter, "Costco CEO Finds Pro-Worker Means Profitability," ABC News Interview (December 1, 2005), abcnews.go.com/2020/Business/story?id=1362779.

3. Allison Schiff, "Reed Hastings explains why Netflix won't sell ads," AdExchanger Interview (January 21, 2020) www.adexchanger.com/online-advertising/reed-hastings-explains-why-netflix-wont-ever-sell-ads/.

4. Lucia Moses, "Netflix ad tier reaches 70 million subscribers," *Business Insider* (January 23, 2025) www.businessinsider.com.

5. Matthew Heller, "Under Armour Fined $9M Over Accounting Trick," CFO.com (May 4, 2021), www.cfo.com/news/under-armour-fined-9m-over-accounting-trick/655654/.

CHAPTER 6

1. "Mr Buffett on the stock market," *Fortune Magazine* (November 22, 1999), berkshirehathaway.com/1999ar/FortuneMagazine.pdf.

2. Andrew Bary, "What's Wrong, Warren?" *Barron's* (December 27, 1999), barrons.com/articles/SB945992010127068546.

3. "The Late 1990s Dot-Com Bubble Implodes in 2000," Goldman Sachs, www.goldmansachs.com/our-firm/history/moments/2000-dot-com-bubble.

4. Berkshire Hathaway annual returns versus S&P 500 (1965–2024), Berkshire Hathaway 2024 Letter to Shareholders, www.berkshirehathaway.com/letters/2024ltr.pdf.

5. Stanley Druckenmiller's $3 billion loss during the dot-com bubble, "Stan Druckenmiller's Worst Mistake Ever," *Novel Investor* (January 9, 2019), novelinvestor.com/stan-druckenmillers-worst-mistake-ever/.

6. Bill Miller, "Bill Miller Archives: Sources of Edge," Miller Value Partners, (May 21, 2015), millervalue.com/bill-miller-archives-sources-of-edge/.

7. Amazon operating margins and stock price data from Amazon 2006 and 2024 Annual Reports.

CHAPTER 7

1. *Fortune*, "Chipotle E. coli Earnings," April 29, 2016. fortune.com/2016/04/29/chipotle-e-coli-earnings/.

2. Reuters, "How Chipotle's E. Coli Outbreak Has Brought the Chain Down to Earth," CNN, (April 29, 2016), money.cnn.com/2016/09/22/investing/chipotle-stock-bill-ackman/index.html.

3. The Motley Fool, "Why 2017 Was a Year to Forget for Chipotle Mexican Grill Inc.," Nasdaq (December 2, 2017) www.nasdaq.com/articles/why-2017-was-year-forget-chipotle-mexican-grill-inc-2017-12-02.

4. Thomas Chua, "Why It's Premature to Cancel Google Search," *SteadyCompounding.com* (March 3, 2025), steadycompounding.com/investing/google-search/.

5. Bill Ackman on pandemic valuation, Pershing Square Holdings, Annual Report 2019, assets.pershingsquareholdings.com/2022/10/07155536/Pershing-Square-Holdings-Ltd.-2019-Annual-Report-Letter-Only.pdf.

6. Netflix 2021 subscriber and revenue data. Netflix 2021 10-K. s22.q4cdn.com/959853165/files/doc_financials/2021/q4/da27d24b-9358-4b5c-a424-6da061d91836.pdf.

7. Netflix 2024 subscriber and revenue data, Netflix 2024 10-K, s22.q4cdn.com/959853165/files/doc_financials/2024/ar/Netflix-10-K-01272025.pdf.

8. Michael J. Mauboussin and Dan Callahan, "The Math of Value and Growth," Morgan Stanley (June 9, 2020), www.morganstanley.com/im/publication/insights/articles/article_themathofvalueandgrowth.pdf.

CHAPTER 8

1. Kara Sprague, "Reborn in the cloud," McKinsey & Company (July 1, 2015), www.mckinsey.com/capabilities/mckinsey-digital/our-insights/reborn-in-the-cloud.

2. Jaakko Nurkka, Josef Waltl and Oliver Alexy, "How Investors React When Companies Announce They're Moving to a SaaS Business Model," *Harvard Business Review* (January 13, 2017), hbr.org/2017/01/how-investors-react-when-companies-announce-theyre-moving-to-a-saas-business-model.

3. Susan Pulliam, "P/Es of Cisco, Others Lead To Stretching of Yardsticks," *Wall Street Journal* (April 12, 2000), www.wsj.com/articles/SB955485845794159366.

4. Jay Greene and Anne Steele, "Microsoft Shares Hit All-Time High," *Wall Street Journal* (October 21, 2016) www.wsj.com/articles/microsoft-shares-hit-all-time-high-1477057103.

CHAPTER 9

1. Hendrik Bessembinder, "Do Stocks Outperform Treasury Bills?" *Journal of Financial Economics*, (September 2018). Updated data available at: wpcarey.asu.edu/department-finance/faculty-research/do-stocks-outperform-treasury-bills.

2. Michael J. Mauboussin and Dan Callahan, "Drawdowns and Recoveries," Morgan Stanley, (May 21, 2025), www.morganstanley.com/im/publication/insights/articles/article_drawdownsandrecoveries_ltr.pdf.

3. Chris Mayer, *100-Baggers: Stocks That Return 100-to-1 and How to Find Them* (Laissez Faire Books, 2015).

4. Martin Whitman quote from Chris Mayer, *100 Baggers: Stocks That Return 100-to-1 and How to Find Them* (Laissez Faire Books, 2015).

5. William A. Ackman, "Letter to shareholders on selling Netflix," Pershing Square Holdings (April 20, 2022), assets.pershingsquareholdings.com/2022/04/20184527/Letter-to-Shareholders-4.20.2022.pdf.

6. Wesley Gray, "Even God Would Get Fired as an Active Investor," Alpha Architect, (February 2, 2016; updated June 14, 2017).

CHAPTER 10

1. Howard Marks, "Fewer Losers, or More Winners?" Oaktree Capital Management memo (September 12, 2023), www.oaktreecapital.com/insights/memo/fewer-losers-or-more-winners.

2. Joel Greenblatt, *You Can Be a Stock Market Genius: Uncover the Secret Hiding Places of Stock Market Profits* (Simon & Schuster, 1997).

3. Burton Malkiel, *A Random Walk Down Wall Street: The Best Investment Guide That Money Can Buy* (WW Norton & Co, 2024).

4. Chris Reining, "Interview with Tom Engle: Investing Legend," ChrisReining.com, chrisreining.com/tom-engle/.

5. Howard Marks, "The Illusion of Knowledge," Oaktree Capital Management memo, September 8, 2022.

6. J.P. Morgan Asset Management study on missing the best days (2004–2024). "Avoiding the Cash Trap" quarterly update. am.jpmorgan.com/content/dam/jpm-am-aem/americas/us/en/insights/market-insights/cash/3q24-update/avoiding-the-cash-trap.pdf.

7. Peter Lynch on market timing and investing at peaks versus bottoms, PBS Frontline interview, www.pbs.org/wgbh/pages/frontline/shows/betting/pros/lynch.html.

CHAPTER 11

1. "Full Transcript from CNBC's 'Charlie Munger: A Life of Wit and Wisdom'," CNBC (November 30, 2023), www.cnbc.com/2023/11/30/full-transcript-from-cnbcs-charlie-munger-a-life-of-wit-and-wisdom-.html.

2. Jeff Bezos, *Invent and Wander: The Collected Writings of Jeff Bezos* (Harvard Business Review Press, 2020).

3. Howard Marks, *The Most Important Thing: Uncommon Sense for the Thoughtful Investor* (Columbia University Press, 2011).

INDEX

D

N

O

P

Q

R

S

T

ABOUT THE AUTHOR

THOMAS CHUA is an investor and author dedicated to empowering individuals to achieve financial freedom. His popular blog, *Steady Compounding.com*, serves as a beacon for those seeking to build wealth through the stock market. After overcoming a challenging upbringing and achieving financial independence at 31, Thomas is passionate about sharing his hard-won lessons and time-tested strategies with others which he sets out in this book, *The Lunch Break Investor*. His unique journey and practical insights make him a trusted voice in the world of investing.